THE
WASTRELS
OF
DEFENSE

THE
WASTRELS
OF
DEFENSE

How Congress Sabotages
U.S. Security

Winslow T. Wheeler

Naval Institute Press
Annapolis, Maryland

Naval Institute Press
291 Wood Road
Annapolis, MD 21402

Library of Congress Cataloging-in-Publication Data
Wheeler, Winslow T.
The wastrels of defense : how Congress sabotages U.S. security / Winslow T.
Wheeler.
    p. cm.
    Includes bibliographical references and index.
    ISBN 1-59114-938-X (alk. paper)
    1. Waste in government spending—United States. 2. United States.
Congress—Appropriations and expenditures. 3. United States. Dept. of
Defense—Appropriations and expenditures. 4. United States—Defenses—
Economic aspects. 5. Patronage, Political—United States. I. Title.
HJ7537.W54 2004
336.3'9—dc22
                                    2004015003

Printed in the United States of America on acid-free paper ♾
11 10 09 08 07 06 05 04   9 8 7 6 5 4 3 2
First printing

*For Matthew, Nate, Owen, and Jack. So that they might
have the Congress they need and deserve.*

Contents

Foreword

With defense spending skyrocketing while America overextends its military reach in the pursuit of security against a dangerous new enemy, the need has never been greater for independent expert views and information that could help avert wasteful spending and policy blunders. Historically, the U.S. Congress has played a key role in safeguarding our democracy against myopic and misguided defense policymaking, but in recent times the legislative branch has failed miserably in this critical responsibility, as this book amply demonstrates.

As *The Wastrels of Defense* makes all too clear, Congress is not the only institution that has fallen down in exercising oversight and steering the nation back on track. The media, think tanks, "watchdogs," and other institutions have collectively failed to hold U.S. defense policymaking accountable to the public interest. However, the pivotal place of Congress in the traditional checks and balances of our democracy makes its failures especially consequential, and deserving of the degree of reproach leveled by the author of this volume, Winslow T. Wheeler.

Winslow spent a lifetime working on defense issues for Republicans and Democrats in the U.S. Congress. His extensive expertise, insider experience, integrity, and an unvarnished nonpartisan candor produce an indictment of unusual power, depth, and clarity. Congress's free-spending ways and reluctance to apply meaningful countervailing pressures on the executive branch and the Pentagon represent an abdication of its responsibility under our constitutional system. Congress has become a bigger part of the problem and a smaller part of the solution, churning out pork to constituents at a furious pace while turning a blind eye to its own excesses and lying low on the policy mistakes of an administration heedless to domestic or international restraint.

This book lays out the indictment in excruciating detail, and its author takes few prisoners along the way. Its diagnosis goes a long way toward finding solutions, and Winslow's keen insight sheds real light on a path out of the morass. This intrepid and wise public servant has produced an indispensable book at a critical time in the nation's history. His unwavering commitment to the public interest that cost him his congressional career—for sharing his views with the media and the public as an anonymous source and writer during his staff days—is on full exhibit in this book. He is single-handedly renewing faith in the power of independent thinking and honesty to rescue a foundering institution, if only it can bring itself to look into the mirror that this book holds up.

Bruce Blair
President, Center for Defense Information

Preface

Sen. Pete V. Domenici (R-N.Mex.) didn't want to make the phone call, but his staff director explained why he had to. Domenici had told the *Albuquerque Journal* he had fired me,[1] but his staff director explained that if he didn't permit me simply to resign, I could make life difficult for the senator. Domenici had been angered by an essay I wrote that had been circulated widely on the Internet and described in various newspapers and journals, some of them national. But to continue to treat me as he had would only provide more grist for the press to cover. Over the years, I had acted as a frequent source to many in the press and in some cases a friend. The senator wouldn't like what some of them might write about my being fired.

Moreover, the press coverage was not likely to be restricted to the *Albuquerque Journal;* it could well be in the *Wall Street Journal,* the *Washington Post,* and other national media that had already written about my offending essay. Now they might draw the nation's attention to my detailed insider's account of how atrociously the Senate had behaved in the immediate aftermath of the September 11, 2001, terror attacks. Examples:

- Senators added $4 billion in irrelevant and useless projects ("pork") for their home states to the defense budget (e.g., the army museum Sen. Robert Byrd [D-W.Va.] added for West Virginia; the parking garages Ted Stevens [R-Ala.] put in for Alaska; and the unrequested career development center Domenici himself added for White Sands Missile Range in New Mexico).

- The same senators stripped $2.4 billion out of the defense bill's accounts that supported military training, weapons maintenance, spare parts, and other military "readiness" items (just the things soldiers need most) to help pay for the pork. This was done just as the first American casualties were coming home from the fighting in Afghanistan, some of them in boxes.

- Sen. John McCain (R-Ariz.) gave an excellent speech railing against all this and then stood quietly by as the Senate voted to add another $387 million in pork to the defense bill. The Senate's self-described "pork buster" was nothing more than a "pork enabler."

If the press woke up to what was going on—and Domenici's firing me could be an alarm bell—there could be some real trouble.

Even so, Domenici was reluctant to make the phone call. I had broken just about every unwritten rule for how congressional staff should behave. I had criticized senators by name and in writing—which I had done not to obtain advantage for my own senator (something that was not merely allowed but encouraged)—and I had attacked all political persuasions. I even made Domenici look bad for not doing his job as a Budget Committee leader who should have stood up for rules that, if enforced, would have stopped some of the bad behavior.

I had bitten the hand that fed me, and I had bitten the hand that fed Domenici. By attacking Sen. Ted Stevens of Alaska, the top-ranking Republican on the Senate Appropriations Committee, I was complicating Domenici's access to pork for New Mexico. An ill-tempered individual, Stevens doled out pork like candy, but only to well-behaved senators. If Stevens associated my criticism with Domenici, he might take it out on Domenici's pork, and that might hurt his reputation in New Mexico where he was known as "Saint Pete" for all the federal spending he brought in. That could spell trouble in the November elections.

Despite all this, Domenici was being told he had to call me and eat his words about firing me. This was turning the Senate world on its head. Senators don't eat humble pie; staffers do, especially miscreants like me.

Acknowledging that he understood what he had to do, Domenici picked up the phone and gruffly told his secretary to get me on the line. By the time the phone started ringing, he had adjusted his tone. "If I had really meant to fire you, I would have told you first," he said in as friendly a voice as he could muster. I responded to Domenici's peace overture in as friendly a voice as I could: "Hi, boss, I appreciate your saying that." Then, I changed my tone, but only slightly. "I think we understand each other," I said. "You'll have my resignation by the end of the month. You won't read any more in the press about all this if I have anything to say about it." The call ended as abruptly as it began, with both of us avoiding saying anything that would disrupt the superficially friendly finale to my thirty-one-year career on Capitol Hill.

As soon as Domenici hung up, I made some phone calls. I told the ABC News researcher I had decided against an on-the-air interview; I told *American Spectator* magazine I didn't want to publish my essay after all. I did not return a call from the *New Republic,* thereby making sure it would not write anything. Domenici had relented; the parting was going to be amicable.

The engineer of the agreeable parting, the Budget Committee's Republican Staff Director, G. William ("Bill") Hoagland, was the man who explained the situation to Domenici before the senator reluctantly made his phone call. Hoagland had also been counseling me.

He was truly the man in the middle. He had feared it would come to this and knew it had when the *Washington Post* printed an article in which Senator McCain had cleverly made the issue not the Senate's, and his own, behavior, but mine.[2] McCain complained that I had used a pseudonym, "Spartacus," when writing the essay and argued it was not "correct journalism" for a reporter to protect my anonymity. Hoagland and I, and almost certainly McCain, knew that in the culture of the U.S. Senate the outing would have serious consequences for me. In fact, as soon as I arrived at work on the day the article that McCain had inspired appeared, Hoagland told me: "You need to get out of your office; you don't want to be able to answer your phone. Go home."

Hoagland had worked for Domenici for twenty years and knew him well; he was sure Domenici would be boiling after reading the *Post* article. He was right. Even though McCain and Domenici were not friendly and Domenici probably relished the scorn my own essay directed at McCain, the *Post* article fingered me as the staffer who was criticizing not just McCain but literally scores of senators, all of whom would resent my descriptions of them. Domenici had to find a way to disassociate himself from what his own staffer had done, and nothing was more effective than a quick and public firing. Hoagland feared Domenici would pick up the phone that very morning to do just that. Hoagland wanted to talk to the senator first and, if he could, change his mind.

Hoagland had a serious problem. This was not the first time I had caused trouble. In the past, I had written various reports and essays using the "Spartacus" pseudonym. Each addressed Congress's or the armed forces' handling of the defense budget. The Spartacus studies were controversial; Pentagon spokesmen usually spurned them as "all wrong." But they were detailed, footnoted, and documented, and the Pentagon's denials were suspiciously data free and self-serving.

It would have been much easier if the senator had been willing to release my studies as official Budget Committee reports, but that was not in the cards. Domenici was certainly not going to release anything critical of his Senate colleagues, Republican or Democrat, and he also had real problems with my criticism of the Pentagon. Domenici carefully nurtured his relationship with top generals and senior civilian administrators there. They were essential facilitators of the pork process that fostered Domenici's "Saint Pete" image in New Mexico. Critical reports from his Budget Committee staff would put sand, not grease, on the pork skids. He wanted no part of that.

Hoagland knew I was writing these Spartacus reports and essays. Any other staff director on Capitol Hill would have prohibited what I was doing, pseudonym or not. But he believed what I was writing needed to be said, and he did nothing to stop me.

But now as "Spartacus" I had pushed things past the limit. The new essay about Congress's post–September 11 behavior was long, detailed, and heavily footnoted, like the earlier reports, and it also used some angry rhetoric. It played on the 1939 Frank Capra movie, *Mr. Smith Goes to Washington* (about homespun political heroics in the U.S. Senate), and was titled "Mr. Smith Is Dead." In the text, senator after senator, regardless of party, ideology, or seniority, was exposed as a hypocrite. The entire Senate Armed Services Committee was termed "The Quintessence of Irrelevance and Self-Protection." Even President Bush was joined with Senator McCain as a "pork enabler." The essay's tone was out of line, but it said things that needed saying. Hoagland believed I should be given a serious talking to, but not a public firing.

When Hoagland met with Domenici to discuss the situation, the senator wanted him to fire me. He refused. It was not in his nature to be argumentative with Domenici, but Hoagland's own sense of decency told him Domenici's bidding was too much. Instead, he suggested a compromise: keep the staffer on for a few months and then let him step down. Domenici was adamant: I was too far out of line. If Hoagland could engineer a quiet resignation, okay, but it had to be soon, not some months off.

After a short hiatus, I did resign, and the press hardly noticed. Senators Domenici, McCain, Stevens, and others went on with business as usual. I found a new job with a Washington think tank, the Center for Defense Information, and wrote this book.

I have described here the "highlights" of my last days as a U.S. Senate staffer because they show what makes people tick on Capitol Hill at the start of the twenty-first century.

When I wrote the essay "Mr. Smith Is Dead" in January 2002, I knew it would cause a problem. I made a conscious decision to detail the atrocious behavior in Congress in the aftermath of September 11, 2001, in the hope that public exposure would cause some elected member to exercise his or her conscience and take up arms—parliamentary ones—against business as usual. My hope was not realized. The Senate's behavior, and that of the House of Representatives, did not improve; it worsened.

For more than thirty-one years, I have watched Congress evolve into a place where ambition and partisanship reign supreme, where members care little for substance and most for appearances.

The effect on our national security may not yet be apparent to most Americans, but it is alarming. Congress is not just dithering with national security—it is trashing it. The military effectiveness U.S. forces have shown in two wars against Iraq is not because of, but despite, Congress's work. U.S. armed forces are not supported at the level most Americans have been led to expect. The leadership in Congress and in the Pentagon work to pursue personal and career agendas, not national security.

Acknowledgments

Writing a book for the first time is a lonely enough task. It could prove impossible but for the encouragement, counsel, and support of friends and loved ones.

This book would not exist were it not for the Center for Defense Information, its president, Bruce Blair, and his able staff, especially Marcus Corbin and Theresa Hitchens. I especially appreciate CDI's neutral outlook on my work. At no time did I sense even the slightest attempt to alter the directions I have taken with my writing or to grind down any of the sharp edges concerning what and whom I have written about. In today's hyper-partisan environment in Washington, D.C., such an attitude is not just rare, it is extraordinary. If such an nonpartisan outlook were just a little more evident in this town, this book would be unnecessary, and the future of our democracy would be secure. I'd also like to give special thanks to the Ford Foundation for their generous support throughout the writing process.

There are others who helped me get started, sustained my efforts, and helped me steer a better course when the road became confusing. These include, but are in no way limited to, the following: Chuck Spinney religiously read chapters in their not-ready-for-prime-time condition and, above all else, kept on telling me what I was doing was needed and important. Robert Coram gave me a brutally honest and accurate critique of an early draft to help me produce a volume that readers might actually get through. He also gave me important counsel on the strange new world—to me—of publishing. George Wilson was always there at the beginning, middle, and end with leathery but good-natured insights on the problems and obstacles I would, and did, encounter; he helped me persevere. Jim Fallows never failed to offer help and encouragement. Jim Stevenson opened a door for me to Mark Gatlin and the Naval Institute Press, where they bothered to read a nobody's manuscript and to react in a way that any unpublished author can only dream about. Still others took the time to read chapters and to give me important comments, needed corrections, and an enthusiastic response; attempting to name them risks an oversight—I thank you all.

There was no more important help than from my wife, Judy, and my younger son, Matthew, to whom I dedicate this book. Patience, forbearance, advice, ideas, encouragement, and an environment where an easily distracted novice at book writing can get his work done day after day do not begin to describe their help and support. My first son, Winslow B., and his delightful wife, Cathy, have given me the three beautiful grandsons to whom this book is also dedicated.

THE
WASTRELS
OF
DEFENSE

I

THE NATURE OF THE PROBLEM

1

WHAT IS THE PROBLEM?

When I first started work on Capitol Hill in the office of Sen. Jacob K. Javits (R-N.Y.), the war in Vietnam dominated the national security agenda in Congress. Like the nation, the Senate was wracked with division, and senators fought hard and long with each other over the war. At the staff level, people working for committees and individual members spent long hours investigating the issues. Staff working for opponents to the war, like J. William Fulbright (D-Ark.), chairman of the Senate Foreign Relations Committee, produced startling reports about the Johnson and Nixon administrations' evasion of laws that were intended to contain the conflict. Staff working for proponents, such as Barry Goldwater (R-Ariz.), produced long treatises on the president's prerogative under the Constitution to pursue the war entirely as he saw fit. Even though this staff work often confronted senators with conclusions they had not been prepared to embrace—such as a president from a senator's own party lying to the public and themselves—individuals like Fulbright incorporated the material into their thinking and their speeches on the Senate floor. Because of this, both the Senate and the nation had an informed and informing debate.

Today, the Senate is a very different place.

One Staffer, Two Senators, and an Investigation

In 1996 Ted Stevens had served as a Republican senator from Alaska for twenty-eight years. Short and scrawny, he was nonetheless one of the "Old Bulls" of the Senate. He rose to the top of the heap in seniority and was a powerful member,* especially on defense issues. He also had a temper, but he knew how to play the Senate game and to keep himself within the confines of what other senators deemed acceptable behavior. Doing so had paid off. Stevens's Republican colleagues had elected him chairman of the obscure but extremely powerful Defense Subcommittee of the Senate Appropriations Committee ("Defense Appropriations"). Defense Appropriations had jurisdiction over 90 percent of the money spent by the Department of

---

* As used in this book and as generally understood on Capitol Hill, the term "member of Congress" ("member" for short) can refer to either a senator or a member of the House of Representatives. The terms "congressman," "congresswoman," and the politically correct "congressperson" refer to a member of the House of Representatives.

Defense (DoD),* and with Stevens in firm control of the subcommittee, there was just about nothing in Congress involving DoD that he did not have a major say in.

Beyond control of the DoD budget, Stevens's colleagues voted him chairman of the Senate Government Affairs Committee. Government Affairs did not have direct control over money, but it could influence policy and the decision-making process in the executive branch. As a result, the committee's jurisdiction was virtually unlimited; it could write legislation that could impact any or all federal agencies. It was a popular committee for senators to join.

On a fall day in 1996, Ted Stevens was having a tough time, his power and seniority notwithstanding. He had instructed the staff of one of the Government Affairs subcommittees, the Permanent Subcommittee on Investigations (PSI), to brief him on what subjects they wanted to look into. The staffers were complying, professionally and—especially with Stevens—respectfully, but he was becoming more and more upset.

The staffers in the room with Stevens were the subcommittee's chief investigator and chief counsel. They explained that they planned to look into an incident that the Air Force had allowed to fester without explaining satisfactorily. In 1994 in Iraq, two U.S. Air Force F-15s had fired on two helicopters, thinking them Russian-built, Iraqi-piloted Hind-D attack helicopters violating the "no fly zone" established over northern Iraq to prevent Iraqi depredations against Kurds after the Persian Gulf War. Sadly, the helicopters, which were hit and destroyed, turned out to be American "Black Hawks," a transport and utility helicopter, and they were filled with U.S. servicemen and servicewomen and civilian Kurds. They were performing authorized transport and liaison duties. In all, twenty-six men and women were killed, fifteen of them Americans. In response to this "friendly fire" incident, the Air Force had been busy in the media trying to blame a junior officer in an Airborne Warning and Control System (AWACS) aircraft that had been attempting to manage events from about three hundred miles away. One thing the Air Force was very definitely not doing was looking at the incident objectively, trying to establish whether its own equipment, doctrine, and/or leadership were contributing, if not controlling, factors.

The subcommittee's chief investigator, Eric Thorson, knew better than to blame the disaster solely on a junior officer in the AWACS aircraft. An Air Force Academy graduate and ex–Air Force pilot, Thorson knew the technology and "rules of engagement" that were in use at the time. As a

---

* The significant parts of the defense budget not controlled by the Defense Appropriations Subcommittee are spending for military construction and nuclear warheads, which separate appropriations subcommittees control.

student of defense issues, he recognized that friendly fire was a serious problem and certainly should not be swept under the rug. Indeed, there was reason to believe that in modern warfare, friendly fire against civilian and "blue force" targets was going to present more and more trouble.

In the Persian Gulf War in 1991, 24 percent of allied casualties were inflicted by our own side. In 1988 the U.S. Navy experienced the problem over the Persian Gulf by shooting down an Iranian airliner climbing out after takeoff, killing more than one hundred civilian passengers. The captain and crew of the USS *Vincennes* interpreted, wrongly, from their advanced "Aegis" air defense system that the airliner was a fighter-bomber diving on the cruiser. The technology for identifying "friend or foe" was so frail in the Vietnam War in the 1960s and 1970s that no Air Force, Navy, or Marine fighter pilot was allowed to fire on any airborne target unless he personally identified it as an enemy type with his own eyes.

By the 1990s, much money had been spent to solve the "identification, friend or foe" (IFF) problem, and far more had been spent on a growing inventory of long-range weapons designed to attack targets "beyond visual range." Unfortunately, the IFF problem was proving far more intractable than some in the Air Force were willing to admit. Blaming the 1994 helicopter tragedy on human error and a junior officer would avoid the need for a lot of difficult explaining to Congress.

Without acknowledging the long history of friendly fire accidents and making it very clear he didn't want anyone under him asking probing questions of the Air Force about its doctrine, procurement strategy, and leadership, Stevens wanted to squelch the investigation the staffers proposed. The senator sharply asked the subcommittee staff whether the chairman of the PSI, Republican Sen. Bill Roth of Delaware, had approved the inquiry. When told he had, Stevens seemed skeptical and set up a second meeting with Roth the next week to confirm what the staffers said.

While almost as senior in years of service and a dyed-in-the-wool Republican, Roth was nonetheless a very different senator from Stevens. Always wearing an obvious toupee and bookish looking, he was regarded by some senators and staff, but not by Thorson, as something of an odd duck. On defense issues, he was very much a maverick, and most senators—Republican and Democrat—who wanted to be known as solidly "pro-defense" did not feel comfortable aligning with Roth. Only on a few occasions did Roth put together a majority in the Senate chamber to win a vote on a major defense issue. On the other hand, as chairman of the Permanent Subcommittee on Investigations, Roth could pursue any matter pretty much as he saw fit, and this presented Stevens with a problem.

At the meeting he called with Roth, Stevens began by asking if Roth had authorized the investigation. His tone implied skepticism that Roth had done so, thereby giving Roth an out, should he choose to shorten a difficult meeting with the irascible Stevens. Oddball or not, Roth was no patsy. The investigation certainly did have his authorization. Not giving up, Stevens then took a different course and asserted in an authoritative manner that because the shoot down occurred in a "no fly zone," the Air Force "had every right to shoot them [the American Black Hawks] down."[1] The intimidation game was still afoot.

Roth looked at Thorson, whom he had invited to the meeting, and nodded, telling him silently it was okay to respond to Stevens—but carefully. Thorson, who knew the rules of engagement operative in Iraq at the time (and with senators), respectfully explained that Stevens had it wrong: positive identification of the target was, indeed, required before anyone was supposed to shoot at anything. Indeed, the rules required identification of both type of aircraft and nation of origin; had the technology and doctrine on the scene been capable of such identification, the tragedy clearly could have been avoided.

Still clearly not liking what he was hearing, Stevens switched tactics again and announced he did not want anyone embarrassing the Air Force because programs, budgets, and senior officers defending them could all be put into difficulty. Thorson responded, again respectfully, that the Air Force would only be embarrassed if it had done something wrong. That got Stevens angry. When Thorson tried to explain the problems pilots historically had had with IFF systems, Stevens, who had been a transport pilot in World War II, snapped at him, "I suppose you're a pilot" in a tone accusing Thorson of being a "know it all." Actually, he was a pilot, Thorson calmly explained, with combat experience in Vietnam.[*]

Stevens's efforts to intimidate Roth and the subcommittee staff out of the investigation flopped badly, and the meeting was clearly over. Moreover, a few weeks later, after the Air Force refused to hand over documents Thorson needed, Roth did something that was almost unheard of on Capitol Hill: he issued subpoenas against five Air Force officials.

But ultimately, the report was never written; in the end, Stevens won. First, the Air Force adopted a particularly adept stalling tactic to kill the subpoenas. It had very probably been tipped off by someone wise in the ways of the Senate, like Stevens or his staff, that in the upcoming January the Senate would reorganize because of the retirement of some senior members. There would be changes in committee and subcommittee leadership. The Air Force seemed to know that it would not need to worry about

---

* Thorson also flew transports, C-130s, in Vietnam.

Roth and Thorson any longer. Second, Roth started receiving letters from his Senate colleagues, both Republicans and Democrats. These letters expressed strong disagreement with Roth's subpoenas against the Air Force: it just wasn't the right way to treat senior officers and civilians in the Pentagon, the letters argued. Some of the letters were especially aggressive— some were almost belligerent.

Roth was willing to stand up to his colleagues' efforts to bully him out of what he thought was his job, but the Air Force's less crude delaying tactic paid off. In the musical chairs operation that took place among the Senate's various committees and subcommittees to fill the positions vacated by retiring senators, Stevens moved up to be chairman of the all-powerful Senate Appropriations Committee: not just the Defense Subcommittee (which he also retained). Roth moved on to the also supremely powerful Finance Committee, which wrote tax and trade law and controlled spending for the federal government's huge health and welfare entitlement programs. A new senator, Fred Thompson of Tennessee, was given the chairmanship of the Government Affairs Committee, and another newcomer, Susan Collins of Maine, was handed the PSI.

At Government Affairs and the PSI, it was clear the new hierarchy had other staffing ideas in mind and no interest in continuing Thorson's work on the 1994 incident. It became time for Thorson to move on; he went with Roth to the Finance Committee. There, Thorson investigated the Internal Revenue Service (IRS) and found major horror stories involving IRS abuses of taxpayers. The result was a series of spectacular hearings that became all the rage on Capitol Hill and in the national press. Major legislation to reform the IRS was declared needed, quickly written, and enacted into law with bipartisan support. The success of the investigations made Thorson something of a star staffer in the Senate.

His successful oversight of the IRS notwithstanding, Roth lost his reelection bid in Delaware in 2000. He was the last of a now almost extinct breed in the Senate who were not afraid to treat misbehavior by senior generals and DoD bureaucrats the same as misbehavior by any other agency. With Roth gone, Thorson retired. However, based on his investigatory success, he was now a frequent lecturer and consultant on how to perform congressional investigations. He was hired by different members of Congress and committees to perform them, but no one seemed interested in using Thorson's talents where they were strongest; he was never asked to return to the subject matter he knew best, defense. It is reasonable to suspect that Thorson's "take no prisoners" attitude toward investigations was okay for many subjects but was too aggressive for the Pentagon. After all, as we shall see later, DoD can be a lot more helpful to members when there are no bull terrier investigators shredding its bureaucratic pants.

The friendly fire problem? It remained alive and well. With no investigation of the Black Hawk incident propelling any solutions, the Pentagon muddled on. The result cost lives. In 2003 in Operation Iraqi Freedom, the Army's Patriot missile shot down two allied aircraft, killing four aircrewmen. Overall, friendly fire incidents resulted in 35 U.S. and allied deaths (most of them from U.S. air attacks), 18 percent of the 189 killed in the first six weeks of the campaign.[2]

It is impossible to say whether a solution to the friendly fire problem could have been secured in the seven years between Thorson's attempt to start an investigation and the second Gulf War in 2003. It is also impossible to hold Senator Stevens personally responsible for the lives that were lost. However, it is possible to say that Senator Stevens actively impeded a solution. His attitude toward a competent investigation says a lot about how Congress does, and does not, exercise its national security responsibilities.

Pork Parade

The press and experts on Congress generally characterize "pork" (the project-specific spending that members of Congress add to spending bills for their home states and congressional districts) as a foolish, marginally expensive pastime of political self-indulgence to impress the voters back home. They say Congress has always done it; it's an unavoidable part of congressional business as usual. They are quite wrong. "Pork" is a core activity on Capitol Hill, and given the way Congress pursues it, it unravels a central responsibility the U.S. Constitution imposes on Congress. In addition, it is far more costly than the experts understand, and it's all getting increasingly worse.

The Constitution gives Congress responsibility to "raise and support armies" and "provide and maintain a navy." An instructive indicator of how current members of Congress interpret those jobs is what changes senators and representatives make in the defense budget the president requests. They do so in the form of legislative amendments, sponsored by individual members or small groups of members. However, to make it through the entire legislative labyrinth, the amendments must—at several points—be endorsed by a majority of the Senate and the House of Representatives. Thus, these amendments become the handiwork of not just the originating members but of most, if not all, congressional members.

One of the defense bills annually debated and passed by Congress "to raise and support armies" and "to provide and maintain a navy" is the National Defense Authorization Act. It is a product of the prestigious Armed Services Committees in both the House and the Senate; it addresses both policy and funding issues in DoD, and it is a major opportunity for members of the House and the Senate to influence national defense each year. For fiscal year 2002, the Senate debate on this bill started on 21 September 2001, just ten days after the terror attacks on the World Trade Center and the Pentagon. It was a particularly cogent opportunity for senators to show what they thought was important to fight a war, rhetorically declared by President George W. Bush in a special joint session of Congress on 20 September—the night before the senators took up the bill. They considered and adopted seventy-nine different amendments. Here is a sample of their priorities: a transfer of land from DoD to establish the Fort Des Moines Memorial Park and Education Center,[3] improvements at the Rocky Flats National Wildlife Refuge,[4] alterations to contract arrangements at the U.S. Army Heritage and Education Center at Carlisle Barracks, Pennsylvania, for design and operation of a museum,[5] and a study of helicopter flights to ferry passengers at Minot Air Force Base, North Dakota.[6] Each one, and many more, were authored and pushed by a senator from the home state that benefited.

In all, of almost eighty amendments adopted, half were completely irrelevant to the war against terrorism and instead sought to increase federal spending in the state of the author of the amendment. More than a score of other amendments did not address themselves to the authors' home states, but they did accommodate the solicitations of one political constituency or another, such as military retirees and their retirement payments. These amendments also made no contribution to the war against terrorism. Another fifteen amendments were in some way relevant to the war, but they were also marginal, such as one to require a report from DoD to Congress on chemical and biological protective gear.[7]

Two months later, in December 2001, the Senate took up the fiscal year 2002 Department of Defense Appropriations bill: a bill different from, and generally considered more important than, the authorization bill debated in September. An appropriations bill actually gives money to DoD to spend. Attached to this one was an "emergency supplemental" to spend an additional $20 billion to prosecute the war in Afghanistan and to provide for homeland security. This time the Senate adopted more than one hundred amendments.[8] Of them, more than two-thirds provided for spending in the home state of the author. The remaining thirty amendments were irrelevancies. We shall look at the details of these parochial and essentially meaningless amendments in chapters 3 and 4.

Moreover, these acts of mal-, mis-, and non-feasance came from Democrats, Republicans, conservatives, moderates, liberals, males, females, and young and old senators. The parade of goodies for the authors' home states and other irrelevancies knew no distinction by party, philosophy, gender, age, or even religion. It was not one part or sector of Congress behaving poorly, it was the entire Congress.

Throughout this process, the aforementioned Ted Stevens was busy. As the top-ranking Republican on both the Defense Subcommittee and the full Appropriations Committee, he had to be consulted on each and every one of these amendments if they were to be adopted without controversy. Given his power and authority in the Senate, not even one would have made it through the process without his explicit approval.

He was also careful to take care of Alaska. In the various defense bills the Senate considered in the year after September 11, one finds Alaska plastered all over the legislation intended to fight the war against terrorism. In addition, it was not war-related items Stevens was stuffing into the bill; it was money for fisheries,[9] gyms,[10] parking garages,[11] and more. A content analysis of the text of defense appropriations bills and of the committee reports that accompany them (that also direct DoD on how, when, and where to spend money) would reveal that the word "Alaska" is almost certainly the most prevalent proper noun used throughout. The only possible competitor would be the word "Hawaii."

In 2001 the Democrats controlled the Senate, and Daniel Inouye of Hawaii was chairman of the Defense Subcommittee. While far more even-tempered and decorous than Stevens, the more "senatorial" Inouye is, nonetheless, not to be outdone as a porker. Into the defense appropriation bill he stuffed things like the "Hawaii Federal Health Care Network"[12] and the "Institute for Tribal Government."[13]

In fact, Stevens and Inouye formed something of a tag team to insert these items into defense bills for their own and others' states. Senators seeking pork don't want a fight; they want their amendments adopted quickly and quietly so that they can beam the good news back home without interference from troublemakers. They don't want anyone in the press wondering why such irrelevant spending should be added to a defense bill in the middle of a war, and they don't want other senators wondering why those items should not be directed at their own states as well. Hence, the authors of these amendments seek the endorsement of both Democrat Inouye and Republican Stevens. If both agree, the amendment is "bipartisan," and if both parties can agree to it, it must also be "noncontroversial." Thus, it is no problem to adopt the amendment in the Senate by a quick "voice vote" (which takes just a few seconds) rather than the arduous (fifteen- to thirty-minute) "roll call vote" that asks each and every senator to individually say "yea" or "nay," to have some idea of what he or she is voting on, and to be recorded for posterity.

Nor are these activities a sideshow. In the case of both the National Defense Authorization bill and the DoD Appropriations bill, pork, irrelevancies, and marginalities constituted almost the entirety of the Senate's legislative business. There were, of course, many speeches given—all of them highly patriotic—but for actual business, the pork and the junk were all they adopted.

As a staffer, I worked on defense bills for most of thirty years. Toward the end of my career, while working for a member of the Defense Appropriations Subcommittee, Senator Domenici, two other members of Domenici's staff empire and I would spend hour upon hour, week after week on Domenici's New Mexico–specific additions for defense bills. This work would normally start in January and end in October. There were weeks when other business would take up more time; there were even some weeks when our pork activity was *de minimis,* but those weeks were all too few. Nor was there anyone else handling more serious defense budget work for Senator Domenici. On Capitol Hill today, pork is a full-time preoccupation for both members and staff.

Costs

Members of Congress add hundreds, nay thousands, of these home state additions, variously called "member adds," "earmarks," "congressional-" or "line-items," "state impacts," or just "pork," to defense-related legislation each year. Sen. John McCain (R-Ariz.) and his staff keep tabs on the dollar amounts. Their estimates of the totals are in the billions for each bill. For the fiscal year 2002 DoD Appropriations bill, when it came to the Senate for debate, McCain estimated a total of $3.601 billion.[14] And, after the Senate finished amending the measure, the bill went up another $378 million.[15] For FY 2003, the pork bill went up to $8.5 billion. The next year, FY 2004, it was at $6.5 billion at the start of the year and sure to go up as it progressed.

That's not the worst of it. The cost of pork is not just in dollars spent. In fact, pork costs do not mean an amount added on top of the rest of the defense budget; instead, much of it is paid for by making cuts in other parts of the defense budget, usually in portions requested by the president and DoD. Worse yet, huge cuts are extracted out of what is called the "Operations and Maintenance" (O&M) budget. O&M is almost certainly the most important part of the budget, especially when it comes to fighting a war. O&M pays for training for troops going into combat, weapons maintenance, spare parts, military exercises, and combat operations themselves.

Reluctant to make obvious what it is cutting to pay for pork, Congress puts the O&M cuts not in the O&M part of the bill but in the back, in the

"General Provisions" section, which most observers, including the press and the experts, pay little attention to. There, for example, in the fiscal year 2003 DoD Appropriations bill passed by the Senate, the curious can find the following:

- Section 8082 extracted $211 million from O&M in foreign currency "savings" that the Appropriations Committee decided were going to occur in the future from the dollar rising in comparison to currencies such as the euro and the yen (a long-range prediction no professional in the financial markets would dare make and which did not in fact happen).
- Section 8097 permitted $68 million in transfers out of O&M that were simply not explained.
- Section 8099 took $8 million out for those railroads at two bases in Alaska.

- Section 8100 was the granddaddy; it declared that DoD would save $700 million in better service contract management, an economy the White House's Office of Management and Budget (OMB) and DoD said was impossible.

These and similar provisions cut a grand total of $1.1 billion in the FY 2003 O&M budget as passed by the Senate. And, just so no one in DoD would get confused, the Appropriations Committee also left instructions that "congressional items"—i.e., pork—are not to be reduced without specific permission from Congress, even if DoD is forced to cut programs that support military readiness. Finally, in the small number of instances that DoD asked for that permission, I am aware of no case where a member of Congress failed to complain about his or her pork being cut out.

With the exception of Senator McCain, the speeches members give never explain what is going on; even official documents don't help. Despite its raid on FY 2003 O&M spending to pay for pork, the Senate Appropriations Committee's report on the same bill stated in its "Committee Priorities" section: "The primary goals of this bill are to ensure readiness and fair treatment of our men and women in uniform." [16]

Benefit

When the Senate debated the FY 2002 DoD Appropriations bill in early December 2001, the fighting was at its height in Afghanistan. When the Senate debated the FY 2003 DoD Appropriations bill in July 2002, the controversy of whether or not to go to war against Iraq was coming to a head. For the FY 2004 bill, the second, deadly guerrilla phase of Operation Iraqi

Freedom was in full bloom. In other words, while U.S. armed forces were preparing for combat or actually fighting, the U.S. Senate decided that the budget accounts that pay for training, weapons maintenance, spare parts, and combat operations should be diminished to help pay for garages, gyms, fisheries, museums, and other dubious impedimenta.

Senators universally think these things are very important. Few are so foolish to think they are important for U.S. armed forces, but they are for re-election. They convey the message to constituencies back home that the senator can bring in federal dollars. In this respect, the defense bill is no different from those for the Departments of Commerce, Labor, Interior, or Health and Human Services, except that the defense bill usually contains more pork than any other appropriations bill.

A small number of senators, usually just one or two, exploit the pork parade a different way. They are the ones who call themselves pork busters. They instruct their staff to tally up all the pork spending, and they give detailed speeches that serve the useful purpose of explaining it all. However, no one ever fully informed the public of what is really going on before, during, and after these speeches. First, even though the antipork speeches are really quite compelling, the legislative actions to give real meaning to the words are left undone. In an institution specifically designed to enable the minority, even of one or two, to effectively encumber the abusive majority, the parliamentary arsenal available to make the Senate's adoption of mountains of pork a process of undying agony for the porkers has never been used. Second, in many cases, individual amendments adding pork to defense bills are brought to the pork busters for their approval—to avoid any unseemly fights. In the vast majority of the cases, the approval is freely given, and the morsel is added to the bill. Third, after the Senate adopts the pork with a voice vote, the pork buster often gives yet another speech about how terrible it is for the Senate to do what he just approved. Like good judo artists, the pork busters work off of Congress's obsession with acquiring pork to pose, but not act, as reformers. In a political sense, it has been a spectacularly successful operation; the press eats it up.

While he sometimes has one or two other senators joining with him, there is really only one pork buster in the Senate, John McCain. He has successfully made himself both the darling of the press and the Sunday morning television talk shows by convincing observers—obviously merely casual ones—that he is a "plain-talking" iconoclast in the Senate who among other things "busts pork."

It is a system where everybody benefits. The porking senators get their goodies and the skids greased for re-election, and the pork busters get a reputation as heroic opponents.

The description here only scratches the surface. There remain depths to the pork system that can turn the skeptics into cynics. We shall plumb those depths in later chapters.

It is also a system that is getting worse.

Spontaneous Degeneration

Just before Congress sends a bill to the president for signature into law or a veto, the bill takes the form of a "conference report" that has two parts. The first is the text of the law as proposed; the second is a "Joint Explanatory Statement of the Committee of Conference" that explains why the final bill language is what it is and adds some additional detail to illuminate congressional "intent." A typical defense appropriations bill conference report of the early to mid-1980s would consist of about ninety pages. Five or six pages would be bill text; the rest was the "Joint Explanatory Statement."[17] Each pork item was described in a short paragraph; the entire bill and explanatory statement might include two hundred to three hundred such items.

An early twenty-first century defense appropriations conference report has grown to 300 or more pages, about 60 of which are devoted to bill text and the rest to the "Joint Explanatory Statement." In those 240 or so pages of "explanation," individual pork items consist of a single line, maybe two, in a large table containing scores, if not hundreds, of such items. These tables occupy the great majority of the "explanatory" statement of roughly 240 pages. There are thousands of pork items in the bill and report. Just like the stock market of the 1990s, pork in defense bills grew several fold. However, unlike the stock market, there are no bears in congressional porking.

It Gets Worse

Oversight of and budget support for the military services are not the most onerous national security responsibilities the Constitution tries to impose on Congress. Congress is also the ultimate authority on decisions to go to war. Ignoring what the Constitution says and what its authors said it means, many think that authority lies with the president, the "commander in chief." We will explore that argument later, but whether it is through the Constitution's delegation of the war-making authority or Congress's undisputed control of government spending, Congress holds the power of life or death over America's military personnel.

In October 2002 Congress debated war with Iraq. When the debate started, then–Majority Leader Trent Lott (R-Miss.) said he wanted the Senate to show why it calls itself "the world's greatest deliberative body." At first, no one took him up on that; not a single senator bothered to talk about Iraq, even inelegantly. Sen. Jim Bunning (R-Ky.) decided he wanted to talk about the Future Farmers of America chapter in Caldwell County, Kentucky. Sen. Barbara Boxer (D-Calif.) addressed herself to the one-hundredth anniversary of the city of Mountain View, California, and so on.

The next day, after still more miscellany, Iraq became a talking point when Sens. Bunning, Carl Levin (D-Mich.), and George Voinovich (R-Ohio) spoke. Later, to an almost empty chamber, senators John Warner (R-Va.) and Robert Byrd (D-W.Va.) argued about the war, rather eloquently but not for long.

On the third day, several senators read staff-prepared texts about war with Iraq and then disappeared, not bothering to listen to others. Interspaced among these scripted flourishes, senators debated one issue rather hotly; it was the question of who speaks next. At one point, the Senate took half an hour to sort out whose turn it was. Sen. Joe Biden (D-Del.) could be overheard mumbling into his Senate microphone, calling it all "ridiculous."

This was not the low point of the debate, it was only the beginning of a "Week of Shame" that chapter 14 addresses in detail. Subsequently, it became clear in the Senate debate that some members had not bothered to read the war-authorizing legislation they were considering, or if they had, they were willing to distort its meaning and effect to justify their position on it.

President Bush was also playing political games with the question of war. The White House submitted its legislation to authorize war against Iraq just before the November 2002 congressional elections. It was clear to everybody on Capitol Hill that Congress was being pressured to show its patriotism just when it was most vulnerable.

In a national dilemma, such as deciding to go to war, there will always be some politicians who exploit the situation for their own benefit, but it is not unreasonable to expect some to rise above themselves. In October 2002 there were a few, but their number was tiny. It has not always been that way.

The Not-as-Hopeless Past

In the past, members of Congress did attempt to grapple seriously with the question of war. Liberals and conservatives stepped out of what was comfortable for them politically, made every effort to hear out all sides of the issue, and extended themselves to breathe life into their convictions and change how America decides to go to war. This effort was in the face of an "imperial presidency" during some of the most difficult years of an ongoing war. It was a clear case of senators acting on a matter of principle and conviction, not at all clearly in their political self-interest.

This occurred in the early 1970s when some in Congress chose to pursue war powers legislation and take it from a quixotic impulse of a small minority to enactment into law over a presidential veto. The pros and cons of Congress's right to assert itself in the decision to make war aside for now, it suffices to say here that in other times some in Congress have operated on a higher plane.

That time is no longer. It is virtually inconceivable to picture any in today's Congress pursuing a fight in the manner Sens. Javits, John Stennis (D-Miss.), and Thomas Eagleton (D-Mo.), the primary authors of the War Powers Act, did in the 1970s.

A senator selected, and then promoted, by his colleagues to oversee the Defense Department who works to prevent oversight. A skilled investigator who is not asked to investigate the one area he knows the best—defense. A constitutional duty to support and maintain the armed forces employed, instead, to raise and maintain politicians' prospects for re-election. Senators posing as pork busters and instead being "pork enablers." Senators who, when asked to decide on the terrible question of war, decide instead to defend their personal political prospects. Led by the U.S. Senate, today's Congress is an institution armed with all the tools to make itself a constructive and effective component of America's national security apparatus. Instead, it has degenerated into a gaggle of wastrels competing for selfish advantage.

We will probe today's depths and yesterday's occasional heights. We will start with an examination of Congress's pork system, which I believe will surprise not just the average voter and taxpayer but also professional observers among the press and the think tank community. But before we probe Congress's obsession with pork, it is appropriate to plumb what is perhaps the deepest pit of them all: congressional egos.

2

Ego Is at the Heart of the Trouble

Inflated egos are not new on Capitol Hill. Representatives and especially senators have always been treated with deference by each other, the public, the press, and, indeed, the entire Washington, D.C., community. Literally and figuratively, doors open for the members, and they are led to the head of the line wherever they go. Their environment trains them to consider themselves special. Rare is the member who does not permit it all to go to his or her head after a few years.

It is very difficult to measure whether today's members of Congress are more self-focused than their predecessors. Descriptions of past senators, such as Robert Caro's biography of Lyndon Johnson, *Master of the Senate*, make it difficult to conceive that any progeny could exceed the egoism of not just Johnson but many in Congress in the past. Moreover, the first member I worked for starting in 1971, Jacob Javits, was notorious for his arrogance. Even ten years after his death in 1986, I continued to hear stories from newer staffers of his pompousness, which they considered extraordinary, even in the Senate.

However, Javits sometimes had the good sense to know some issues and circumstances were even more important than his own personal standing. For the frequency with which he did rise above himself, and for his brilliance, those of us on his staff respected and even loved him. We didn't like him, but we did love him. In a tribute to him after his death, a former legislative director correctly, but with affection, called him "pompous, aggressive, brilliant and, as a legislator, effective."[1] However, as I said, there were times when, like members today, Javits was happy to use others to elevate himself.

Capturing the Captive Nations

An annual drill in the Senate during the 1970s was "Captive Nations Week." As a junior member of Javits's staff, I had the task of writing up a short statement for him to insert, without its actually being spoken, into the *Congressional Record*. We enclosed reprints of the statement in letters to constituents who wrote to Javits about such issues. The statements directed rhetorical flourishes at the Soviet Union's occupation of Eastern Europe and the yearning for liberty of the oppressed Poles, Romanians, Bulgarians, Hungarians,

Czechs, and Slovaks, among others. Some of the stranger objects of these statements, I thought, were the nascent nations described inside the Soviet Union that also yearned, I wrote, for national independence. An independent Ukraine? A new nation of Byelorussia? Not likely, I thought. Surely, these statements were nothing more than appeals to the ethnic groups in the United States and the votes they could cast in elections. Surely, there was no real prospect that any true nation would ever emerge—with or without a Soviet Union to oppress them—from these ethnic regions inside Russia that were culturally distinct, but surely not unborn nations.

History has proven me utterly wrong.

Even though I considered writing the statements bothersome, I nonetheless religiously produced them. If I didn't, the ethnic groups in New York would notice; they would complain to Javits, and I would definitely hear about it.

By 1978 I wasn't such a junior staffer for Javits any more, and I decided it was time to make my views known to him. On 18 July, in the middle of the day, I took him a copy of my ritual statement for Captive Nations Week, 1978. I handed it to him in his private office on the first floor of the Capitol Building and told him I didn't think the statements served any worthwhile purpose. I urged him not to put the statement in the *Congressional Record*. He did not seem to want to talk about it, took the written statement, and said he would think about it.

That evening, I attended a reception celebrating the very same Captive Nations Week. It was in the historic Caucus Room on the third floor of the Russell Senate Office Building just around the corner from Javits's office suite. I was on my way out of the building at the end of the day and walked by the Caucus Room. I was hungry; they had hors d'oeuvres and an open bar. I put on a name tag identifying myself as a Javits staffer and went in. Munching, drinking, and talking to one of the ethnically Lithuanian hostesses of the reception, I busied myself trying to impress her with my position as one of Javits's foreign policy staffers responsible for Captive Nations issues. I did not notice Javits come in; he did not notice me either.

Someone asked Javits to address the throng in the room. He told them that he had talked with a staff aide that day about Captive Nations Week. He said the staffer had told him that Captive Nations commemorations were "out of date—old hat." The Lithuanian hostess gave me an icy stare. Then, Javits laid it on thick: his response to the aide was "not on your life—those who hold these nations captive count on the fact that we will be unable to run the course. So I beg you, dedicate yourselves to their struggle for freedom—not only during my lifetime and yours, but thereafter. It may take a long time, but justice will triumph if those who believe in justice persist."[2]

As the throng applauded, I tried to make myself as small as possible as the Lithuanian hostess smirked at me in derision.

As I made my way to the door, trying hard to attract no attention, Javits was momentarily standing alone. I went over to him and said in a voice trying to make a joke of it, "I guess you made up your mind." He looked at me briefly, saying, "Oh, Win, I didn't know you were here." That was all. I left.

My comments to Javits earlier that day had given him fodder to inflate himself for the Captive Nations commemorators in the Caucus Room. As the loud applause at the reception and an article in the next morning's *Washington Post* made obvious, he successfully scored points with them. The staffer served the senator, not as an adviser but as a prop to garner applause, and maybe a few votes, from an ethnic group.

My being Javits's fall guy for an evening did not, however, fool everybody at the reception. One woman in the room, whom I never met, told the *Washington Post:* "I come here every year to some kind of party for the captive nations. We have drinks and everybody talks, but I always have the feeling that they only come to get the ethnic vote, but they don't do a damned thing about it."[3] She had it quite right.

Sometimes, the consequences of taking liberties with another as one's fall guy, as in my case with Javits, are inconsequential; in others, they can be significant. Such a case is next.

Honor as a Sometime Thing

After Javits, working for Republican Sen. Nancy Landon Kassebaum of Kansas was a breath of fresh air. Friendly and kindhearted to her staff, she usually tried hard to be genuine in both her private and public personas. However, sometimes she did not try hard enough.

My first few years working for her were immensely successful. On both foreign affairs and national defense issues (my portfolio on her staff), she was having a major impact on President Ronald Reagan's policies—and for the better, according to my biases. She was forcing the State Department to pay attention to human rights problems in El Salvador, where right-wing thugs in and out of the government were making it easy for the communists to make headway in the civil war there. On national defense, she was jarring the eyeteeth of defense secretary Caspar Weinberger's proclivity to shower the military services with national treasure for high-cost, ineffective weapons.[*]

She was not a "knee-jerk" liberal opponent to defense spending, and she was not an automatic conservative proponent of more and more—the

---

[*] In sharp contrast to his moniker "Cap the Knife" when he was Richard Nixon's secretary of Health, Education, and Welfare, we called Weinberger "Cap the Ladle" at Defense.

two points of view that had dominated the debate in Congress. Kassebaum focused on "military reform"; she was a "cheap hawk" trying to make U.S. defense more effective at less expense. Making a name for herself, she was offered the co-chairmanship of an obscure caucus in Congress, the Congressional Military Reform Caucus. That gave her a platform to offer still more commentary and legislation advocating Pentagon reform and to help propel a national debate. Both the Kansas and national press were intrigued by her criticism, and that of other Republicans, of the Reagan-Weinberger defense program. The Kansas press began to routinely cover her actions and statements,[4] and it gave her highly favorable editorial commentary.[5] She knew she hit the big time when the *New York Times* started boosting her political profile in feature stories with titles like "From 'Nice Little Nancy' to 'Effective'" and "New Breed of Military Reformer."[6] The more coverage she and the other reformers received, the more other members of Congress started to support her initiatives, and that in turn got her more coverage. The news stories evolved to show that she was not just thinking and doing interesting things but was also accumulating a base of power in defense affairs. The Pentagon and the defense-business-as-usual crowd in Congress increasingly had to pay attention to her and fellow reformers. Stories with titles like "Pentagon Worried: Military Caucus' Mission Causing Stir"[7] and "Caucus Is Slicing Pentagon into Itty Bitty Pieces"[8] began to appear.*

Politically, it was all "manna from heaven." However, none of it had sprung forth Athena-like from Kassebaum's head, or from the head of any other member of Congress. Nor did it spring from my own. It came from a small group of men who were both geniuses and deeply committed to the goal of fundamentally changing the way America fought its wars. A retired Air Force colonel, John Boyd was the leader and mentor; he and his cohorts had an immense impact on the hardware and thinking of the military services. He and his allies forced the Air Force to improve its design for the fighter airplane that became the highly successful F-15. Dissatisfied with the results, he then forced the Air Force to acquire an even better and cheaper dogfighter, the F-16. Boyd and his associates also played key roles for the Navy's F/A-18 and the Air Force's A-10.

---

* The quote, "Caucus Is Slicing Pentagon into Itty Bitty Pieces," was from the Under Secretary of Defense for Research and Development, Richard DeLauer. In an associated article in the Associated Press, he stated of Kassebaum: "I can't talk to Nancy Kassebaum. I talk right by her. Her eyes glass over when I talk about trade-offs between survivability and capability and sophistication." (This article appeared in a newspaper on 27 December 1983, titled "Military Caucus Turns Pentagon's Head," by AP writer Jim Drinkard; the identity of the specific newspaper is not included on the xerox copy in the author's files.) As a cogent example of the ethical level at which defense debates can occur, when Under Secretary DeLauer made that statement, he and Senator Kassebaum had never met. They did shortly after—at Kassebaum's invitation.

Even so, their talents went well beyond combat aircraft design. They were also the godfathers of a new land warfare doctrine for the Marine Corps and the Army, used in Operations Desert Storm and Iraqi Freedom with greatly acclaimed success. Boyd[†] also wrote an analysis of warfare itself that many continue to study today.

He and his closest friends also had ideas to change how the Pentagon armed and supported U.S. armed forces. One of the ideas that Kassebaum and the Military Reform Caucus picked up was better weapons testing. She threw her support to a bill introduced by Sens. David Pryor (D-Ark.) and Bill Roth (R-Del.) to establish a new Pentagon office to run combat-realistic testing, known as operational testing, and make it independent of the military services and others who designed and developed the same weapons. As Pryor put it, the bill prevented the students from grading their own exams.

The bill became law over bitter opposition from the Pentagon. The hostility continued after enactment, and Secretary of Defense Weinberger professed he was unable to find anyone to run the new office the bill established. He asked Kassebaum to recommend a candidate. With my assistance, Kassebaum conducted a search and ultimately accepted a recommendation from John Boyd to put forward the name of an Air Force colonel, James Burton. He had been running various weapons tests, insisting that they be realistic and that the results be accurately reported, which—to put it mildly—did not make him popular with weapons advocates in DoD. Kassebaum felt, however, that he was, in her words, "ideal."

Burton had not asked for the job for himself and knew some in the Pentagon would be more than a little upset about Kassebaum's nominating him. To help protect him from retaliation, Boyd asked Kassebaum for a favor before she put forward Burton's name as her candidate: namely, that Weinberger be asked to ensure that if Burton were not selected for the position, he would be allowed to complete his current assignment testing the Army's Bradley Infantry Fighting Vehicle. Kassebaum agreed.

On 24 April 1984, she sent a letter on her personal stationery to Weinberger and followed it up with a personal phone call to him. Although Weinberger's staff failed to give him the letter and tried to discourage Kassebaum from talking to Weinberger about Burton, they did eventually connect after Kassebaum persisted. She asked for the assurance Boyd requested but got no promise from Weinberger in return. Weinberger did interview Burton for the job, but then things quickly went downhill. A different

---

[†] There are two biographies about Boyd: *Boyd: The Fighter Pilot Who Changed the Art of War* by Robert Coram (New York: Little, Brown & Co., 2002) and *The Mind of War: John Boyd and American Security* by Grant T. Hammond (Washington, D.C.: Smithsonian Institution Press, 2001).

candidate was offered the job, and, as feared, the Pentagon bureaucracy went after Burton.

And for good reason—Burton was driving the Army crazy with his efforts to test the Bradley. The Army had promised Congress that the Bradley could fight on the European battlefield and effectively protect the crew and infantry squad carried inside. Burton was trying to find out if the vehicle was truly capable of doing so. He wanted the vehicle realistically loaded with fuel and ammunition to determine how vulnerable it was to hostile fire and explosion; the Army wanted the flammables removed. He wanted to use Soviet RPG-7 antitank rockets (which were then and remain today the world's most prevalent antiarmor weapon); the Army wanted to use a much less common, and weaker, Romanian weapon. Burton wanted soldier dummies inside the vehicle; the Army wanted them watered down with a hose first. And so on. He fought the efforts to phony up the tests at every turn, and the vehicle was tested much as he insisted. The results were disastrous. The Bradley proved to be extremely vulnerable to the RPG-7, and other weapons as well.

As the fights over the Bradley tests progressed, the Army decided to solve its problem creatively—by getting rid of Burton. Senior Army generals spoke with Burton's superiors in the Air Force. Together, they found a solution. Congress had passed legislation to require DoD to reduce overhead by 5 percent. Five percent in the office where Burton worked meant one position. One slot was already vacant in the office; Burton was the only Air Force representative there, and the Army had three. Burton was, of course, selected for elimination. As an Air Force general explained to him, none of it was personal, but if he did not want to be reassigned, he could always retire from the Air Force.

I explained it all to Kassebaum.[9] To my very great surprise, she felt no compunction to do anything to help Burton. While Burton himself steadfastly refused to ask her to intervene, Boyd met with her to do so, and I, as her staff, urged her to. I believed it was a question of honor to protect someone whose name she had put forward to a hostile Pentagon and who was quite obviously being punished for the "crime" of realistically testing military equipment—an issue Kassebaum had used to help make a name for herself. Instead, she chose to parse the situation legalistically: Burton was not being punished because she had nominated him for the testing job; he was being punished for insisting too aggressively that the Bradley be tested realistically, she argued. Therefore, she was not responsible for his being punished and had no obligation, moral or otherwise, to help him.

Burton made himself available to her when she had asked. He was being victimized for trying to do his job in a manner consistent with what she said was her agenda for the Defense Department. It was her own nominee being trampled by the unrepentant DoD bureaucracy. The people who had helped her become a national figure on defense issues were asking for help. None of it mattered.

I was never able to discern if there was some other reason for Kassebaum's inaction: whether Weinberger asked her to lay off; whether she had grown wary of Burton's, Boyd's, and the other reformers' uncompromising approach to defense issues, or what. I seriously considered resignation but talked myself out of it. My relationship with Senator Kassebaum became one that included an undertow—never fully articulated—that made the relationship polite but never again so successful or satisfying.

Things turned out better for Burton, temporarily at least. Although they had not, like Kassebaum, taken the lead in advocating Burton to Weinberger, other members of Congress—Sens. David Pryor (D-Ark.) and Charles Grassley (R-Iowa), and Reps. Denny Smith (R-Ore.) and Mel Levine (D-Calif.)—were incensed at the Pentagon's behavior. They wrote to Weinberger and caused enough of a public stink that DoD was embarrassed into inaction against Burton. On his part, Burton continued to insist on realistic Bradley testing, and major modifications to improve survivability for the crew resulted. Indeed, when the Army was preparing for Operation Desert Storm in 1991, the U.S. commander, Gen. Norman Schwarzkopf, learned that the Bradleys sent to him in Saudi Arabia were not the models that were modified after Burton's tests. He had them all replaced with ones that were.

By then, however, Burton had left the Air Force. By being so uncompromising, he made too many enemies in high places in the Army. Discussions again occurred with senior Air Force generals; Burton was forced to retire.

As they say, "politics can make strange bedfellows"; it also makes impermanent bedfellows. According to the thinking of many senators, such alliances are not only temporary, they run in just one direction.

The $40 Billion Ego

He had just cast an extremely difficult vote; I was proud of him and knew that day, 12 October 2000, was one I would remember. Sen. Pete Domenici (R-N.Mex.) knew others would remember it, too: he would take a lot of political heat for what he had just done. However, the proposal was tremendously expensive, and the Armed Services Committee had presented it in an underhanded way.

The issue was health care for military retirees. After spending twenty or more years in the armed services, military retirees had to rely on Medicare when they turned sixty-five. That made them unhappy. They were promised free health care when they enlisted. Moreover, they had paid for free health care with their blood. Medicare was not just a lousy system, they said; it also cost them their own money. It was a politically powerful argument: the nation was not treating military retirees with the respect they deserved. It was also irresistible; a large and vocal constituency, military retirees, was applying the pressure. In a system where senators are attentive to small groups of constituents, the 1,900,000 military retirees nationwide easily commanded members of Congress's adoring attention.[10]

The retirees' proposal to solve their problem was expensive. It gave them a whole new health care system. It was to be called "Tricare for Life." The Congressional Budget Office said it would cost more than $40 billion in the first ten years.

The arguments against Tricare for Life were neither simple nor superficially compelling. The costs would put a big squeeze on the other parts of the DoD budget, especially its already high weapons and readiness accounts. It could be a mistake to single out the military retiree population with a plan that other elderly citizens could not receive. Nonmilitary civilians would ask why should DoD give its retirees three health care systems (at military facilities, Medicare, and Tricare) while everyone else received only the unsatisfactory Medicare program. The costs of giving Tricare to everybody would be gigantic. Some said that it was baloney that servicemen had been promised "free healthcare for life"—the glib promises of recruitment officers were not legally binding. One senator, Bob Kerrey (D-Neb.), made the comment that the Navy must owe him many airline tickets because when he enlisted he was told, "join the Navy, see the world."[11]

None of these or any other concerns received any real attention because of the way the Senate Armed Services Committee handled the issue. The committee's chairman, John Warner (R-Va.), did not hold serious hearings to examine the pros and cons of the various plans. When the Senate considered the committee's annual National Defense Authorization bill, he put forward a very strange proposal. It paid for the "Tricare for Life" program for just two years and then directed that the program self-destruct. But Warner was describing his plan as if it were permanent.

The reasons for the truncated program in the bill were obscure but simple. Warner was circumventing the Senate's budget rules. One of those rules puts a limit on the amount of spending for new entitlement programs the Senate could consider. The extra costs of any new program for the first ten years had to be offset with savings. If they were not, the proposal was subject to a "point of order" that made the idea nondebatable. It took sixty votes to waive the point of order. Warner could not find all the savings needed to offset the $40 billion "Tricare for Life" program, and he did not want to face the need for sixty votes to waive the budget rules. Thus, he decided to have his political cake and eat it, too: he limited the life of the new program to the number of years for which his staff could find the off-sets to pay for it, two meager years. That technically avoided the budget point of order and the need to find sixty votes. Later, he could add a provision making the whole thing permanent. After perfunctory discussion, Warner had the Senate ram through his bizarre amendment with a "voice vote."

Warner had a ways to go to get through the legislative labyrinth. His amendment was adopted only for Senate passage of the National Defense Authorization bill; the House had adopted no such amendment and an entirely different bill altogether for the overall fiscal year 2001 defense program. This and hundreds of other differences had to be resolved in a House-Senate "conference" consisting of the senior members of the House and Senate Armed Services Committees.

After weeks of wrangling over all the issues, the conferees decided to give permanent life to the Warner proposal. Unfortunately, however, this brought back the immense costs and the possibility that some senator would object under the budget rules and force Warner to find sixty votes when the bill came back to the Senate for final approval. Warner's staff bragged to me that no one would commit "political suicide" by taking on the politically active military retirement community and challenging their $40 billion program. No one on the Armed Services Committee had those guts; so surely no others would. They had also done their homework and pointedly told me the 20,266 military retirees in Domenici's state of New Mexico would appreciate his support. "Be smart," I was told; encourage Domenici to over-look the budget rules—it was "good politics."

When the high-cost political steamroller came back to the Senate in the form of a "conference report" for final approval, we knew at the Budget Committee that we had a problem. The $40 billion cost was immense (it later was apparent this estimate by the Congressional Budget Office was too low); other parts of the budget might be depleted to pay for this program, and if it were seen as a model for others, Medicare costs would explode even more in the future than they were already programmed to. As the chairman of the Budget Committee, Domenici would be expected to express himself if there were any serious concerns, and there were plenty. However, how could any "smart" staffer tell his boss to stand in the way of this steamroller, and how could any "good" politician take such advice?

We obtained more cost data from CBO; we collected arguments on the implications for the future from the Congressional Research Service (CRS) and from other professional staffers on the Budget Committee, and we even tried, unsuccessfully, to get Secretary of Defense William Cohen to utter a whimper of concern about the costs. The Republican staff director of the Budget Committee, Bill Hoagland, and I took the data and the arguments to Domenici. He did not like the costs or the implications either. He also believed the federal government had to do something about health care for retirees, military and otherwise, but this was not the way to do it. Domenici had decided to take the rocky high road. He supported a budget point of order against the Warner proposal.

By contemporary Senate standards, there was a pretty good debate. Both sides made their points, substantive and political, and there was a real back and forth—not the usual scripted speeches seriatim. Nonetheless, Domenici and a few other senators were creamed. Not only did we fail to get to the ostensibly obtainable forty votes needed to win, we got only a paltry nine.

Immediately after the vote, Domenici and I were on our way back to his office in the Hart Senate Office Building, where his press secretary was waiting—nervous and unhappy—to help us put together a press release explaining why he had just voted as he had. Domenici was not happy either; he knew he had done the right thing, and now he had to pay the price.

Other senators did not see it quite that way.

The elevator doors opened in the basement of the Hart building for Domenici and me to get to his office. Already in the car were a bunch of senators, smiling and laughing. There were several, but I only specifically remember one. "Come on in, Pete, there's room" someone said. I wedged myself in as well. There was banter about the vote the Senate had just held.

"Boy, that was the worst vote I ever cast," one of the other senators said with a loud laugh. I looked to see who it was. At first, I did not recognize him; he was young, not like most senators, and handsome. It was John Edwards (D-N.C.). Edwards was only a freshman, but he was no political novice. He was already being talked about as a Democratic Party possibility for the presidency or vice presidency. He had voted in favor of the Warner proposal but apparently had done so to curry favor with the military retirement community. I felt both surprised and disgusted that a senator would say what Edwards had just uttered in the circumstances.

With those words, Edwards spoke volumes about Senate politics and national defense. He had just spent $40 billion on a program that needed much more scrutiny. He made it clear to me he knew that, but that did not overcome his apparent compulsion to do the "smart," and easy, thing. To me, it seemed that the question in Senator Edwards's mind was, Should the nation endure a dubious and expensive proposal, or should Edwards's political comfort be disrupted?

How Ninety-nine Senators Saved the Republic

Sometimes, the Senate sinks to unintended humor.

From 18 to 28 June 2002, the Senate was debating the National Defense Authorization Act for Fiscal Year 2003. The debate was desultory; the bill had become the target of senators eager to add the usual projects for their home states and of senators trying to make some sort of broader point, but not one related to defense. One amendment that took two days to debate was from the 2002 chairman of the Budget Committee, Kent Conrad (D-N.Dak.), to insert a congressional budget resolution into the defense-spending bill. It had no business being a part of that bill, but in the Senate, you can at least try to add anything to anything. Then, Sen. Kay Bailey Hutchison (R-Tex.) threatened an amendment on the marriage penalty tax. Senators Tom Daschle and Trent Lott, the Democratic and Republican leaders, put their collective feet down and demanded only "defense-related" amendments for the rest of the Senate's time on the bill.[12]

Immediately thereafter the Senate spent several hours debating the important "defense-related" subject of abortion (for military personnel). The next amendment addressed U.S. female military personnel being forced to wear scarves (abayas) in public in Saudi Arabia. Then, they moved to an amendment favored by labor unions to reopen privately contracted DoD work for federal employees. All this occurred without a peep from Senators Daschle and Lott.

The National Defense Authorization Act was continuing on a slow track to nowhere, despite the fact that the United States was fighting a war against terrorism and threatening an invasion of Iraq.

Then, the U.S. Senate collectively leapt into action to defend the republic. Sen. Bill Nelson (D-Fla.) made an announcement with a "heavy heart."[13] Sen. Tim Johnson (D-S.Dak.) felt "shock and dismay."[14] Sen. Joe Lieberman (D-Conn.) expressed "outrage and amazement."[15] Deputy Minority Leader Harry Reid (D-Nev.) called it "senseless."[16] Leader Daschle said it was "nuts."[17] Sen. Robert Byrd (D-W.Va.) announced, "I, for one, am not going to stand for this."[18] Armed Services Committee Chairman Warner said, "I join my friends in expressing our grave concern."[19] That opened the door for action; it was his bill the Senate had been debating. Thereupon, the Senate took up and passed, by a vote of 99–0, a measure—drafted and agreed to by both parties in a matter of minutes—to deal with the matter.

What was it? Word of a new terrorist attack? Did an enemy develop a surprise weapon?

It was the news that a three-judge panel of the U.S. Court of Appeals of the Ninth Circuit had ruled the phrase "one nation under God" in the Pledge of Allegiance unconstitutional. Knowing easy political meat when it was on the table, the senators rushed to the chamber to express their outrage. So heartfelt was their concern that even after their unanimous vote, many (Leahy, Daschle [for a second time], Bennett, Feinstein, Levin, Burns, Allen, Brownback, Sessions, Clinton, Smith, and Hollings) kept on talking about it until there was, almost literally, nothing more to say.[20]

And, what did they do to end this grave offense to the nation? They passed what is called a "simple" Senate resolution, which had no legal force, to express that "the Senate strongly disapproves of the ninth circuit decision."[21] The staffers on the back benches in the chamber were unsurprised by the comic opera, but the amount of eye rolling reached near record proportions.

And, what of the National Defense Authorization bill they had been debating? They got back to business as usual. The first action after the eruption cauterizing the wound inflicted by the Court of Appeals was to adopt a "managers' package" of amendments, containing forty-eight different parts, consisting of spending for projects in the home state of the authors or proposals that were altogether irrelevant to the war against terrorism.

Arrogance of this sort is difficult to measure over time. I cannot say that the level of what I observed at the end of my career was higher than what I observed at the start. However, it does seem the self-inflating behavior has grown more corrosive. In the past, it mostly expressed itself as a matter of style, or in Senate business only at intervals; moreover, at least some could rise above it. Today, arrogance, in the form of self-directed benefit with no heed for the consequences, is a constant expression of public business that no one seems to rise above. It is almost that the Senate has institutionalized the behavior.

That is a tough accusation to make. However, a detailed inspection of Congress's behavior in the aftermath of September 11 will reveal the extent of members' self-preoccupation and how it degrades U.S. national security. We will now turn to that discussion. Up to now, we have only scratched the surface.

II
Pork: It's Worse Than You've Been Told

3

War Is Not Hell: It's an Opportunity

The sequence of the September 11 terror attacks and Congress's subsequent passage of national defense bills demonstrates how members of Congress believe they should respond to a crisis and support U.S. armed forces in a new war. To understand, defense legislation basics require some explanation.*

The Legislative Framework

Each year, Congress handles three major bills that support the Department of Defense. They are

- The Department of Defense Authorization bill, which consists of hundreds of pages codifying a myriad of major and minor defense policies and programs, ranging from how to structure a national missile defense to whether to extend "multiyear" procurement contracts for medium-sized trucks. This bill is the major annual work product of the House and Senate Armed Services Committees.
- The Department of Defense Appropriations bill, which sets the level of funding for programs and the terms and conditions upon which that money may be made available. This bill is one of several major appropriations bills; it emanates from the Defense Subcommittees of the House and Senate Appropriations Committees.
- The Military Construction Appropriations bill, which does the same thing as the DoD Appropriations bill but only for DoD's facilities in the United States and abroad. The House and Senate Military Construction Subcommittees of the respective Appropriations Committees draft this bill.

Each year, usually in February, the president submits his request for these bills, and in the subsequent months—ideally before 30 September when the new fiscal year starts—they make their way through the legislative process.

---

* This and the next chapter are based in part on the author's 2002 essay "Mr. Smith Is Dead." As explained in the preface, the essay resulted in the author's resignation of his job with the Senate Budget Committee. The original was written during the holiday congressional recess of 2001–2, immediately after Congress completed its action on the FY 2002 defense bills. It was widely distributed on the Internet in 2002 and published by the Center for Defense Information in October 2002.

In 2001 President George W. Bush submitted only a preliminary request for DoD authorizations and appropriations in February; his requests were incomplete until July, thereby delaying the process. As a result, both the House and Senate had not considered their various bills until *after* September 11. This permitted Congress the opportunity to incorporate into each bill any and all reactions members had to the September 11 terrorist attacks. The sequence of events presented virtual test-tube conditions to explore members' collective and individual values on defense in a circumstance where one would hope to find the members at their best.

To Each According to Status

Of the three annual defense bills, the Military Construction Appropriations bill is the smallest and the simplest. It consists of just a few pages, and it provides roughly $10 billion for building facilities and housing on U.S. military bases. The House debated and passed this bill on 21 September by a vote of 401–0; the Senate handled it on 26 September and passed it by a vote of 97–0. The House and Senate resolved their differences and acted on a "conference report" on 18 October with votes of 409–1 and 96–1, respectively. Congress then sent it to the president, who signed it into law on 5 November. Note that a grand total of 2 members of Congress, out of a possible 535, expressed any unease with the bill by voting against it.

Bush originally requested $9.8 billion for the bill. Congress appropriated $10.5 billion. Not bad, a $700 million increase. Surely, Congress was augmenting the U.S. base infrastructure to help fight the war. Probably adding things like more and better training facilities and augmented protection against terrorist attack, right?

Not exactly. Congress did insert training facilities and a new security-related construction project, but they totaled just 3 of the 120 projects Congress added. The balance constituted a hodgepodge, including plans for a new museum, a new chapel, gyms, warehouses, fire stations, water towers, land acquisition, day care centers, National Guard armories, and much else. They were all routine additions and were typical of the pork Congress adds to peacetime military construction budgets every year.[*]

The additional projects cost more than the $700 million Congress added to the bill. To wedge them in, the Military Construction subcommittees used two gimmicks: first, they decided that in fiscal year 2002 the value of

---

[*] In 2002 Sen. John McCain's Web site included a formal definition of pork at http: mccain.senate.gov/pork02.htm. Hard copy is in the author's files. Put simply, "pork" is a spending project not requested by the president in his budget nor by the Joint Chiefs of Staff in their back door "wish lists," discussed later. In addition, "pork" is usually, but not always, directed at the state or congressional district of the member seeking to add it to authorizations or appropriations bills.

the dollar would increase over foreign currencies for the costs of military construction projects in foreign nations by $60 million—this despite the absence of any such predictions by independent economists, such as the Congressional Budget Office. Second, the subcommittees wrote into the bill a 1.127 percent "across-the-board" reduction which arbitrarily deemed any and all projects, regardless of their priority or whatever overfunding—or underfunding—they might actually contain, to cost that much less. With the help of these alterations, the extra projects fit like magic within the $10.5 billion allocated by the chairmen of the House and Senate Appropriations Committees for military construction. The two devices made another $200 million available for the added projects.

The locations of the projects added were even more interesting. Eleven states received added projects totaling $25 million or more. The number one beneficiary was California: it received eight projects that were not requested by the president; they cost $144 million, or 16 percent of the $900 million added by Congress. Next was Texas: ten new construction projects with a value of $86 million, 9 percent of the additions. Not coincidentally, senators from these two states served in the Senate Appropriations Committee as the chairman and ranking minority member* of the Military Construction Subcommittee. They were Sen. Dianne Feinstein (D-Calif.) and Sen. Kay Bailey Hutchison (R-Tex.), respectively. Feinstein's priorities included accelerated environmental cleanup at Hunter's Point Naval Shipyard and McClellan Air Force Base, a new barracks complex at the Monterey Language Institute, and a new fire station at March Air Force Reserve Base. Hutchison added upgrades in air conditioning and water facilities at Corpus Christi Naval Air Station, new water treatment facilities at Fort Bliss, a new gym at Sheppard Air Force Base, and $6 million in airfield lighting at Kingsville Naval Air Station.

Environmental cleanup, gyms, fire stations, and lights are all nice things to have, and the recipient bases very probably benefited from them. But, is this the best Congress can do to sharpen our armed forces to fight more effectively against terrorists and governments that harbor them?

The pattern continued. The third-biggest winner was West Virginia, for which the president had requested no military construction projects but for which the appropriators added five, including a new Army National Guard armory at Williamstown and plans to renovate an Army museum at Martinsburg. These and three other projects cost $44 million. West Virginia

---

* A ranking minority member is the member from the party in the minority in the House or Senate who is the most senior member of that party on a committee or subcommittee. Were that party to become the majority party in the House or Senate, that member would become chairman.

just happened to be represented by Democrat Robert Byrd, who also happened to be the chairman of the full Senate Appropriations Committee. Not far down the list was Alaska, with three projects for $29 million, which just happened to be represented by Republican Ted Stevens, the most senior Republican on the Appropriations Committee. And so it went; in all, the top eleven benefactors for their states and congressional districts were senior Democrats and Republicans in the House or Senate who just happened to be the sitting chairmen or ranking minority members of the Appropriations and Armed Services committees and subcommittees that handled the Department of Defense and its military construction budgets.*

Altogether, these eleven states and their senators and representatives consumed $511 million in new, unrequested projects: put another way, 22 percent of the states got 57 percent of the money Congress added to the Military Construction bill. Conversely, the thirteen states receiving the smallest add-ons—just $10 million or less—were, with one exception,† represented by senators or congressmen who had no senior position on the committees or subcommittees overseeing DoD or military construction.‡ In those cases, 26 percent of the states got a total of $56 million, or 7 percent of the add-ons.

In distributing additional military construction projects, the thing that matters in Congress is who you are. If you are a senior member of the Appropriations Committee or its Military Construction Subcommittee or the commensurate structure in the Armed Services Committees, you get the goodies. If you are not in this hierarchy, you do not.

The Mismatch of Words and Deeds

When the Senate debated the Military Construction bill, one finds pages in the *Congressional Record* replete with rhetorical flourishes about how dutiful

---

* There was one exception to this rule: number eleven was the state of Nevada, which had no top of the heap representation on DoD or military construction committees or subcommittees. However, Sen. Harry Reid (D-Nev.) was the Majority Whip of the Senate, and he was the chairman of the Energy-Water Subcommittee of the Senate Appropriations Committee, which handles Department of Energy nuclear weapons matters.

† Wisconsin, represented by the ranking Democrat on the House Appropriations Committee, David Obey.

‡ One might argue that members with large and numerous military bases in their state or congressional district would tend to sit on these committees and subcommittees and therefore properly add proportionally larger military construction budgets. This is frequently not the case. For example, West Virginia, Florida, Alaska, New York, and New Jersey, which have relatively few and small military bases, persist among the top military construction recipients. It is also true that members not on the military construction subcommittees also represent districts and states with large military bases. For example, the list of <$10 million "losers" includes North Carolina and Kansas, which have substantial military bases. A statistical analysis will show that senior membership on military construction subcommittees correlates significantly more with added projects than do states with large military bases.

senators found themselves meeting the nation's needs as it went to war. The Military Construction Subcommittee chairwoman, Senator Feinstein, was at the head of this procession:

> Given the events of the past few weeks [i.e., September 11 and its aftermath], and the events that we expect to unfold over the coming weeks and months, this bill could not be more timely. This bill was reported out of the full Appropriations Committee only yesterday. We moved it to the floor today in acknowledgment of the pressures under which we are currently operating. Our men and women in uniform cannot afford delay in getting these projects under way. We have a duty to provide better for the members of our military and their families, especially at a time when the president has ordered them to "be ready" for war.[1]

Having laden the bill with $144 million in pork for her own home state and doing virtually nothing elsewhere in the bill to aid the war against terror, Feinstein was posturing that her handiwork was both relevant and urgent. She may have been in a hurry, but rushing help to the troops in the field was not manifest in her actions, as opposed to her words. Feinstein was not alone.

The Quintessence of Irrelevance and Self-Protection

On 21 September, just ten days after the terror attacks, the Senate started its debate on the National Defense Authorization Act for Fiscal Year 2002. The chairman of the Senate Armed Services Committee, Sen. Carl Levin of Michigan, and the ranking Republican, Sen. John Warner of Virginia, made moving statements about September 11 and the importance of their bill.

> **Levin**: [T]his is no ordinary time in our country. . . . [O]ur fellow citizens continue to sift through the ruins left by the most deadly attack ever against the United States. Our fury at those who attack innocents is matched by our determination to protect our citizens from more terror and by our resolve to track down, root out, and relentlessly pursue the terrorists and those who would shelter or harbor them.[2]

> **Warner:** Today, as the Senate turns to the consideration of our national defense authorization bill for the year 2002, in this time of national emergency, it is time we provide our President and the men and women of the Armed Forces, and the thousands of civilians who support those men and women, the requirements that they have for the coming fiscal year as best we can judge them.[3]

The Senate debate on this bill took seven days. The body considered and adopted seventy-nine different amendments. Very few had much to do with the war against terrorism, declared rhetorically by the president in a special joint session of Congress just the night before the Senate took up the bill. A few amendments did relevant things, such as make available Arabic language training at the Defense Language Institute's Foreign Language Center, an amendment offered by Democratic Sen. Jeff Bingaman of New Mexico, or provide for training of reserve personnel for incidents involving weapons of mass destruction, an amendment jointly offered by Sens. Kit Bond of Missouri (a Republican) and Byrd of West Virginia.[4] However, far more were either irrelevant or pure pork, or both. In all, of the seventy-nine amendments adopted, thirty-eight directly increased spending for the state of the amendment's author for an unrequested project; another twenty-six did not appear to address the author's home state, but they were in no way relevant to the war against terrorism or the September 11 attacks.

Fifteen amendments were in some way relevant, but they were also marginal. In addition to the Bingaman and Bond-Byrd amendments cited above, a relevant amendment by Warner authorized payment of hostile fire pay to certain civilian employees of the federal government who were attacked on September 11.[5] Virtually none of these or other amendments was urgent or important to the war.

A senior and respected defense correspondent, Pat Towell, of the usually dry and unopinionated *Congressional Quarterly,* expressed a surprisingly negative assessment of the Senate's action on this bill:

> Each year, Congress' defense authorization bill moves on its own clock, seemingly unconnected from world developments.
>
> That has never been more clear than it is this year. The current war on terrorist forces in Afghanistan—what Joint Chiefs Chairman Gen. Richard Myers on October 18 called the most important task that the military has been handed since the Second World War—is affecting the legislation only at the margins. . . .
>
> Overall, the bill that would authorize one-third of a trillion dollars for national defense in fiscal year 2002 is likely to be remarkably unaffected by the Sept. 11 terrorist attacks and the U.S. response.
>
> The most contentious issue before the conference [appointed to resolve differences between the House- and Senate-passed versions of the bill] is Bush's request—supported by the Senate and adamantly opposed by House Republicans—for a new round of military base closings in 2003.[6]

Indeed, the president's request to permit DoD to stop wasting money on unneeded military bases and to consolidate activities on remaining bases absorbed more time and energy during Congress's consideration of this bill than any other issue. It provoked a major debate in the Senate, and it caused a contentious argument consuming several weeks of sporadic meetings of the House-Senate conference committee that was attempting to resolve differences in the legislation.

Military base closings are dreaded in Congress. Even if it means that DoD can save money and make the military services more efficient, and even if studies have shown that a locale cannot just recover from the lost jobs but grow economically by converting a closed military facility into an industrial park or other commercial enterprise, members of Congress almost universally believe that closing a military base in their state or district is terrible news. The immediate local reaction is always negative, and constituents look to members of Congress to protect them. A member who fails to do so is seen as ineffective and/or insensitive to local needs and could be vulnerable in the next election. To a member of Congress, the most important thing to remember is that a base closing can cost people jobs, not just those of the folks back home but also the member's.

As a result, many of the Senate Armed Services Committee conferees to the DoD authorization bill were eager to overturn behind closed doors in the House-Senate conference their body's decision in a 53–47 vote to endorse a new round of base closings in 2003. However, as the reversal was being contemplated, Secretary of Defense Donald Rumsfeld found out about it and informed the conferees that if they undid the new round of closings, he would recommend that Bush veto the entire bill. Because Rumsfeld's public performance in response to the September 11 attacks had so favorably impressed the press and the public, the politicians on Capitol Hill knew he had the weight to make the veto threat stick.

The members of Congress caved to Rumsfeld, but they added a catch. They retained the base closing provision, but they delayed it until 2005. That was a convenient date: not only would that be just after, not before, a congressional election, it was also far enough into the future that during the intervening time some helpful member would have the opportunity to repeal the unwanted provision, thereby showing how much he or she cared for their district.* Rumsfeld very probably knew he was being had. After the 2005 deal was announced, he told the press he was "very disappointed," adding: "What that means is that the United States will continue to have

---

* That effort did, indeed, occur in 2003; it failed, however, after Rumsfeld made another veto threat. The effort repeated itself in 2004. As this book went to press, the result was undetermined.

something like 20 percent to 25 percent more bases than we need. We will be spending money . . . that is being wasted to manage and maintain bases we don't need. Given the war on terror, we will be doing something even more egregious, and that is we will be providing force protection on bases that we do not need."[7]

He went on to say he wanted to "sleep on" whether he would still recommend a veto. Probably realizing that in Washington a spurned compromise—even a bad one—can lead to an ugly fight, Rumsfeld did not recommend a veto. The president agreed and signed the bill into law on 10 January 2002.

Just like the Military Construction bill, the FY 2002 DoD authorization bill passed by Congress was indistinguishable from a peacetime bill. There were no major changes to the pre–September 11 request from the president except to riddle the bill with pork, irrelevancies, and marginal provisions and to delay by two years any effort to save money, or divert it to other defense programs, by closing excess military facilities.

Hard-Core Porkers

Defenders of Congress's actions in the aftermath of September 11 might argue that the criticism here is inappropriate because Congress withheld its constructive response to September 11 for a specific measure, which addressed the president's request to rebuild after the attacks and to pursue the war against the Taliban in Afghanistan and al Qaeda. That measure is the 2002 Department of Defense Appropriations bill and an emergency supplemental attached to it.

This bill, H.R. 3338, provided $317 billion for the Department of Defense for all of its programs and policies, except military construction, for FY 2002. In addition, both the House and Senate attached an "emergency supplemental" amounting to an additional $20 billion specifically to help recover from the attacks on New York and the Pentagon, to strengthen homeland security against further terrorist attack, and to fight the conflict in Afghanistan.* The House passed its version on 28 November. The Senate took it up on 6 December and on 7 December, which being Pearl Harbor Day was a particularly cogent anniversary.

Most of the Senate's debate involved the Democrats' contention that the $20 billion was insufficient. The chairman of the Appropriations Committee

---

* This $20 billion emergency supplemental completed action on a $40 billion supplemental the president requested in September immediately after the attacks. The first $20 billion emergency supplemental is not assessed here—other than to say that it specified only in the vaguest terms how the money was to be spent and does not constitute the basis for an appraisal of Congress's values and behavior other than to hand the president a virtual $20 billion blank check.

and the generally acknowledged master of Senate parliamentary procedure, Byrd led the effort, seeking to add another $15 billion. That exercise ran its course and lost its steam after the Republicans found enough votes to hold the line at $20 billion. The maneuvering on this matter also entailed an Inouye-Stevens substitute (discussed below) that replaced and redistributed the $20 billion emergency supplemental sought by the president.

While this legislative-political wrangle was being worked out, Sen. John McCain (R-Ariz.) interjected himself to object to the pork that the Appropriations Committee had larded into its substitute measure. His staff had found no less than $2.144 billion in unrequested, unjustified state-specific additions in the regular DoD portions of the bill and another $1.457 billion in the emergency supplemental parts. His speech was impassioned and compelling: "In provisions too numerous to mention, this bill time and time again chooses to fund porkbarrel projects with little, if any, relationship to national defense at a time of scarce resources, budget deficits, and underfunded urgent defense priorities."[8]

While this speech was being offered in front of the Senate's C-SPAN cameras, an on-the-scene observer would have noticed a constant level of activity in the off-camera recesses of the Senate chamber. This action was the staff of senators conducting their bosses' business. Were they rushing to extract their state's pork and other venal provisions from the bill having been embarrassed by the ever-aggressive, "pork-busting" McCain? Were they rushing to inject new ideas and money to fight the war in Afghanistan to make up for previous inadequacies?

Not exactly. In fact, the Senate's reaction to McCain's "pork-buster" speech was to increase the pork in the bill. The staff activity before, during, and after McCain's speech involved cutting various deals with the Appropriations Committee to add scores of additional state projects. Senators and staff were acquiring the consent of Senators Inouye and Stevens to add new amendments to the bill. This occurred quietly in what are called "managers' packages," packages adopted by a voice vote with no record of who supported and who opposed the various provisions, and with little or no discussion of the content. The curious among the public can uncover the contents the next day when the texts of the various amendments are printed in the *Congressional Record*.

The managers' packages were a thing to behold. They consisted of 111 separate amendments.[9] According to one analysis, they added another $378 million in pork to the bill,[10] thereby bringing the grand total to $4 billion.

About 72 of these amendments were typical pork for the home state of the author: grants to non-defense corporations, additional long-term research for obscure labs, public health research, and more.[11] The rest, some

30 amendments, were irrelevancies: aid to small businesses,[12] an increase in the number of general trustees for the John F. Kennedy Center for the Performing Arts,[13] loan guarantees for Alaskan fisheries,[14] and instructions to change rules for using funds to operate federally owned buildings.[15]

All of this was much like the shenanigans performed on the DoD authorization bill. However, there was more of it on this appropriations bill; it was all done immediately after one senator had objected to precisely this behavior, and it just happened to be 7 December, Pearl Harbor Day.

For the U.S. Senate, war is not hell; it's an opportunity.

Kicking It Up a Notch

Some senators were out for bigger game.

One of the indirect effects of September 11 was to depress not just the air travel industry but also the U.S. airliner production industry: i.e., Boeing. Some believed Boeing needed a bail-out package, and one was put together. Almost certainly, it exceeded Boeing's wildest dreams.

Ted Stevens wanted to help Boeing, but in a specific way. He was an advocate of hardware acquisition for DoD not just through normal procurement, where the rules required all the money to be paid "up front"; he also liked the idea of leasing hardware. Leasing had two advantages to Stevens's type of thinking: first, it is paid for out of DoD's O&M account, rather than the Procurement account. This had the benefit of not using up what he believed to be scarce procurement dollars and permitted more dollars for additional hardware. It did not seem to trouble him that O&M also paid for training, spare parts, depot maintenance, and other "readiness" activities and that these accounts would be pinched by converting O&M into a second procurement account.

Second, if the congressional and executive budget rules could be bent just a teeny-weeny bit, a lease could be paid out "incrementally" during its course, rather than using "full" (up-front) funding as required by guidelines from the Office of Management and Budget (OMB) and the Congressional Budget Office (CBO). With "incremental" funding, the cost impact for the initial years of a "lease purchase" is reduced, and money is freed up—but only in the beginning—to start up or continue other hardware programs.

Shortly after September 11, Stevens called the Air Force. He told them he wanted a proposal using "creative funding" to acquire new Boeing aircraft to replace part of the aging KC-135 air-tanker fleet.[*] He was ignoring the fact that the Air Force had deemed KC-135 replacements as so low a priority that it failed to include such procurement in its just completed

---

[*] These aircraft refuel others in mid-air. In doing so, they significantly extend the radius of action of both tactical fighter-bombers and long-range bombers.

"Quadrennial Defense Review" to reconsider how the Air Force should "transform" for the twenty-first century. He was also obviating a study the Air Force had been planning in 2002, called Analysis of Alternatives, to determine when it would be best to buy KC-135 replacements and what aircraft to buy. Stevens wanted those decisions accelerated; in fact, he had already made them;* he told the Air Force it was going to get the Boeing 767 aircraft (the line that would otherwise close down because of the airliner cancellation orders) and "creative funding" meant leasing.†

The compliant Air Force began littering Congress with briefings advocating two decisions. First, without performing any "Analysis of Alternatives," it decided the Boeing 767 was the replacement for the KC-135, and it needed one hundred of them.‡ Second, the Air Force announced it did not want to buy these one hundred aircraft; it wanted to lease, and then purchase (hence "lease-purchase") them. The proposal under discussion would cost $20 million per aircraft per year for ten years for $20 billion over the term of the leases. At the end of ten years, the lease could be extended, or the Air Force might be able to buy the aircraft for $1 each. Boeing was cogitating that. Sound like a good deal?

Not exactly. For a normal cash purchase, each 767 tanker was assessed at the time to cost $150–160 million, or $15–16 billion for all one hundred.§ That's $4 to $5 billion less than the lease. Using alternative methods to calibrate the costs, the results came out the same. With "nominal" dollars (calibrating the value of dollars to when they would actually be obligated),

---

* Not all of this decision-making may have been Stevens's. In 2003, *Defense Week* reported that about a month after Stevens made this phone call to the Air Force, he went to Seattle for a fundraiser the Boeing Company held for him. There, executives for Boeing's commercial aircraft lines, especially the 767, gave Stevens $22,000 in campaign donations. Stevens asserted that these donations came after his decision to advocate the deal, and there was no impropriety. However, it is also possible that Boeing first contacted Stevens, informed him what it needed, and asked for help. What explicit or implied promises of help were made for Stevens are unknown. (See "Boeing Payments to Senator Raise Questions," by John M. Donnelly, *Defense Week*, 2 September 2003.)

† Senator Stevens's "instructions" to the Air Force were described to the author by senior representatives of the Air Force, members of Senator Stevens's staff, and members of two Senate committees' staffs.

‡ The 767 is an excellent candidate for the air-tanker mission, but there are also compelling arguments for the Boeing 757. Its lower cost would mean a larger number of refueling aircraft. Thus, even though the 757 carries less fuel, a larger fleet of 757s could refuel more aircraft at one time than could a smaller fleet of bigger 767s, an important tactical consideration. There are other factors for and against the 757, and there is a third option that might be the most compelling—a mixed 757/767 fleet. We may never know; the Air Force decided it already had the answer to a question it had not studied.

§ Later, a study by the Institute for Defense Analyses found that an appropriate cost for the 767s as tankers would be $120.7 million per copy. (See GAO letter to Sen. John W. Warner, chairman, and Sen. Carl Levin, ranking member, Senate Armed Services Committee, 14 October 2003, GAO-04-164R Military Aircraft, p. 1.)

OMB estimated the purchase at $15.1 billion and the lease at $22 billion. That's $6.9 billion more for the lease. Under "net present value" calculations, OMB gave the purchase an almost $1 billion advantage.[16] Calculations inside the Office of Secretary of Defense gave an even larger cost advantage to buying, not leasing. DoD's Cost Analysis Improvement Group found a 15 percent cost advantage for a purchase and that a lease would exceed a purchase by almost $12 billion in nominal dollars over time.[17] CBO also performed a preliminary analysis of the different costs showing a major advantage for the purchase over the lease; however, fearful of retaliation from the irritable Stevens, CBO did not permit its analysis to be used publicly.[18] Later, CBO released several studies; in 2003 it found the savings from a purchase to be $5.5 billion.[19]

In addition to the higher cost, there still was another disadvantage to Stevens's lease-purchase. He would need not just fifty-one votes in the Senate to pass it; he would need a "super-majority" of sixty. Under Budget Act scoring rules enacted in 1990 after years of lease-purchase problems, OMB and CBO had been scoring all "budget authority" for a lease purchase when the government makes the commitment to acquiring the asset. According to a 2 November letter from OMB Director Mitch Daniels to the chairman of the Budget Committee, Sen. Kent Conrad, $13 billion would be needed in 2002 to cover the lease-purchase proposal according to OMB rules.[20] However, that is exactly what Stevens wanted to avoid; he wished to stretch out the payments into cosmetically more digestible— but ultimately more costly—payments, otherwise known as incremental funding. This was exactly the abuse the OMB/CBO scoring rules sought to obviate.*

In past years, when Republican Pete Domenici chaired the Senate Budget Committee, that committee frequently enforced the lease-purchase upfront scoring rule. Now Democrat Conrad was chairman; he had not been an activist in enforcing that particular rule, and he just happened to have in his state a squadron of KC-135 aircraft that might eventually be replaced by the new Boeing 767s. Boeing and Stevens's staff approached Conrad,

---

* The federal government has a lot of experience with incremental funding; none of it good. As Director Daniels said in his letter to Senator Conrad, in the past "[incremental] scoring hid the fact that these [lease] agreements had a higher economic cost than traditional direct purchases, and in some cases allowed projects to go forward despite significant cost overruns." That is why OMB and CBO insist on knowing and scoring the total cost of the lease-purchase commitment up front. Director Daniels is not alone; since 1996 GAO and other research organizations have produced at least eight studies on incremental funding, saying, for example, that it "erodes future fiscal flexibility," "limits cost visibility and accountability," and contributes to "cost overruns and schedule delays." (See Budget Issues: Incremental Funding of Capital Asset Acquisitions, U.S. General Accounting Office, Letter to Hon. Pete V. Domenici, chairman, Budget Committee, 26 February 2001, GAO-01-432R Incremental Funding of Capital Assets, p. 3.)

who was considering what he should do about the scoring rule. They made the senator an offer. The OMB and CBO scoring rules were different for "operating" leases, as opposed to lease purchases. Under a lease-purchase, the government is basically acquiring the item for its permanent use. Under an operating lease, the government is just making temporary use of the item, after which it will be returned to the original owner. They made a deal, whereby the lease-purchase of the one hundred 767s was rewritten as an operating lease. Scoring rules for such leases permitted the stretched-out (incremental) funding that Stevens wanted. Everybody was happy. Stevens got his incremental funding. The Air Force got its airplanes, and the new chairman of the Budget Committee got adherence to the OMP and CBO scoring rules.

There did remain one small problem. To transform the lease-purchase into an operating lease required changing the already bad idea into a truly horrible one. Under CBO's rules, there were three characteristics that distinguished a lease-purchase from an operating lease: one, the item in question had to be commercially available; two, the cost of the lease could not exceed 90 percent of the purchase price; and three, the item had to be returned to the original owner in its commercially available configuration at the end of ten years. This meant the 767 deal would have to go through some real contortions. First, the Air Force would have to lease a 767 airliner from Boeing, not an air tanker. Then the Air Force would have to pay (Boeing) to modify the airliner into an air tanker (cost: $30 million). The Air Force could then operate the aircraft for no more than ten years, not the forty-year operating life the aircraft should have. Moreover, finally, before being returned to Boeing at the end of the lease, the air tanker had to be remodified (by Boeing) back into an airliner (for another $30 million). According to OMB calculations, this increased the total cost of the lease to $26 billion,[21] while also decreasing the availability of the aircraft to the Air Force from forty to ten years.

This change was just fine with everybody involved. For reasons we will explain later, even the former Budget Committee Chairman and past opponent of such games, Domenici, enthusiastically endorsed it.[22]

The proposal did finally find two critics when the Senate debated the DoD Appropriations bill on 7 December. McCain included a cauterization of it in his "pork-buster" speech: he called the operating lease "a sweet deal for the Boeing Company that I'm sure is the envy of corporate lobbyists from one end of K street [in downtown Washington] to the other."[23] Sen. Phil Gramm (R-Tex.) said, "I do not think I have ever seen a proposal that makes less sense economically . . . and I have been here . . . for twenty-two years."[24] Given the strong rhetoric, one would expect some strong action, right?

Not exactly. McCain and Gramm did offer an amendment to modify the 767 deal. Stevens accepted it without debate. He was smart to do so. As he privately explained to Gramm and McCain,[25] the terms of the amendment changed nothing, and he would accept it for that reason. The amendment was pure cosmetics, but now McCain and Gramm could claim they did something.

Shortly after this, the Senate passed the bill and sent it to conference with the House to conform the two bodies' different versions of the entire legislation into one. It was a new opportunity for creative thinking.

Why Stop with Just One Bad Idea?

It looked like the 767 deal might encounter trouble when the Senate-passed DoD Appropriations went to conference with the House. The defense subcommittee of the House Appropriations Committee had expressed strong opposition to exactly the kind of gimmickry Stevens had authored. The only difference was that the House critics focused on incremental funding gimmicks in Navy programs. They argued:

> The committee is also dismayed that the Navy continues to advocate the use of alternative financing mechanisms to artificially increase shipbuilding rates, such as advanced appropriations, or incremental funding of ships, which only serve to decrease cost visibility and accountability. . . . [T]hose Navy advocates of such practices would actually decrease the flexibility of future Administrations and Congresses to make rational capital budgeting decisions. . . . Accordingly, the committee bill included a new general provision (section 8150) which prohibits the Defense Department from budgeting for shipbuilding programs on the basis of advanced appropriations.[26]

This was pretty stern stuff, and the same complaints applied—in spades—to the Stevens–Air Force lease proposal that added high cost and truncated use to the tricks the Navy was trying. Surely, the lease deal had finally met a stone wall.

Not even close. With nary a whimper, the House members of the conference committee accepted every word of the original Stevens–Air Force operating lease deal. They also agreed to take the whole thing a step further. The House conferees agreed to lease under the same arrangements four additional 737 (Boeing) aircraft. These are not to be air tankers to assist future combat aircraft engaged in military operations, they are what DoD likes to call "CINC Support" aircraft. They are otherwise known as "VIP transports," and it is not just military dignitaries who use them; members of Congress also routinely fly in them. Neither the House's bill nor the

Senate's had included these four 737s, but the White House, Speaker of the House Dennis Hastert, and Vice President Dick Cheney's office were reported to have urged the addition of them.[27] Doing so stretched Senate Rule 28 that purported to bar the adoption in conference of anything that neither the House nor the Senate had endorsed in their initial bills. The rules, the cost, and the embarrassment notwithstanding, the VIP transports were added to make the atrocious 767 deal even worse. Staff wags have a term for such proposals emerging out of nowhere in a House-Senate conference committee: they are called "immaculate conceptions."

No Merit in This Pork?

The question occurs, Is there no merit whatsoever to these items added to defense bills at various stages of the legislative process? Even if they won't help the war, is there not merit in the environmental cleanups Feinstein added for Hunter's Point Naval Shipyard and McClellan Air Force Base? Byrd's museum at Martinsburg, West Virginia, may be excessive, but what about a bioterrorism lab Reid added for Nevada? Some even say the VIP transports are a good idea; the existing ones are old, and the transports make travel more efficient for decision makers and their staff. Some of these proposals are easy to criticize on their own face; some are not.

When these items are added to defense bills, very few in Congress know what they are, and even fewer, if any, have weighed their pros and cons. Either because no one submitted them for review or because they flunked, deservedly or not, the items did not make it through the review process in the executive branch and were not included in DoD's budget request. Nor do the items go through any rigorous analysis when their proponents bring them to senators and representatives. There are almost never any hearings to assess the merits. (And, if there are, they may be a setup by the proponents.) A review by the Government Accounting Office (GAO), CBO, CRS or any other objective entity is virtually unheard of. As I discovered in some cases, even the members and staffers pushing the items barely understand what they are pressing. In most cases, they will know only the arguments for the item, having been fed that side only by the advocates. Members and staff will rarely know what case might exist against the items. They also believe it means a certain amount of jobs or corporate cash flow in their state or district as well. However, as we will discuss later, these data often vastly overstate whatever economic benefit might pertain. In short, virtually no one on Capitol Hill has rigorously been through the pros and the cons. Some items may have merit; some already have a few strikes against them and probably would flunk another review, but no one really knows. They are genuine "pigs in a poke."

One of the Many Costs of Pork

If all Congress did was add pork to defense bills, the problem would just be a question of finding the additional money to pay for it. Unfortunately, that's not the way the House and Senate Armed Services Committees and the House and Senate Appropriations Committees fund their pork. Instead, they use money from existing programs, including the accounts in the DoD budget most directly related to fighting the war against terrorism. Knowing that being found to do so might be embarrassing, they use numerous devices to cover up the raid.

The first gimmick used in 2001 was to simply misstate what they were doing. The chairmen and ranking members of the various committees and subcommittees involved claimed they were increasing 2002 funding for military "readiness" funded by the O&M account.* For example, Rep. Bob Stump (R-Ariz.), chairman of the House Armed Services Committee, claimed the DoD Authorization bill, as sent to the president in final form, "substantially increases critical readiness accounts."[28] Carl Levin, chairman of the Senate Armed Services Committee, said his bill "includes a major victory for good government and for the readiness and transformation [of] our military forces," and, "This bill makes significant contributions to the readiness of our military."[29]

How could this be? The 2002 DoD Authorization bill actually reduced the funding requested by Bush for the O&M account. The president requested $125.7 billion; the final version of the bill authorized just $123.3 billion, a reduction of $2.4 billion. The explanation is simple. In referring to an "increase," these members were addressing the change in the O&M budget from the last year of the Clinton administration. The final, anemic FY 2001 Clinton budget for O&M had been $113.2 billion. The FY 2002 authorization bill provided $123.3 billion; thus, an almost $10 billion "increase," which was dutifully headlined in the press releases. Those same press releases and speeches did not point out that the president had requested $125.7 billion—$2.4 billion more than was allowed in the bill. Had the politicians been willing to be complete and accurate, they would have included both terms of reference. Being unwilling to fully explain themselves, they excluded a key point of reference.

That was hardly all. A review of the text of the final legislative product for the O&M account shows an O&M budget laced with still more state-specific projects added by the Appropriations Committees. The reports of

---

* The O&M account funds many things, including the Defense Health Program, base repairs, counter-drug activities, DoD's civilian employees, and much else. Readiness is just one of the myriad activities funded in O&M.

the House and Senate Appropriations Committees and their final, joint Conference Report add item after item of state-specific projects to the O&M budget, many—again—having nothing to do with the war on terrorism or even war in general. The list includes not just repairs and operating expenses for specifically designated bases, but also acquisition and research and development projects, which belong in other accounts.

Some examples: $1 million for buying MBU-20 oxygen masks and another $1 million for an alternative fuel program at Hickam Air Force Base, Hawaii,[30] $2.5 million for the Philadelphia Naval Business Center,[31] $3.4 million for a landfill relocation,[32] $4.9 million for a Northwest Environmental Resource Center,[33] $5 million for a Center of Excellence for Disaster Management and Humanitarian Assistance,[34] and $2 million for Rock Island bridge repairs.[35] It goes on in three Appropriations Committee reports. Moreover, because of directions contained in the final, authoritative Conference Report, each of the three reports adds to the projects designated by the other two.

The impact is not to add new funding; the money used for these projects displaces the money intended for the regular purposes of the O&M budget. According to McCain, these earmarks for pork in the O&M budget in the preliminary Senate Appropriations Committee Report alone totaled more than $400 million.[36]

However, the pork earmarks that displace normal O&M spending are the lesser of the obscure mechanisms to reduce O&M spending below apparent levels. In the back of the authorization and appropriations bills in the "General Provisions" sections, one finds more bites out of O&M. Some of these are just more pork; others have more elegant justifications.

For example, in the final DoD Appropriations Conference Report, Section 8062 of the General Provisions Title uses $10.2 million of O&M funding to realign railroad track at Elmendorf Air Force Base and Fort Richardson, Alaska; Section 8136 takes $2.1 million for a Lafayette Escadrille Memorial; Section 8138 takes $4.2 million for the battleship *Alabama* museum and memorial; Section 8139 takes the same amount for the USS *Intrepid* museum and memorial; Section 8140 takes another $4.2 million to relocate a school at Fairchild Air Force Base; and Section 8141 takes $3.5 million for a special needs learning center for the Central Kitsap School District in Washington state.

Different provisions take larger chunks. Section 8095 in the same General Provisions Title of the bill reduces O&M by $240 million to "reflect savings from favorable foreign currency fluctuations." Section 8102 takes out $262 million to restrict travel of DoD personnel. Section 8135 extracts $105 million "to reflect fact-of-life changes in utilities costs." Section 8146 takes $100 million "to improve scrutiny and supervision in the use of government credit cards." Section 8123 is the granddaddy: it reduces O&M by $1.650 billion for "business process reforms, management efficiencies, and procurement of administrative and management support."

Some members of Congress call these "good government" provisions, but they are mostly phony. They pretend to assume reforms and savings—even to force them to occur—but as the committee members are acutely aware, they are not going to happen. As they have been told time and time again by the Defense Department and OMB, these mandated reductions involve unrealistic assumptions about DoD's ability (and willingness) to adopt management reforms within the fiscal year; they make unjustified economic assumptions regarding foreign currency exchange rates. The members assume that in a time of war DoD is going to reduce travel costs, and they pretend that defense contractors can and will adopt efficient business practices despite decades of obstruction to full and open competition. Numerous times during the House and Senate consideration of the DoD appropriations bill, both bodies were told these reductions in O&M were unrealistic and, more important, would hurt real defenses. On 28 November OMB told the House Appropriations Committee:

> [T]hese reductions were based on unrealistic assumptions about achievable FY 2002 savings—primarily from reductions in consultant services, headquarters staff, and A-76 studies. . . . [T]he real effect of the House's deep O&M reductions would be to undercut the President's plan to address readiness shortfalls and competitive sourcing, and reduce funds available for military operations and support.[37]

On 6 December, OMB told the Senate Appropriators:

> The Committee has made reductions to Operations and Maintenance (O&M) programs, based on unrealistic assumptions of how much savings could be achieved through reductions in consultant services, foreign currency fluctuation account balances, and travel. These reductions would undermine DoD's ability to adequately fund training, operations, maintenance, supplies, and other essentials. They would seriously damage the readiness of our armed forces and undermine their ability to execute current operations, including the war on terrorism.[38]

And yet, the House and Senate appropriators persisted. Not only did they refuse to eliminate the phony cuts—totaling more than $2 billion—they also refused to take care that the cuts they were requiring did not come out of the key training, spare parts, maintenance, or operating expense accounts of the O&M budget: something they could have easily done by prohibiting such cuts in those places. To do so would have been contrary to the goal they had quietly established—to lower spending in the O&M budget in order to increase it in the procurement and R&D budgets, which they had already also laced with their state-specific add-ons.*

Just to make it all worse, they also explicitly stated that none of these cuts in the O&M budget was to be taken out of the "line item" pork they added to the O&M budget. Offered the choice to load up the bill with pork projects for the members' home states and districts or to load up the combat units of the armed forces with extra training, spare parts, and other necessities for going to war, Congress opted for more pork and less military readiness.

Endgame

At the end of the process, when Congress's handiwork was presented to the executive branch for either a veto or approval, both Secretary of Defense Rumsfeld and President Bush blinked. When he was confronted with the FY 2002 DoD Authorization bill with its prolongation of unneeded, wasteful military bases, almost $3 billion in pork, and $2 billion in cuts in the O&M budget, Rumsfeld withdrew his threat to recommend a veto.

When he signed the FY 2002 DoD Appropriations and Emergency Supplemental bill into law, President Bush said the bill "provides approximately $2 billion less than requested, the Act does not adequately fund all my critical priorities, specifically the readiness of our forces. The $2 billion reduction is largely achieved by cuts to operation and maintenance programs. . . . As a result, these cuts will place our military forces in the all too familiar predicament of having to choose either to sacrifice near-term readiness or to forego critical repair of family housing, defer important depot maintenance of our weapon systems, and reduce base operations."[39]

Bush chose not to force Congress back to the drawing board with a veto; instead, he signed the bill into law. He used words not actions to address Congress's self-centered priorities and, thus, enabled, rather than opposed, the substitution of pork and irrelevancies for better support for the soldiers and aircrew he had sent to fight and perhaps die in Afghanistan.

Even though Congress had already delayed the passage of the 2002 defense bills until three months after the start of the fiscal year,† neither Rumsfeld nor Bush was willing to delay things for a few more days, or even weeks, for Congress to be instructed to revise its priorities and bring its wartime actions into conformance with its wartime rhetoric.

---

* It is also notable that these reductions in buying power, especially the $1.65 billion "procurement reform" reduction, occur in the O&M accounts, not in the procurement or R&D accounts, where much of the buying actually occurs.

† Interim funding for ongoing operations had been provided through an appropriations vehicle known as a "continuing resolution."

In my thirty-one years of working for Congress, I had never seen its members behave so badly, and so consistently badly, in the face of a crisis. Afterwards, I would witness even worse from the collective body, but that comes later. First, it is appropriate to assess the words and actions of some individual members, especially those who would have you believe they oppose what has been described here.

4

Mr. Smith Is Dead

The more you scratch the surface of Congress's behavior in the early twenty-first century, the worse it gets. If Hollywood made a movie about today's Congress, the producers would have a hard time understanding how things have changed since the classic *Mr. Smith Goes to Washington*. Appearances haven't changed, but the reality has.

Frank Capra's 1939 vignette on American politics depicts an honest and stalwart Sen. Jefferson Smith (Jimmy Stewart) standing up against a crooked political machine that owns newspapers, a governor, and another U.S. senator. Goodness and the American way triumph (and Stewart gets his girl) when the hero filibusters and defeats the machine's corrupt land deal buried in the back of a badly needed depression-era "relief" bill.

The movie presents a popular American paradigm: politics includes some dirty business, even at the lofty level of the U.S. Senate; however, our constitutional system empowers stalwart heroes with the tools to defeat debased politicians, and the American way of life produces enough champions to get the job done. *Mr. Smith Goes to Washington* offers a reassuring image, but for the role that Congress plays today in national defense, it is a false image from the past, and no one in Congress, not even the few who pose as reformers, has any regrets.

Jefferson Smith versus John McCain

One of the standard rituals of modern Senate passage of a defense authorization or appropriations bill is a short speech by Senator McCain. He gives them after his staff identifies all the "pork-barrel" spending they find in the bill.* The speech is usually impassioned and—for those depressed by even a cursory review of the contents of these bills—uplifting. McCain often applies harsh, but entirely appropriate, language to what his staff uncovers. One can sense some other senators' staff silently cheering in the back of the chamber as McCain nails the junk his senate colleagues stuff into the defense bills. The speech usually takes about fifteen to twenty minutes and comes with the insertion into the *Congressional Record* of tabulations of the

---

* Senator McCain's definition of "pork" is forgiving; it does not consider pork to be any program requested by the Department of Defense. If anything, McCain's tabulations of the dollars spent on pork understate the problem.

pork items, letters from outraged organizations, newspaper articles identifying wasteful provisions, etc. It is all quite impressive, but only up to a point.

The speech McCain gave on 20 December 2001, when the Senate was about to vote on the final version of the FY 2002 DoD appropriations bill, is a typical example. The House-Senate Conference Committee took the Senate-passed DoD appropriations bill McCain had so bitterly cauterized on 7 December and made it worse. They eliminated the cosmetic amendment he had added regarding the 767 air-tanker lease, and they added the unrequested, superfluous VIP transports. They included the hundreds of pork add-ons of both the House- and Senate-passed bills, and they added a few more.

One of these late additions was from Tom Daschle (D-S.Dak.), the Senate majority leader. According to OMB staff,* this item "would transfer unprecedented and virtually unlimited liability for environmental cleanup and tort claims to the American taxpayer, even where the liability is unrelated to action of the U.S. government."[1] It was for the Homestake Mine, one of numerous gold mines owned by a multibillion-dollar corporation with operations in the United States, Canada, South America, and Australia. The mine shaft in the town of Lead in Daschle's South Dakota was more than a mile deep. This made it a candidate for a research facility for subatomic neutrinos because the depth rendered it unaffected by other subatomic particles. The new facility could mean jobs in South Dakota. The only problem was Homestake demanded release from any liability for cleaning up cyanide and other pollution from 125 years of gold mining before it was willing to hand over its shaft for conversion into the research facility. While the liability the Daschle amendment handed to the federal government was unlimited by the text of the amendment, in an act of generosity, CBO scored it with a de minimis $50 million cost.

There was this and more. According to McCain, several hundred million had been added to the emergency antiterrorism supplemental for highway spending, the Olympics in Salt Lake City, making Route 61 in Mississippi wider, capital grants to the National Railroad Passenger Corporation, the Woodrow Wilson Bridge in the Washington, D.C., area, and more.[2]

---

* Technically speaking, this Daschle amendment was not added de novo in the House-Senate conference. It was, in fact, added during the Senate's consideration of the bill on 7 December; however, the addition was performed after a total of seven words of explanation from Senator Inouye ("an amendment for Senator Daschle on mining"), and it was the last amendment in the last managers' package adopted on the night of 7 December. (See Congressional Record, 7 December 2001, p. S12664.) When the existence and nature of the amendment became clearer after the text of the conference report was made available on 20 December, I and other staff assumed it was added only in the House-Senate conference.

Describing the new layer of junk added to the rest, McCain turned on the rhetorical afterburners; he found all this "incredible."[3]

> [T]he Senate Appropriations Committee has not seen fit to change in any degree its usual blatant use of defense dollars for projects that may or may not serve some worthy purpose, but that certainly impair our national defense by depriving legitimate defense needs of adequate funding.[4]
>
> This system has run amok. . . . The Senate ought to look at itself. What are we doing?[5]
>
> This kind of behavior cannot go on. . . . You will lose the confidence of the American people. . . . This is called war profiteering.[6]
>
> You read these things. First you laugh, and then you cry.[7]

The stage had been set. The Senate had taken its egregious, pork- and irrelevancy-laden defense appropriations and emergency supplemental bill and had made it even worse. Moreover, McCain had the Senate at a highly vulnerable moment. Senators were eager to finish the bill and adjourn for a recess. It was 20 December, and, under ideal circumstances, they would have finished their business when the new fiscal year started on the first of October, but September 11, the war in Afghanistan, and a labyrinth of tax and spending politics had intervened. Now the senators "were smelling the jet fumes" of airliners to take them home for Christmas, Chanukah, and local—career-lengthening—politics. With a war going on, the defense bill was "must" business. It would be too impolitic to depart Washington with the bill unpassed after all this delay. A filibuster or other delaying tactic unless and until some concessions were made in favor of a better bill would have come at an exquisitely painful moment. The time to wring concessions out of the grisly appropriators had arrived.

Any number of parliamentary maneuvers by McCain could have stymied the passage of the bill. Just starting a good old-fashioned Sen. Jefferson Smith–type filibuster would have given rise to ninety-nine audible senatorial groans. When they realized the "problem" senator was serious and they would otherwise have to tell their personal secretaries to cancel their flight reservations, a delegation would almost certainly have been sent to ask what concession he required to desist. Or, if McCain had no energy for an old-fashioned filibuster, he could have exercised his right under the rules to demand that the Senate's clerk be forced to read aloud every word of the 127-page conference report. Or, he could have demanded that a quorum call of absent senators be continued again and again, a device that can end up taking hours. Or, he could have exercised one of the various Budget Act points of order that the conference report was technically vulnerable to, thus requiring further debate and roll call votes. These and other actions were all available to McCain, if he wanted to require some improvement in the legislation he had so appropriately characterized as bringing any real patriot to the brink of tears.

He chose to do nothing. He talked for a short time and told the Senate: "I know the hour is late. I apologize to my colleagues if I have inconvenienced them."[8] He then yielded the Senate floor and disappeared. After a few more senators gave speeches about the wonderful things they were doing for national defense and a few others inserted into the text of the *Congressional Record* typed statements that were printed to appear as if they were actually given as speeches, the Senate voted on the conference report. The vote was 94 to 2: McCain and Gramm voting in opposition. The bill went to the president who signed it into law on 12 January 2002. The deed was done.

The Night Pork Didn't Die

A few months later, Congress took up the next fiscal year's defense bills and yet another emergency supplemental. What I saw and heard in the Senate chamber on the night of 6 June 2002 was one of the last things I observed, up close and personal, in my congressional career. It was a fitting and proper end.

Just before midnight, the press gallery was almost empty. The Senate had been working hard to pass the new FY 03 $27 billion emergency "Supplemental Appropriations for Further Recovery from and Response to Terrorist Attacks on the United States," which the president had requested in March. Earlier that day, by a vote of 87 to 10, the senators had even invoked "cloture" on themselves to prevent any filibustering. Now, the Senate was getting down to the endgame for the bill. Normally, at this point on a big bill—even if it is close to midnight and members are tired—there is a sense of accomplishment that things are getting done.

And yet, there were no positive feelings this time. In fact, many senators were pretty angry. Red in the face, my own boss, Senator Domenici, told the rest of the Senate, "What happened to me should not happen to any of you."[9] Almost yelling, he violated Senate tradition and called another member by his proper name, not "respected colleague" or some other elaborate honorific. Then, Domenici spat out to that same member, "You can smile if you like, but there is nothing to smile about."[10] The target of this outburst, Senator McCain, took seriously the senatorial insult of being called by his own name and demanded a "personal privilege [to speak out of turn] since my name was used."[11] Before he could start, however, Domenici had stormed out of the chamber.

Others were cantankerous as well. Sen. Byron Dorgan (D-N.Dak.) said that what happened to him was "not . . . fair" and "arbitrary."[12] Oregon's senators, Republican Gordon Smith and Democrat Ron Wyden, thought the problem might cost lives.[13] With a cold stare about her predicament, Sen. Mary Landrieu (D-La.) said, "There is no way to correct this."[14]

Why all the hot tempers? Had someone eviscerated the emergency appropriations bill? Was the nation in danger? Were lives really threatened? Not quite. The senators were being forced to follow their own rules.

As they all knew, when the eighty-seven senators invoked cloture on the bill, they voted to limit further debate and other parliamentary shenanigans to just thirty hours. In addition, the vote meant they had to restrict the subject matter of their amendments; "post-cloture" amendments must be "germane"; that is to say, they must directly relate to a specific subject already in the bill. And, the senators do not get to play with the rules: the Senate's parliamentarian determines germaneness, and he was not playing favorites.

What terrible things were the rules imposing on the senators?

- Domenici was not being permitted to add to the antiterrorism supplemental a $50 million loan guarantee for the developer of a small, civilian passenger jet from his state of New Mexico.[15]
- Dorgan was denied an "earmark" of $400,000 for power transmission studies that would address his home state of North Dakota.[16]
- The two senators from Oregon were unable to prevent the Air Force Reserve from moving a helicopter unit out of their state.[17]
- Landrieu could not change a funding formula to permit thirty-seven states, including her own Louisiana, to retain Department of Health and Human Services funds they had been overpaid.[18]

In each case, the amendment would have introduced a new subject to the bill and was, therefore, "not germane." All it took was for any senator to ask the parliamentarian if they were or were not germane; if they flunked the test, they became dead parliamentary meat. Because McCain was willing to ask the question, the rest of the Senate was unable to ignore the rules by remaining silent and obviating any unsolicited parliamentarian judgments.

That was not all. Earlier that week, McCain announced to the Senate: "The worst damage, the worst pork-barreling, the egregious stuff done around here is in managers' amendments."* He said he was going to "go after this porkbarrel spending and we are going to go after it and after it

---

* As explained earlier, "managers' amendments" or "managers' packages" are groupings of amendments that are usually adopted en bloc by unrecorded voice votes at the instigation of the Democratic and Republican "managers" of a bill. The managers are usually the chairman and ranking minority member of the Senate committee that authored the bill being debated.

and after it." He was going to exercise his right as a senator to demand separate roll call votes on each and every amendment in any package of managers' amendments. Thus, every senator would be "on the record" in favor of or opposed to pork. Also, because managers' packages typically consist of twenty or more amendments and because each roll call vote takes at least fifteen minutes, McCain was going to inflict some temporal pain on the Senate if it wanted to lard up the bill. Just so no one missed his point, he made it explicit that "there is going to be plenty of votes."[19]

The next day, it got worse. McCain submitted twenty of his own amendments, each one removing a morsel of pork already inserted into the bill by the Appropriations Committee.[20] And, he repeated to the Senate a day later, "We will not have one of these deals that we have seen in the past so many times where at the very end—maybe at 10 or 11 o'clock at night—there is a unanimous consent agreement that a managers' package be accepted. We are not going to do that."[21]

My phone started ringing. "Winslow, he's doing it. He heard you loud and clear," one colleague from the Congressional Research Service told me, referring to my January 2002 essay. Others called to congratulate me for embarrassing McCain into actually doing something. I had no idea whether McCain was taking these actions because of my essay, but I was glad to see him do it—someone had to.

Then, McCain started offering his amendments. The first was to remove from the bill $2 million for a new specimen storage facility for the Smithsonian Institution. The next was to extract $2.5 million for mapping coral reefs near Hawaii. The third would cut $50 million for Agricultural Research Service buildings in Ames, Iowa.

The arguments against McCain's amendments were hilarious. According to the chairman of the Senate Appropriations Committee, Sen. Robert Byrd (D-W.Va.), new specimen storage for the Smithsonian was an urgent homeland security need.[22] Sen. Daniel Inouye (D-Hawaii) argued that his amendment was not pork because the award of the money for spending in Hawaii was to be selected competitively.[23] Even if a firm from another state were to have been selected (an improbability to the point of an impossibility given how such things work), the money was to benefit Hawaii, and the senator was sure to claim credit. Sen. Tom Harkin (D-Iowa) said: "Keep in mind, this is a national laboratory. It is not an Iowa lab [to be built in Iowa]."[24] Ergo—he was trying to say—federal money spent in Iowa is not pork.

Huh?

The Empire Strikes Back . . .

Through no fault of his own, McCain lost on his three amendments with at least sixty senators voting against him each time.[25] Were three-fifths of the Senate such dunderheads that they bought the arguments against McCain? Of course not. Most senators are pretty smart. They know babble when they hear it. They also knew that if McCain were able to knock out someone else's pork, they might be next. It was not stupidity that won against McCain; it was an unspoken, mutual pork-protection pact.

But wait! Was McCain's losing, but very laudable, effort the harbinger of his deciding that the time had come to be a reformer in word *and* in deed? Was Sen. Jefferson Smith rising from the dead to actually fight Congress's exploiting defense legislation to buy heaps of pork?

Let us not get carried away here, folks. Remember, we are talking about senators.

Hero Joins Empire

Sadly, McCain's praiseworthy antipork offensive not only fell apart, it reversed course. After those first three votes, McCain realized the futility of his amendments and picked up, instead, the germaneness tool the Senate had handed him when it invoked cloture. But, given the way he used it, he helped pork more than he hurt it. Here is what happened.

The emergency supplemental appropriations bill the Senate was debating addressed the broad subject of homeland security. That meant there were many agencies and programs already in the bill, not just DoD. These included the departments of Agriculture, Commerce, State, Justice, Energy, Labor, Health and Human Services, Treasury, Housing and Urban Development, and Defense. Before cloture had been invoked, several programs were added by virtue of amendments: AMTRAK, federal aid to highways, the Smithsonian Institution, the U.S. Fish and Wildlife Service, and more—all at an additional cost of $3.9 billion.[26] Thus, the sandbox the senators were playing in was already large when cloture closed the door for new, "non-germane" subjects.

McCain did keep some items that transgressed the germaneness requirement out of the bill, but other senators were busy cramming germane stuff in. In all, forty-two germane amendments were added. They included:

- Sen. Kay Bailey Hutchison's "technical change" to enable $10 million in agricultural aid for her own state of Texas.
- Sen. Jim Bunning's (R-Ky.) $1 million in water services for Kentucky.
- The Oregon senators' (Wyden and Smith) $500,000 to reduce West Coast fishing capacity.

- Senator Stevens's exemption for Alaska from certain unemployment taxes, $464,000 for vocational training for specific Alaskans, altered requirements of the Alaska Native Claims Settlement Act, and altered mail delivery in Alaska.[27]

And so it went. There were a few amendments relevant to homeland security and the war in Afghanistan, such as a nonbinding "sense of the Senate" amendment from Sen. Bill Nelson (D-Fla.) on how the FBI should reorganize, but of the forty-two amendments added, just nine were in any way relevant. The rest (thirty-three) were either meaningless, irrelevant, or pork.

This trash was not being adopted behind McCain's back or even over his objections; he was an active part of the approval process of each and every amendment. It was a process that was exercised on other bills that McCain had criticized as laden with pork. One by one, or in bunches, the amendments were shown to him and his staff and were explicitly approved by them. Possibly tired of the hypocrisy, two senators made public what was going on. Assistant Majority Leader Harry Reid said on the Senate floor: "Senator McCain and Senator [Phil] Gramm* have been going through it [a managers' package] for about three hours." This produced a list of amendments "that have been accepted" by McCain and Gramm.[28] Stevens also wanted to make sure everyone knew what was going on: "Those [McCain and Gramm] that sought to review the list had no objection to the amendments on the list."[29]

That review by McCain and Gramm had little to do with pork; all they were doing was determining, with the help of the parliamentarian, which amendments were germane and which were not. Germaneness was culling the amendments not their porcine nature. Indeed, if amendments were found to be non-germane, McCain and Gramm were permitting the authors to modify their amendments—no matter how porky—to enable them to comply with the germaneness rule.

For example: An amendment from Sen. Susan Collins (R-Maine) was made acceptable by eliminating the Department of the Interior as an actor in the $4 million conversion of a "Naval Security Group" in Winter Harbor, Maine, to a research and education center for Acadia National Park, Maine.[30]

Another amendment from Robert Byrd of West Virginia increased from $10 million to $32 million an earmark for West Virginia and other states for Corps of Engineers work.[31]

---

* As they had on previous occasions, Senators Gramm and McCain had joined forces, but Senator McCain was clearly the leader.

There were plenty more.

Then, McCain made no objection when Stevens and Inouye asked for "unanimous consent" (meaning any one senator can object and deny the request) to permit the managers' package to be adopted, en bloc, by a single unrecorded voice vote.[32] After the group of amendments was adopted that way, McCain stood up and said, "We should not be doing this," and gave another speech about the evils of pork and how the Senate shouldn't be adopting managers' packages.[33] McCain was giving a speech about how terrible it was to do what he had just helped get done.

What happened to the threat to force the Senate to vote on each and every amendment in any managers' package? There were twenty-five in the one just adopted; voting on each could have dragged the Senate through about six mind-numbing hours. It would not have helped McCain win any popularity contests in the Senate, but it would have told the feasting senators that while they may have had the votes to add junk to bills, doing so would not be painless.

Return to Peaceful Coexistence

After this episode, the Senate returned to cramming defense bills with senators' home state goodies without the complications of germaneness. When the fiscal year 2003 Department of Defense appropriations bill came up for debate on 31 July, there were four managers' packages totaling more than fifty amendments and more than $200 million. It was the usual combination of a few relevant but mostly pork-ridden amendments. McCain did nothing about them.

The bill was also yet another true horror for the O&M budget and the readiness funding in it for U.S. armed forces. As in the case of the FY 02 bill, the General Provisions section in the back included sections reducing spending in the O&M accounts. As explained earlier, they included

- foreign currency "savings" the Appropriations Committee decided were going to occur in FY 2003; this time $211 million.*
- $68 million in transfers out of O&M that were simply not explained.
- $8 million for railroads at two bases in Alaska.
- $700 million in better service contract management in O&M.

---

* In FY 03, the dollar fell sharply against the euro and the yen.

As we know, the Senate has been through this "savings" game before. These and similar provisions amounted to $1.1 billion and were, in reality, cuts in the O&M budget.

By the time the House and Senate Appropriations Committees had completed their handiwork on the new bill, they had increased the pork from 2002's total of $4.0 billion to a new record total of $7.4 billion.* The new record did not, however, inspire Senator McCain to action. Indeed, on the day the Senate held its final vote on the conference report for the FY 03 DoD Appropriations Act and sent it to the president for signature, Senator McCain missed the vote; he had left town for New York, where he was scheduled for a final rehearsal for his appearance that following weekend on the television show *Saturday Night Live*.[34] He had his statement inserted in the *Congressional Record* as if it he had delivered it in person, but he was 210 miles away.

The Press Takes a Snooze

But you know about all this, don't you? You read in your newspapers all about the posturing against pork while approving it, the mismatches between words and deeds, and the hilarious arguments against pork. Right?

Neither did I. The most I was able to find was a minor blurb in the *Washington Post*. The following appeared under the heading "Pork Roast" in a 10 June 2002 article: "Sens. John McCain (R-Ariz.) and Phil Gramm (R-Tex.) smelled pork and decided to root it out. Tempers flared as McCain blocked amendment after amendment, including one from fellow Republican Sen. Pete V. Domenici (N.Mex.) on loan guarantees for small jets that had been rejected by McCain's Committee on Commerce, Science and Transportation. Domenici, furious, chastised McCain for smiling during the exchange, and McCain angrily demanded time to respond. . . . When the bill finally passed, it was without Domenici's proposal."[35]

Okay, that is part of the story. What about the rest? Where is the discussion of all the pork amendments McCain approved—which was perfectly clear in the publicly available *Congressional Record*? What about McCain's speech that the Senate should not be doing precisely what he had just helped it do? And, what about the unfulfilled threat to require time-consuming roll call votes on each and every managers' package amendment? Instead of reporting the whole story, the *Washington Post* reported a simplistic half-truth instead.

The ongoing joke on Capitol Hill is that there are two things one should never see in the making: sausage and legislation. Usually, when a particularly

---

* When the pork in the FY 04 Military Construction Appropriations bill was added, FY 04 came to a total of $8.5 billion.

disgusting bill or amendment is passed, Capitol Hill staff assuage their consciences by knowingly joking to each other that "the sausage factory"—the U.S. Senate—has been at work again. It's as if there is forgiveness in at least having the knowledge and ethics to appreciate that the legislation is loaded with garbage.

It's a little more complicated than that. After the House and Senate passed the legislation discussed here, the bills went to the president and they were signed into law. Then things started to happen, or not happen. Programs that neither needed nor deserved the money got the money, and programs that did, didn't. An international gold mine conglomerate got unfettered protection from lawsuits; the American nation got the shaft. While soldiers deployed to war with reduced training budgets, Congress increased pork for itself. Members of Congress were trying to make themselves look good by behaving atrociously.

Senator McCain is not part of this crowd. He insists that his staff ferret out the junk in Congress's defense bills. Almost without fail, he marches to the floor of the Senate to rail against it. What his staff finds never ceases to amaze even the most jaded in the congressional staff, and his speeches never fail to aggravate the perpetrators for being found out so easily or to give a lift to an unknown number of staff—and perhaps even a senator or two—who have grown disgusted with business as usual.

But there is a point beyond which Senator McCain is clearly unwilling to go. He gives the good speech, expresses his outrage, lectures his colleagues, and stirs up the place with an occasional, short delay. But then he walks away. When it comes to action—meaningful action—Senator McCain is among the missing.

In a constitutional system specifically designed to equip a minority—even a minority of one—with the parliamentary weapons to bring the system to a crashing halt unless and until the minority receives some satisfaction, Senator McCain has unilaterally disarmed himself. From the large menu of tactics available to him to bring the Senate into legislative agony—tactics many others have used to achieve their own ends—Senator McCain has selected to sit on his hands.

His doing so is all the more remarkable because more than any other senator, he has informed himself of the garbage packed into Congress's defense bills. Knowing at least as well as any other just what is going on, he finds it somehow too extreme to use the tools at his disposal against it. By assuming this role—i.e., the self-anointed, but also self-disarmed, crusader against pork—Senator McCain has made himself not the Senate's "pork buster" but its "pork enabler." If the worst the Congress's most outspoken opponent of pork is going to do is give a speech, there is clearly no meaningful downside.

In the final analysis, McCain sinks to the level of the rest: he seeks to be accepted for something he is not. He has the potential to tower above the other ninety-nine senators, but by failing to act—even to deliver on his own words—he denies himself real stature.

In the movie *Mr. Smith Goes to Washington,* not knowing whether he would win and not caring that he was utterly alone, "Senator" Jefferson Smith took on the good fight and—much to his own surprise—prevailed. Today, the 1974 Budget Act and other measures adopted after 1939 expand the armory of any member of the Senate who wants to impede the actions of an abusive majority. But there is no Mr. Smith available to use those tools. Today, Mr. Smith is dead.

5

Confessions of a Pork Processor

As one who helped Congress acquire billions of dollars in pork with as little delay as a few short speeches, Senator McCain was just one person in a system that engages all 535 members of Congress, thousands of staffers on Capitol Hill, civilian bureaucrats in the Defense Department, senior officers in the military services, corporate executives, university professors, Washington lobbyists, and others.

Sometimes the press takes notice of parts of what is going on, but, unfortunately, most journalists consider their own limited understanding of the process to be complete. They seem to think "porking" on Capitol Hill is a marginally costly and harmful and sometimes comedic waste of money. Journalists are missing a fundamental story that has far more serious consequences than they appreciate; most do not even understand the process.

Christmas Comes but Twice a Year

After it passes the final appropriations bills for the new fiscal year (typically in late October or early November), Congress usually adjourns for the rest of the year. Things stay pretty quiet until January. Before Christmas, there are some holiday parties for defense staffers thrown by defense manufacturers, their associations, and the military services. Between Christmas and New Year's Day, most offices either close or subsist with a skeleton crew. In the first full week of January, Congress will convene, and if it's a new Congress, newly elected or re-elected members of the House and Senate will be sworn in, taking an oath to "support and defend" the Constitution. Except for another round of parties to honor the new members, things usually remain slow until the president's State of the Union address at the end of the month. That speech engages the legislative gears once again.

Toward the end of the down period, in early January, the phones start ringing. For defense staffers, it's probably not a constituent complaining about jet noise at the local Air Force base, and it's not the boss calling to wish everyone a happy New Year. It's the nice man or woman from Boeing, or Lockheed, or Honeywell, or the state university, or the mom-and-pop shop near that local Air Force base, or anyone else—government or private sector—who has had in the past, or wants in the future, a piece of the defense budget. They may politely wish the staffer the best for the New Year and ask how the holiday was, but that's not why they are calling.

The new pork season has begun, and those familiar enough with the process to get in on the ground floor are calling to tell Santa—or rather their representative or senator—what goodies they're wishing for in the new fiscal year that starts nine months away on 1 October. Santa's elf (the staffer) will start making a list. It will include whoever has been nice, but it will also include whoever has been naughty, or rather failed to perform on previous government contracts. Indeed, if the list failed to include the naughty defense contractors, it would be pretty short, and by the time the list is finished, it's going to be very long.

Most think Christmas comes only once a year, but if you feed at the federal trough through the defense budget, and if you are wise to the ways of Capitol Hill, you know that the gifts on 25 December are the little ones. The big ones start arriving on or about 1 October when the DoD and Military Construction appropriation bills for the new fiscal year start the money flowing.

Just about the only people not calling are senior officers at military bases; their superiors order them not to initiate the grubbing for add-ons to the DoD budget; so most of them don't call. The staffers have to call them. However, once the two parties are in contact, the staffers get all the cooperation they need to add several military construction projects at the local bases to their "pork list."

If you're a regular calling into the senator's office, you may not need much more than that first phone call to get the process started. You will need to tell the staffer what you're after, how much it will cost, and where in the Defense Department budget it belongs. Cost might be just a few million dollars if you're a professor after another university research project or a contractor looking to add a few baubles to your laser facility's test program. If you're a four star general who wants a new VIP transport for his personal travel—a perennial favorite—you may need $30 to $60 million. If you're looking for bigger game, such as a few more transport aircraft than DoD asked for that year (for instance, the grossly overpriced Lockheed C-130J) you may need hundreds of millions. If the member of Congress you're calling is one of the "old bulls" in the appropriations committee, like Senator Stevens, or one of the power elite, such as Sen. Trent Lott when he was the Republican leader in the Senate, the cost of what you may be after could be in the billions.

If you're a newcomer to the process, you need to do more than just call. You may need to come into the office and meet the staffer to brief him or her on whatever you want. If the morsel you're after has any significance—political, monetary, or career-enhancement for some staffers—

you may also have to meet the boss. Not to worry. If you get into the senator's or representative's office, he or she will be fully briefed and after a few objective sounding questions will be quite accommodating, unless you really blow your presentation.

Newcomer or regular, at the front end of the process you will be providing paperwork to explain and justify the spending you want. You will also need to contact other Hill offices: the other senator from your state regardless of his or her political party or ideology (pork is, after all, a tag team operation) and staff of the Armed Services and Appropriations committees, if you are a big enough deal for them to return your call. If you have money to burn, you will hire a downtown Washington lobbying firm to tell you what you need to do; if not, the congressional staffer will tell you free of charge. In most offices, but not all, the written material you hand over will be read; in some, it will be understood; in fewer still—only a very few—it will be studied.

The staffer will use this written material to petition the morsel to the Armed Services and Appropriations Committee staff. He or she might also use it for background in hearings with DoD officials, if the senator or representative is on a defense-related committee. Hence, the member can sound like he or she knows what they're talking about when they pose questions to DoD witnesses and prompt them to say wonderful things about the project at hand. (Of course, those questions should only be asked if DoD has already made it clear the questioner will get the right answers; only a rank newcomer with a clueless staff would ask such questions without knowing what the response will be.)

You might be wondering whether there is something missing in this early part of the process: Aren't staffers reviewing the requests for a few million dollars, or a few hundreds of millions, or billions, to see if they have any merit? If the requester is warm-blooded, a request will pass muster in most offices. The simple answer is that at this point in the process there usually is very little, if any, review. Most politicians' offices are not in the business of saying "no" to constituents, especially ones who can make more money flow into the state economy and into re-election campaigns. Any real review will come later, and others will do it. That way it will be easier for a member a member of a senator's staff to give a requester bad news if the project craps out: someone else can be blamed.

In a very few offices—one colleague guesstimated 10 percent, and that sounded high to me—the staffer you contact will have enough knowledge to have some insights about your project and the energy and willpower to look further into it. In those cases, the assessment might involve a review of any available GAO reports about your project and discussions with experts in the Congressional Research Service or colleagues on the Armed Services or Appropriations Committees. It would certainly include a chat with someone in DoD. Sometimes these inquisitive staffers end up with negative views about the request, but that does not always mean you are a dead duck. You will find out one way or another about these negative views, if not from the staffer, then perhaps from the relevant DoD project manager giving you a "heads up." You may have to drum those silly notions of lack of merit out of the staffer's head, but if you fail, you should know that staffers can be, and frequently are, overruled by their chiefs of staff and their members. Sometimes you need just one call, from you or someone else, to the chief of staff or the member with a few reminders about how many voters will find jobs and how many dollars will flow—into the state economy, of course. In giving this information to the top dogs in a congressional office, accuracy and completeness are definitely not de rigueur: your data will almost never be checked in any meaningful way.

Of course, there are also the odd requests that are so outrageous that they could constitute an embarrassment to any member sponsoring it; although in some quarters, this test does not seem to apply. Or your own or your hired lobbyist's presentation could be so inept or so inappropriately articulated that you simply alert the congressional listeners that an association with you can be problematic. This is a more common test on Capitol Hill than any merit, or lack of it, your proposal might have. Most politicians and Hill staffers have a good nose for people who will get them into trouble. For example, offering campaign contributions during these meetings is definitely verboten. That is supposed to remain unsaid. Later, when you do make a contribution or offer some other form of political help—and you probably will—it will be both noticed and remembered, especially for the next year when you come back for more. Going beyond campaign contributions or other legal forms of help will get you a quick escort to the door . . . most of the time.

In any case, the total number of requests that just about any office turns down can be counted on the fingers of one hand. To count on fingers and toes the number most Senate offices will add to their "pork list," an excessively digited freak of nature is required.

Pork Eruption

For the Capitol Hill power elite and the appropriations "old bulls," the pork process does not wait until January; it starts earlier, when the new defense budget is assembled inside DoD before Christmas. If DoD fails to wedge into its budget whatever additional spending an elite member deems necessary, there can be trouble.

In a case the press noted, three major shipyards were vying for expansion of their naval shipbuilding in the FY 1998 budget.[1] These yards were in Virginia, Louisiana, and Mississippi, which just happened to be the home states of Sen. John Warner, the chairman of the Senate Armed Services Committee, Congressman Bob Livingston, the chairman of the House Appropriations Committee, and Sen. Trent Lott, the majority leader of the Senate: a fairly heavy-duty combination of power elite and old bulls. The Virginia shipyard had won contracts for new nuclear-powered submarines that many analysts had dubbed relics of the cold war. In a surprise decision for what Congressman Livingston called "the contract of the decade," the Louisiana yard won a contract for new LPD-17 amphibious warfare ships for the Marines, costing more than $9 billion.[2] But the Ingalls Shipbuilding unit of Litton Industries in Pascagoula, Mississippi, was left holding the bag. They had to subsist just on the billions in contracts the yard had already won; there was nothing big and new in the FY 1998 stocking.

Mississippi's Trent Lott was outraged. He threatened to cut funding for the Navy's F/A-18 fighter, which, of course, was built elsewhere. He threatened to deep-six the Navy's futuristic new "Arsenal Ship," for which Pascagoula had little chance. The *Wall Street Journal* reported: "Sen. Lott hit the roof. . . . Word went out on Capitol Hill [from Lott's office]: the Navy had insulted the majority leader and would live to regret it."[3] In an unusually crude exercise, Senator Lott's staff sent a memo to the Navy specifying what it should do, as the memo said in an underlined conclusion, "to make an unhappy man happy."[4] The memo included a list of demands Lott wanted for Pascagoula at the expense of other yards, including the construction of DDG-51 destroyers and design work for several types of future ships, all costing billions of dollars. In addition, there were rumors on Capitol Hill (almost certainly spread from Lott's office) that if the demands were not met, other Navy programs would be cut and future promotions of Navy officers, presumably those making the offending shipbuilding decisions, would be held up when sent to the Senate for their constitutionally required confirmation.[5]

In some Hill offices, such tactics, especially dumb ones that made it easy for the Navy to leak embarrassing documentation to the press, would be cause for acute mortification. The imperious behavior of Senator Lott and his staff drew muttered grunts of derision among the Senate staff and the non-Hill professionals I worked with.

The Navy found itself in a political, if not moral, crisis, and it did what it judged was the only right thing. It decided not to shift shipbuilding and design work from other shipyards (that would infuriate the other power elite) but just to build more ships, something the Navy is always in favor of.

The Navy achieved this by simply winking and nodding while Congress added more Pascagoula-built ships to the budget: one DDG-51* destroyer in 1998 for $720 million and more in the later years, plus an unrequested LHD-8 amphibious assault ship for which Congress spread the funding stream over several years.†

Senator Lott and his staff were finally sated; they dropped their threats and moved on to other things.

Making a Little List

In most Hill offices, the pork process works at a much lower profile. While Senator Lott was extorting billions out of the Navy, I and staffers for other members were quietly making lists. These tallied the various requests from the diverse supplicants that called and came into our offices.

The lists were long. Even if the senator in question represents a state with just modest spending for defense contracts and only a moderate sprinkling of military bases, such as New Mexico, the list can go on for scores of items and hundreds of millions of dollars. Our list extended into the most obscure items, such as university research for "Phyto-Extraction Technology" or unheard-of satellite systems, in one case a project called "GLINT" being worked on in a lab in a local military facility. The list also included buildings on military bases that the Defense Department did not see fit to request but a local base commander said he wanted, additional spending for research on programs the Air Force supported but not at the level the contractor desired, new ideas from the state universities in areas where they claim expertise, and new "centers of excellence" in areas that caught on recently, such as land mine detection, border security, or explosives sniffing. Such lists also included things that have little, if anything, to do with defense: spending for breast and prostate cancer research, youth programs, counter-drug activities, and environmental programs, among others. For FY 2003, I prepared—as I did each year—a spreadsheet to help me and my colleagues keep track of the requests Senator Domenici had gathered by June of 2002: it identified only programmatic and budget essentials and continued for

---

*   It is a minor footnote, but the DDG-51 would strike some as a strange ship to buy more of in the post–Soviet Navy world. The heart of the DDG-51 is its Aegis radar and air defense system that was designed in the 1970s to defend against massed, Soviet air raids on aircraft carrier battle groups on the high seas. In the late 1980s, I participated in a GAO study of the effectiveness of the Aegis system against very simplistic simulations of Soviet tactics. The results of this operational testing were mostly classified but very much did not support the premise that Aegis was extraordinarily effective.

†   The LHD-8 became the brunt of Senate defense staffer jokes as it endured cost overruns and devoured seemingly endless clumps of annual funding in hundred-million-dollar bunches after this episode. The money-hungry LHD-8 became known as "Senator Lott's LHD-8."

twenty-three pages covering eighty-eight separate items. Moreover, this list was just for the defense-related bills. Staffers handling other areas had different lists, all of them long.

When he was a member of the Senate Armed Services Committee, Sen. William Cohen (R-Maine), complained that senators not on the committee had sent such lengthy, item-filled letters asking for additional spending for their states that it took not one, but two, fat loose-leaf notebooks to hold them.[6] Senator Cohen also noted that these requests flooded in whether the requesting senator voted to increase the overall defense budget or to cut it. Porking is an activity that knows no party, ideological, religious, ethnic, gender, racial, or planet of origin boundaries in Congress.

Although the Armed Services Committee does get these letters and although the bill and report that the committee produces do contain thousands of modifications to accommodate these "member requests," the money does not flow unless and until the Appropriations Committee, and its bill and report, endorses them, and the committee's bill becomes law. If an item is "authorized" by the Armed Services Committee but not included in an appropriations bill or report, that item is out of luck. However, if Congress does not authorize an item but does include it in an appropriations bill or report, the money will flow. The Appropriations Committees in the House and Senate are the center of pork activity.

The Envelope, Please

Because they are the primary mechanism for delivering pork and because they receive thousands of requests from members, the House and Senate Appropriations Committees have adopted a routine. In the Senate in early March, the staff of the Defense Subcommittee notify the staff of senators when their "member request letters" (i.e., their pork lists) are due to permit time for subcommittee staff to process the requests. The subcommittee staff will also tell senators' staff what format to use in their letters and an accompanying spreadsheet that is needed to make processing feasible.

Several weeks later, usually on the day before the Defense Subcommittee will meet to "mark up"* the Department of Defense appropriations bill, the subcommittee staff will again convene the staff of senators. At that meeting, subcommittee staff will briefly summarize the major provisions of the bill the chairman is recommending to the Defense Subcommittee, and the

---

* A "markup" is a committee or subcommittee meeting to consider a draft bill. The meeting will proceed through the text of the bill considering both it and amendments. Even though hundreds of billions of dollars are at stake, a markup of the DoD appropriations bill in the Defense Subcommittee, and then again in the full Senate Appropriations Committee, typically takes no longer than an afternoon.

subcommittee staff will hand out large envelopes. The senators' staffers rip open the envelopes and pore over the contents, the first tranche of that year's goodies from the Appropriations Committee.

In addressing the contents of the envelopes, the top Republican and Democratic Defense Subcommittee staffers in the Senate will invariably explain that no member got everything he or she wanted, and no member got nothing. Frequently, there will be two factors explained to control how well each member did: 1) the availability of funds, and 2) whether a senator did or did not vote for the subcommittee's last defense bill. One subcommittee staff director was sometimes uncommonly clear about it: "If you helped us, we helped you." Some might call that extortion.

Getting More Bites Out of the Apple

These envelopes are not the end of the process; they are just the beginning. That afternoon and evening, senators' staff will busy themselves comparing their original pork lists to the contents of the envelopes. Staff will identify where they lost and where their member should try for another bite out of the apple. That is often accomplished with a call from the disappointed member to either the staff director of the subcommittee, or directly to the chairman or ranking member, depending on the supplicant's party. That conversation might consist of a presentation on why the member needs some additional largesse for a specific project for political or economic reasons, and sometimes reasons outlining how the project might assist the national defense. If the call is to the staff director, he or she will always be polite, offer explanations about the shortage of money, and promise to raise the matter with the boss: for Republicans, Senator Stevens, and for Democrats, Senator Inouye. If the call is directly to the chairman or ranking member, the response will often be that they will "think about it" or they will "do what I can."

That evening, Senators Stevens and Inouye will be doing a lot of "thinking about it." They and their staff will have received many calls from senators' offices, more than one from some offices. They will give their consent to several of these requests. Sometimes they will discover more money to pay for the project. Sometimes they will agree to a no-cost solution, which may outlay nothing in the year under consideration but will constitute a commitment for funding in subsequent years. Sometimes they will agree to "report language" that will state how wonderful the idea is and how the Defense Department should find the funds to pay for it. The various agreements for the additional "member items" will be written up in the form of amendments to the bill, or just to the report. At the markup meeting the next day, they will be offered by the chairman as a managers' package that he or she will announce at the meeting and that the subcommittee will, invariably, unanimously adopt.

In addition, at the markup meeting, individual senators may offer separate amendments for projects not included in the managers' package. They may be adopted by prior arrangement with the chairman and ranking member (going that route can sometimes make for a better press release for the offering member). Alternatively, if the answer the offering member already received was a "no," he or she may be fishing for a better answer. Or, that member may simply be demonstrating their stalwart commitment to the beneficiaries of the project back home (which also makes for good press release material). Sometimes, the persistence will pay off, and the sponsor will get some sort of accommodation for their efforts, but if the member is smart, he or she will desist short of aggravating their chairman or ranking member: when pushed too far, an old bull can get nasty—and, more important, stingy.

Just One More Bite

The process will repeat itself for the markup of the full Appropriations Committee, which usually occurs a day or two after the Defense Subcommittee markup. Senators and staff who remain frustrated will persist in their calls to the committee staff and the chairman and ranking member. If they have been rejected more than once, their chances are low, but they may have summoned some new evidence to substantiate their case, or they may have brought in heavier guns.

"Heavier guns" come in many forms. It may be a new letter from the base commander stating why "military necessity" really requires that new parking garage, water tower, or fence. It may be the president or chief executive officer of a major corporation, which just might have a corporate presence in the state of the requesting senator. Rarely will the corporate leader be so crude as to hint about future campaign contributions deriving from the chairman's decision, but if the thought is not present at both ends of the phone line, one or both are not thinking very clearly. Some things simply do not need to be articulated to be fully understood.

At the full committee markup, there will be another managers' package consisting of leftovers from the subcommittee markup and new proposals latecomers to the process have dreamed up. These may be from senators not on the Defense Subcommittee but on the full Appropriations Committee. Senators who are not members of either the Defense Subcommittee or the full committee will act through Appropriations Committee members who are friends or allies, or they will contact the chairman or ranking member directly. The Appropriations Committee chairman and ranking member will accommodate a number of these additional requests. The staff will rewrite the bill and its report to incorporate the additions, and the committee will report the bill to the full Senate for it to consider.

Guess what happens there.

And, Another Bite

Appropriations Committee chairmen like to have their bills debated by the full Senate very promptly after the committee reports the bill out of the Appropriations Committee. Too long a delay will give beavering staff ample time to imagine ways of amending the bill with new, or old, ideas. Too many amendments make for an agonizing experience on the floor for everybody, especially the staff and members managing the bill through the Senate. Invariably, there will be amendments, however, such as the 108 offered to the FY 2002 Defense Appropriations bill, or the more than 50 offered to the FY 2003 Defense Appropriations bill. Many, if not most, of these will be some form of pork, some of it the same project that got a "no" in the subcommittee and full committee markups; some of it something new. The ones deemed acceptable by the chairman and ranking member (for it to be included, both have to approve) will be incorporated into a third and perhaps subsequent managers' packages, after the two adopted in the committee proceedings. The Senate will adopt the new packages with an unrecorded voice vote, and the presiding officer will ask for those in favor and those opposed to register by voice. If he is in the room, Senator McCain will customarily voice-vote no, but the rest will say "aye." It is usually here that Senator McCain will give one of his speeches (usually rather good) about how tawdry the contents of the managers' package are and how someday this behavior should be stopped—presumably by someone other than Senator McCain who has the spine and brains to stop the pork parade as it grunts and snorts without serious opposition through the Senate.

After a day or two of speeches and managers' packages, the Senate will pass the Defense Appropriations bill and send it to a House-Senate Conference Committee to work out the differences between the two bodies' bills.

If you have been paying attention, you know what will happen there.

And Another Bite

When a Defense Appropriations bill is about to go into a House-Senate conference, Senate staffers who are on their toes will contact their House counterparts in the offices of members from the same state, especially if they work for members who are on the House Appropriations Committee. When I worked for Senator Domenici, there would invariably be such a meeting, or phone calls, with the staff of Republican members of the New

Mexico delegation. We would share the identity of those projects we would want to protect in the conference and also, of course, of the projects we wanted to increase. We would also make sure we did not duplicate efforts: the House staffers would focus on certain projects, and I and the other Senate staffers would focus on the remainder. Thus, we could avoid wasteful, redundant staff effort and maximize the number of projects for New Mexico.

If there were projects that had thus far crapped out and received zero funding in both the House and Senate bills, and if any member or staffer felt they deserved yet another try, both sides would work on it. However, in these cases, the rules presented an obstacle. Senate Standing Rule 27 says that new items—that is, items that appear in neither the House nor the Senate bill—cannot appear in a conference report. Those may be the rules, but the phenomenon is frequent enough to have its own name, "Immaculate Conceptions," which do, indeed, occur—such as the four Boeing 737 VIP transports added to the FY 2002 Defense Appropriations bill when it was in conference.

Not everybody can perform immaculate conceptions. They will not occur without the blessing of the chairman and ranking member of both the House and Senate Appropriations Committees. But given the specific individuals involved in the late 1990s and early 2000s, the occurrence of these divine interventions was frequent enough that they would provoke little beyond a smirk among the staff. They would require member-to-member phone calls and, in rare instances, memos or evidence to support them. If the member seeking divine intervention was in the good graces of one or two of "the Big Four"—the chairmen and ranking minority members of the House and Senate Defense Subcommittees—and if the member didn't ask for such special favors too often, the chances would be decent. Depending on the starkness of the new addition, it would violate Senate Rule 27, but rules require someone to enforce them. In the modern Senate, there usually is no such person.

If for some reason a project a member desires has fallen through all the cracks, fear not. In a few months there will probably be a supplemental appropriations bill to augment the regular DoD appropriations bill. There, the process will get started all over again. If you can't make it through these large, low hoops on a second round, it's probably time to give up.

Press Releases

At each and every one of these stages in the process, there is an opportunity for the member to broadcast to the voters back home what a great job he or she is doing bringing home the bacon. The press releases start when the defense budget first goes to Capitol Hill. If the opposing party occupies the White House, the press release will bemoan what a lousy job the president has done to take care of the state (and national defense), but, not to worry, the senator will fix things and obtain more spending for the state. If the president is of the same party, the press release will say that the president's request for the state—and national defense—is a good start. But, not to worry, the senator will improve things and get more for the state.

During the rest of the fiscal year, there are recurring opportunities for more of the same. Additional press releases will invariably be beamed back home informing the voters what bacon the senator has procured as the defense bills squiggle through the legislative process. Long and detailed releases identifying each and every project's funding status will be sent to the state newspapers once

- the Armed Services Committee sends its bill to the Senate for debate;
- the Senate passes the Armed Services Committee's bill;
- the House-Senate Conference on the Armed Services Committee's bill is finished;
- the Defense Appropriations Subcommittee marks up its bill;
- the full Appropriations Committee marks up the Defense Subcommittee's bill;
- the Senate passes the Appropriations Committee's bill;
- the House-Senate conference is finished on the defense bill; and
- any other opportunity seized by a creative press secretary or defense staffer, which of course includes all of the above stages for the Military Construction Appropriations bill.

Some members will anxiously await the response of the state newspapers to these press releases. They are not taken lightly. If the papers fail to mention the senator's actions to procure goodies for the state, that day in the office might not be a pleasant one, especially for the press secretary. Alternatively, if the defense staffer failed to get the information in time for the next day's newspapers, the unpleasant day might pass to him or her. The worst-case scenario is for the newspapers to mention the state's other senator, but not one's own boss. Remember, while one senator's staff is generating all of these press releases, the staff for the state's other senator is doing exactly the same thing, and the exercise will normally be quite competitive. It is not a question of party politics; most senators will find it just as aggravating that a senator from the same party has seized credit for procuring pork as a senator from the other party.

Indeed, regardless of political party, both senators are likely to claim credit for whatever morsels land in the state. In some cases, it will be a bipartisan team effort, and both will deserve credit. In other cases, the bacon will be the work product of mostly one senator, but the other will likely not hesitate for a nanosecond to include that morsel in their own press release, implying it was all his or her work. Woe to the staffer responsible if their own senator deserves the credit for a morsel, but the other senator gets the credit.

Only rarely does the press expend the effort to sort out who did the heavy lifting. In my own experience, the senator with the politics that the paper's editorial board prefers will get most of the credit. During my six years with the Senate Budget Committee, I saw Senator Domenici really angry only twice: the first time was when the New Mexico press failed to give him credit for pork he had added to the Defense Authorization bill and, instead, gave it to the state's Democratic senator, Jeff Bingaman. The second time, which also involved pork and Domenici's angry rebuke to Senator McCain on the Senate floor, is described in the previous chapter.

Who Approves Pork

From the foregoing, it might appear that the say-so for the thousands of "member items" added to defense authorization and appropriations bills comes from the chairmen and ranking minority members of the House and Senate Armed Services, the Defense Appropriations Subcommittee, and the full Appropriations Committees. However, that approval is only one step.

If you are not in the committee leaders' good graces—for example, if you voted against the last DoD Appropriations bill—you are not going to do particularly well by Stevens. Senator Byrd is rumored by staff familiar with his work to keep a list tacked to the back of the door in his private office in the Capitol building. Pork-hungry senators do not want to be on that list; it is rumored to consist of those who, one way or another, have transgressed Byrd and have not yet regained his good graces. Perhaps the senator voted against something that Byrd considered important; perhaps he or she said something at which he took personal offense.

At the other end of the spectrum, if you are a "cardinal" (one of the chairs of the Appropriations Committee's fourteen subcommittees), or if you are a cardinal in waiting (a ranking minority member of the same), or if you chair another Senate committee, such as Armed Services or the all powerful Finance Committee, or if you are one of the power elite (such as majority or minority leader), you will almost certainly do very well with the Appropriations Committee leadership.

Thus, the first test is, "Who are you?" If you are somebody worth helping in the eyes of the Appropriations Committee leadership, you will get some help. If you lack status, and especially if you have offended the wrong senators, your pork requests will not do well.

That is hardly the end of the process. If only requests from members who had managed somehow to offend certain senior appropriators flunked, the rest would be unaffordable. Gluttonous members on the A list would find no limit to their appetites, and non-offending, non-cardinal, non-power elite members would join in on the feast. Some way to filter the billions of dollars worth of outstanding requests is needed. Moreover, Congress needs some way to make it "fair" so that members who fail the test don't revolt.

It's simple. After the "Who are you?" test comes the "Does DoD want it?" test. After they receive the scores of letters requesting thousands of items, the staffs of the Armed Services and Defense Appropriations Committees busy themselves communicating with the Defense Department. They won't be calling any central office and almost certainly no one in the Office of the Secretary of Defense (OSD). They will be calling hundreds of different program offices, often program managers in the military services. If, for example, Senator X wants to add $100 million to an existing program, such as the Air Force's Airborne Laser program, the Senate Defense Appropriations Subcommittee staffer will be asking the Airborne Laser program manager, "How much more do you really want?" If Senator Y wants to start up a new university research program, such as one on Army information warfare, the staffer will ask the appropriate Army office, "Does this thing make any sense?" or "Do you want it?"

If the civilian bureaucrat or the uniformed "milicrat" on the other end of the phone says he or she wants it, congratulations—your pork request just made the grade. The amount of money might, and probably will, be pared down to ensure that both your projects and everybody else's can be wedged into the budget, but once your pork has been blessed by someone in DoD, you might as well write up your final press release. If the DoD bureaucrat is uncertain, the pork request might turn slowly in the wind for a few days or weeks as the appropriators sort out how much money they have to throw around; once that is decided, the questionable projects will be addressed. Some will live, and some will die.

One of the ironies at this point of the process is that the Armed Services or Appropriations Committee staffer might very well be checking out whether DoD wants the pork request with the same individual who got it started in the first place. Those university professors, defense manufacturer lobbyists, military lab scientists, and others did not dream up their ideas entirely on their own. When they call or come into the senator's or congressman's office to state their requests, they often have already been in contact with DoD's bureaucrats and milicrats to figure out what projects and how much money both sides think are reasonable. Alternatively, the supplicant to the senator's or representative's office is the DoD contact. The committee staffer's phone call to check on the project is sometimes simply completing a circle.

In the cases in which the contact in DoD says "no" (i.e., when the pork project is not DoD's baby, and no one there wants it, not even a little), you have a problem. If you're seeking approval from the Senate Armed Services Committee and if your project is rejected by DoD, you're a dead duck. The staff on that committee is known for taking its pork orders directly from its masters in the Pentagon. Just about the only way to turn around a "no" from that committee is to find someone else in the Pentagon to say "yes." In one case, a colleague who had gotten a "no" from the Armed Services staff for a pork request found out that the committee staffer had called the wrong DoD contact, and as soon as the right contact (the DoD sponsor) expressed the right view, the "no" became a "yes."

In the Appropriations Committee, it's a little less clear-cut, but just a little. If the DoD contact gives the committee staffer a "no," your project is in deep trouble, but it may not be completely dead. If you are in the good graces of the committee leadership, if your boss is a cardinal or one of the power elite, you might get a few million, or just a few hundred thousand, to get your project started in order to find out next year if someone in DoD can learn to love your pork. Your chances to overcome reluctance from DoD will probably depend on your senator's making a personal appeal to Senators Stevens or Inouye, or to their top staff. Even then, you'll get half, probably less, of a loaf. But, to receive pork not already endorsed by an official in DoD is climbing a steep grade. The system works easiest when everybody plays by the rule: if DoD wants it, it's okay.

Consequences

Congress is preoccupied with pork to the exclusion of far more important defense issues, especially military readiness. In addition to the backdoor raids on the O&M budget, where training, maintenance, spare parts, military exercises, and combat operations are indirectly tapped to permit more spending on pork (as discussed in chapter 4), Congress sometimes makes direct front-door raids on readiness to enable more pork. Of course, the authors of such maneuvers do not make their actions obvious, but they do sometimes leave a trail, which, sadly, the press often fails to follow.

On 8 June 1999, Senator Stevens shepherded through the Senate an amendment by Senators Kit Bond and John Ashcroft, both of Missouri, to buy four additional F-15E fighter-bombers in the FY 2000 defense appropriations bill for $220 million.[7] The aircraft were not in the DoD budget, but the Air Force was happy to have them. Senator Bond and his sidekick, the junior senator and future attorney general, were also eager to keep the F-15 plant in St. Louis in operation, thereby saving jobs. A member of the Defense Appropriations Subcommittee, Senator Bond took the lead in claiming credit and, predictably, notified the *St. Louis Post-Dispatch*, which dutifully printed an article announcing the good news that the Boeing (formerly McDonnell-Douglas) plant would be able to take a "big step" in keeping the production line open.[8] It was a standard exercise: senator gets additional spending at local plant; local press announces the great success to the workers and voters; senator gets credit; and his staff makes a note to remind everybody at the next election.

Senator Bond did not put in his press release where the $220 million to pay for the aircraft was coming from. As the text of his amendment made clear, $70 million was taken out of the Air Force's account for "Spares and Repair Parts," $50 million was taken out of the Navy's "Spares and Repair Parts" account, $50 million was taken out of equipment purchases for the National Guard and Reserves, and another $50 million was extracted from Research and Development for missile defense.[9] The trade-off was distinct; take $120 million out of spare parts, $50 million away from the perennially under-equipped National Guard and Reserves (as a friend and colleague pointed out, "curiously, Senator Bond is co-chair of the Senate National Guard Caucus,"[10] which was organized to boost the National Guard budget, not raid it), and take another $50 million out of the erstwhile Republican party priority—missile defense. It was a heavy price to pay for four aircraft the Air Force couldn't convince the secretary of defense to buy.

The *St. Louis Post-Dispatch* reported nothing about the readiness and other accounts that Bond and Congress raided to pay for this "good news." It is unclear if the reporter for the story did not bother to obtain and read a copy of Senator Bond's amendment, or having read it deemed a more complete story not the kind of news that his readers needed to know about.

In addition, as the floor manager for the defense appropriations bill who accepted this Bond amendment, Senator Stevens should have known better. Earlier that spring his own staff and I had listened to GAO brief us on a study that Senators Domenici and Stevens had requested. It explained that a major factor causing retention problems in the military services was, among other things, overwork of maintenance personnel and the non-availability of spare parts. In sum, Senator Stevens was permitting the exacerbation of a problem that he helped to expose.

All of this was explained in painful detail in an e-mail message sent by a friend and colleague, Chuck Spinney, to his reader list, which included hundreds of individuals and a few score journalists. As far as I know, not one journalist picked up the news item and wrote about it. The facts were easy for the press to check, especially in the *Congressional Record,* and Spinney even gave them the date and page numbers to look at. It could have made for an interesting news item, especially since the United States had just completed an air war against Serbia over its province of Kosovo. During those operations, spare parts had been a serious problem, and many Air Force and Navy aircraft were cannibalized (stripped of parts and made unflyable) to help keep other aircraft operating. Spare parts were clearly a worsening problem to anyone paying the slightest attention.

Dud Pork Bombs

Sometimes an unfortunate string of events makes it impossible to deliver the bacon in time for an election. This is precisely what happened in late October 2002, just after Congress authorized President Bush to go to war against Iraq. Congress did manage to pass and send to the president the Defense and Military Construction Appropriations bills for the fiscal year 2003, and members were happy to send home the good news. For example, Congresswoman Shelley Moore Capito (R-W.Va.) told the *Morgan Messenger* for tiny Berkeley Springs, West Virginia, that the defense bill would pay $5.2 million for a project entitled "Mustang Survival" in the state.[11]

Unfortunately, however, members of Congress had a serious problem that October with the other appropriations bills. While they had been able to get their act together to pass the DoD and "Mil-Con" appropriations bills, they had not passed any of the other appropriations bills necessary to keep the government operating. Agencies like Veterans Affairs, Transportation, Justice, Education, Treasury, State, and Commerce were all without money and the earmarks and line items that made the pork, and everything else, flow. Congress passed instead a continuing resolution to keep agencies subsisting on the level of funding appropriated the previous year. Unfortunately, however, continuing resolutions contain no line items or earmarks to enable pork to flow. Anxious to get home and campaign for re-elections, the members left Washington—promising to pass the real appropriations bills when they came back the following January. The great tragedy was, however, that there was no pork news to beam home for eleven appropriations bills just before elections.

This was serious. It took quick thinking to avert the crisis. The members wrote the press releases announcing pork goodies and sent them home nonetheless. Each announced project after project just as if the bills had cleared Congress and were law. Congressman Joe Knollenberg (R-Mich.) announced "Federal Funds for [a] SSO Demonstration Project;" Henry Bonilla (R-Tex.) announced $675,000 for Texas A&M's International University; George Nethercutt (R-Wash.) announced federal help for the Boys and Girls Club of Spokane, and so on.[12] Significantly, the members were not announcing what was in any appropriations bills that were becoming law; they were announcing what was in bills as drafted by the House Appropriations Committee but had not yet passed either the House or the Senate and wouldn't be law until the following January, at the earliest.[13] The pork was not in the frying pan; it was still on the hoof awaiting slaughter by Congress when it reconvened in January.

These actions make clear why members of Congress chase pork. Because there was no hard news to report in time for the elections so the voters could thank the members on election day, they were given instead what had queued up in an early stage of the legislative process, and the status was left ambiguous. Pork is not just an act of federal largesse for senators' states and members' districts; it is an integral part of any sitting member of Congress's re-election campaign. Not only do members take credit for the same piece of pork for political purposes, they also take credit for pork they haven't even delivered yet.

Wish Lists and Control of the Budget

Beyond all this congressional pork, there is yet another form—Joint Chiefs of Staff (JCS) pork. It comes in the form of what is known on Capitol Hill as "wish lists" that are submitted each year by the JCS.

Each year the JCS and the House and Senate Armed Services Committees go through a little charade: after the defense budget has been formally submitted to Congress and the hearing process has started, the chiefs of each of the military services are among the first witnesses to appear at Armed Services Committee hearings. Invariably, the committee chairmen ask them, "If you had some extra money, what would you spend it on?" Invariably, the chiefs will respond, "I just happen to have a little list," and they hand over lists that are anything but little. They amount to billions, sometimes tens of billions, of dollars.

These are what the joint chiefs like to call their "unfunded requirements." That name makes them sound as if they have been through some sort of formal review process. In truth, the military services cobble them together independent of any meaningful review. The other military services do not review them; neither the secretary of defense nor any staff in his own offices reviews them, and certainly neither the OMB nor any other non-DoD entity reviews them. The requirements consist of what failed to pass muster when the budget was put together, plus a few extra goodies that clever military staff and commanders dream up.

Just like Congress's pork, the contents of these lists are exempt from any serious review by any objective party, and just like any other pork, they may have good, bad, or indifferent ideas behind them. The problem is, no one really knows. Just like the rest, they are a "pig in a poke."

Sometimes the lack of serious review by anyone is painfully obvious. New VIP transport aircraft for senior military commanders as well as members of Congress frequently appear on these lists. Another favorite is additional ships, such as those requested by Senator Lott, and increases in the production rates of aircraft already in the budget, such as the F/A-18. The overpriced C-130J transport, sometimes in the configuration of a tanker for the Marines, is another favorite. Because most on Capitol Hill, including Senator McCain, do not define the contents of these lists as pork, putting items on these lists is particularly useful. If a member adds money for a wish list program that just happens to be built in his or her state, the item will not be called pork, and the sponsoring member will not have to endure listening to Senator McCain tell the Senate what a useless pile of junk their project is.

Only the JCS control wish lists. Secretaries of defense are neither consulted nor informed about the contents of the lists. One year, when the joint chiefs submitted their wish lists to Congress, the staff of the Defense Department's comptroller—who is supposed to have final approval authority over any and all budget requests—had to call me to obtain a copy of the lists. They did not know the contents, even after they came over to Congress.

The implications for civilian control of the Pentagon is obvious: the department's core management device, the budget (as submitted by the secretary of defense and the president) is incomplete as far as the JCS are concerned. Two secretaries of defense, William Cohen in the Clinton administration and Donald Rumsfeld in the George W. Bush administration, tried to assert civilian control. Both failed miserably. In 1997, shortly after he was sworn in as the new secretary of defense, William Cohen, a former senator and member of the Armed Services Committee who knew quite well how the game was played, told Congress he "would look unfavorably on the traditional [JCS] military strategy for garnering new funds" by submitting wish lists.[14] Days later, in a brazen act of defiance, the joint chiefs each submitted their lists, totaling for that year $11.45 billion. Cohen's own former colleagues on the Senate Armed Services Committee solicited them to do so. Signaling capitulation to the real masters of the Pentagon, Cohen did nothing in response.

In January 2001, after Bush was declared to have won the election but before his inauguration, the military services saw an opportunity. They began to circulate on Capitol Hill their new FY 2002 wish lists. These were breathtaking, totaling about $90 billion. This was in the face of candidate Bush's statements during the election campaign that he would seek an increase of only $45 billion in the defense budget, and that would be over ten years. Hearing about these bloated wish lists, a colleague and I requested the military services to come by our offices to brief us on them. Service representatives were eager to do so, and we scheduled meetings. I then contacted a member of the staff of the secretary of defense–designate (Rumsfeld had not yet been confirmed by the Senate and sworn in) and asked him if he was aware of what the military services were doing. He was ignorant, but he also agreed they were making a mockery of Rumsfeld's authority. I waited. In a few days, the military services called me to cancel their briefings; Rumsfeld shut them down, and for the first time in years, it appeared that civilian authority might be back in control of the Pentagon. At least, I had the luxury of thinking so for a little while.

By late that spring, after Rumsfeld had submitted a revised 2002 defense budget, the joint chiefs communicated to the Armed Services Committees that they were ready to be asked "the question." They were, and they answered it, this time with wish lists totaling $32.4 billion. The chiefs repeated their control a year later, but their aspirations for 2003 were "limited" to "just" $25.4 billion. Control by civilians over the defense budget was a short-lived thing in the second Bush administration.

Under the U.S. Constitution, Congress holds the power to spend revenues as it sees fit, and the modern Congress has exercised that power by delegating it to the JCS and hundreds of faceless mid-level officials, in and out of uniform, in the Pentagon. These civilian bureaucrats and uniformed milicrats exercise more control of the billions spent on pork than do the secretary of defense and even the most authoritative old bulls and power elite in Congress. They and the rest of Congress are just facilitators for pork.

Beyond this abdication of responsibility, there are other more subtle, but even more troubling, attributes to the pork system. In one sense, there is less to pork than appears; it holds less benefit for home states and districts than most believe. On the other hand, there is yet more to it than appears—its consequences go well beyond what is addressed here. It permeates members' decisions on far more important national security issues than just how to spend a few billion dollars each year. We will turn there now.

6

Pork Lows and Highs

There is nothing new about members of Congress pursuing pork, so why all the focus on it here? What was once a predictable but part-time activity has become a full-time preoccupation that permeates Congress's activities and members' decision-making processes. Ironically, this occurs even though there is less selfish benefit to pork than most members of Congress and their staff think, and they are ignoring an approach to pork that could prove far more beneficial to their self-interest than business as usual.

Pork thrived even before there was a United States. Some of the American revolutionaries' complaints about the British parliament included that body's preference to aid members' own boroughs and districts in England, rather than the colonies. During the constitutional convention in 1787, still before there was a Congress, James Madison believed that "[a]rtful legislators 'with interested views' could always find ways to sacrifice 'the interest, and views, of their Constituents' for their own purposes, and then to have their 'base and selfish measures, masked by pretexts of public good and apparent expediency.'"[1] He understood clearly what pork was and is; that it was not just goodies for the folks back home but instead an act by a politician to pander to constituents with an action that he believes will gain himself favor, whether it does or does not in reality benefit the district, let alone the nation. Moreover, even in those cases where it begins to become apparent that the actions benefit very few, or none at all, the politician continues the ruse on the understanding that constituents will remain deceived and express their appreciation with votes and contributions. That is one reason why politicians do not want any serious, objective review of pork: too many times, the public would learn that the effects are hollow or negative.

Early Pork Compared to Modern

An early pork favorite, as today, was shipbuilding. The most expensive weapon system of the early-nineteenth century was "ships of the line" followed by battleships and later nuclear-powered aircraft carriers, which today exceed $10 billion for each. After the War of 1812, Congress authorized nine "ships of the line" to be built in shipyards all along the East Coast.

Four were completed by 1820, and the remaining five entered a creative form of perpetual construction. Each year a small incremental payment was made, but for election years, the funding—and presumably jobs—increased. Forty-one years later, at the beginning of the Civil War in 1861, three of these five ships were still under construction. By then obsolete and useless despite a huge cost that had accumulated, they were more or less finished and then docked and retired or used as prison ships.[2] Whatever funding, construction crew, and operating personnel they absorbed could certainly have been more usefully devoted to up-to-date ships, or anything else the war effort actually needed. These naval dinosaurs were no benefit to the North's cause; they retarded it.

When I started work in the Senate in 1971, the Appropriations Committee was, as now, one of the most powerful committees in the Senate. However, the time and energy senators and their staff spent grubbing for morsels in appropriations bills was a small fraction of what they invest today. In the early 1970s, it was a minor part-time job for me and other staff to follow a few requests through the process. With Senator Javits in the 1970s and Senators Kassebaum and Pryor in the early 1980s, I would occasionally be required to harass the staffs of the Armed Services or Appropriations Committees for some parochial item for New York, Kansas, or Arkansas. Members, of course, wanted pork for their states, and they certainly touted whatever items they won, but the limited effort was the beginning and the end of it.

When I came back to the Senate in 1996 after nine years at GAO, I was horrified to find that just the defense pork in Senator Domenici's staff operation required one individual on Domenici's personal staff, who spent the vast majority of his or her time on defense pork every single day of the week: myself on the Budget Committee, where depending on the time of the year I would spend very little or a great deal of time on Domenici's pork, and yet another staff member on the Budget Committee, who did nothing but follow all appropriations issues, as they pertained to the budget process, and—more often—Senator Domenici's pork requests for all appropriations bills.

I also quickly found out that Domenici's operation was not an exception. Many senators' offices had at least one full-time person handling just pork requests to the Appropriations Committee with help from individual legislative assistants on an as-needed basis.

Moreover, when I would go to the Senate chamber to monitor the progress of defense bills through the Senate, other staff were always busy there handling issues and amendments their senators were interested in. In the past, it was the rare amendment that dealt with pork, and seasoned professional staffers would sneer at them and their staff authors in thinly veiled derision. In the early-twenty-first century, the rare amendments to defense bills were the ones that did *not* deal with pork, and all staffers knew the business was all too serious. Some deeply resented that fact and bemoaned their fate; they thought when they came to the U.S. Senate to work as legislative assistants for national security that they would be involved in important defense and foreign policy issues, but now they found themselves chasing down garbage.

Attitudes and the level of preoccupation also changed outside Congress. In the 1970s, just four defense contractors had any real presence as lobbyists in Senator Javits's office. I would frequently talk, meet, or, as I called it, "be bought for lunch" with lobbyists from Grumman and Fairchild on Long Island, Bell Aerospace from the Buffalo area, and GE from Syracuse and Schenectady. For Kansas, defense lobbyists came from Boeing, Beech, and Cessna. If any smaller subcontractors, representing just a few dozen jobs, wanted to influence Senator Javits's activities and votes (such requests were uncommon), we would always be polite and take note of their concerns, but it never required a building up of one's courage or a major decision in the office to vote or act against the grain of their corporate interests and requests. It was just when there were hundreds or thousands of jobs at issue that caused us to stick our snouts in the trough. Things changed dramatically by the mid-1990s. Small subcontractors and subcontractors to subcontractors maintained a constant flow of requests to Senator Domenici and to the vast majority of staff colleagues I knew in other offices. Not to favor virtually every request they submitted, and to act and vote accordingly, was just about unthinkable.

Consequences

Working for pork requires more than just time and energy—it requires a suspension of principles, especially good government. Repeatedly, I encountered situations where members and staff compromised their better judgment to push pork. Ironically, a good example of how pork can corrupt staff involves an example of Senator Domenici doing the right thing.

In 1997 the Navy and several of its shipbuilders were pushing the Armed Services Committees to employ some back-door funding to permit the purchase of several logistics ships. The Navy wanted the ships but could not fit them into its official budget, so it lobbied together with the American Shipbuilding Association to fund the ships behind the back of Secretary of Defense William Cohen. Their plan was to buy the ships in small annual allotments of funding, rather than to pay all construction costs up front. This incremental funding extracted a commitment from Congress and the executive branch to acquire the ships with only a small and seemingly painless down payment.

History has amply demonstrated that this was an atrocious way for the government to buy things; once the government was committed, costs tended to grow well beyond the original estimate, and because the funding came in annual allotments, not everyone on Capitol Hill would detect the cost growth. As a result, "full funding"—paying all procurement costs up front—became the accepted practice, and various forms of incremental funding, such as the lease-purchase of Boeing air tankers described earlier, were deemed a violation of the Budget Act and made subject to a "sixty-vote point of order."*

When the House and Senate Armed Services Committees were meeting to complete their conference on the FY 1998 Defense Authorization bill, I learned that the senators and congressmen from shipbuilding states were arguing for the worst possible form of incremental funding—through a lease-purchase. I sent memos to Senator Domenici with data on the additional cost beyond normal "fully funded" purchases and argued against the bad precedent the proposed deal would set for other defense procurement. Domenici instructed me to draft a letter to the chairmen and ranking members of the House and Senate Armed Services Committee telling them that if their final bill contained the lease-purchase, their entire bill—and year's effort—would be vulnerable to a sixty-vote point of order in the Senate. Without saying so directly, the letter also hinted that Senator Domenici might raise the point of order himself, which was highly unusual for him on a defense bill. The bill came out of the conference without the funding scam, and Senator Domenici was credited (some would say blamed) by the press for killing the bad idea.[3]

Then, I received an interesting phone call. It was from a staffer on the Senate Armed Services Committee who was sympathetic to what I had helped Senator Domenici accomplish. He was giving me a friendly heads-up. It was not the shipbuilders after my skin (their lobbyist had always been professional and correct in her dealings with me) but a House staffer. This staffer had been pushing the incremental funding very hard and was irate it was defeated. He was also boasting he would take revenge against me. As it turned out, nothing happened to me, but I did learn later that the House staffer took a job with the shipbuilding industry. It was clear to me he had curried favor with the proponents of the bad idea of lease-purchasing ships

---

* As explained earlier, such points of order force the proponents of a ruse to acquire not just the normal majority of votes to win, but sixty of the Senate's one hundred votes to overcome the rules imposed by the Budget Act to permit the provision that violates the Budget Act to be debated further.

in order to advance his personal agenda. Pushing pork can increase more than government spending; it can also increase personal income.

Consequences: Robbing Peter *and* Paul

Another consideration is the programs that do not receive funding but should. The consequences for military readiness have already been explained. Former senators Warren B. Rudman (R-N.H.) and Gary Hart (D-Colo.) explained another consequence on the op-ed page of the *Washington Post* on 5 November 2002. In a piece titled "We Are Still Unprepared," Rudman and Hart explained that they had chaired a 1990 commission on national security that warned that terrorism was the most serious national security threat of the future and the United States was vulnerable and unprepared. Of course, September 11 followed. More than a year later, the two former senators warned again: "But more than a year has passed since the 9/11 attacks, and basic security priorities have not been met. . . . If funds for these tasks do not exist, authorization and appropriation of funds must be made the immediate priority of a post-election, lame-duck congressional session."[4]

Congress convened that lame-duck session, and it did finally pass the Homeland Security bill that created the new Homeland Security cabinet department. However, Congress failed to appropriate any new money for the agency and left town for the holidays. When reconvened on 7 January 2003, it did rouse itself to consider the FY 2003 appropriations bills it had left unpassed before the holidays.

It takes little imagination to surmise what Congress did. At the recommendation of Senator Stevens, the Senate produced a bill that cut homeland security funding to permit budget room for still more "member items."

Consequences: Collectively and Individually

A novel event occurred when the Senate Democrats took both notice and offense at Senator Stevens's excessive member items in the 2002 homeland security legislation. They offered amendments to restore homeland security funding for the $5 billion extracted out of local fire and police departments, food safety, the FBI, nuclear power plant protection, and port, border, and airport security.[5] Stevens angrily threatened to restore the homeland security funding by taking out of the bill the thousands of member items he had put in. To their shame, the Democrats, led by Senator Byrd, shrank in horror, and the Senate did not even debate any amendment to trade pork in for more homeland security funding.[6]

Such manipulation works individually as well as it does collectively, and the threats do not always have to be explicit, or even stated. When word of the Boeing 767 tanker deal first started to hit Congress's hallways in October

2001, I asked the CBO to prepare a cost estimate, and I asked a friendly budget examiner in the OMB to send me his cost estimates. Both calculations showed the lease purchase to cost billions more than a purchase, no matter how it was scored (current year dollars, constant year dollars, net present value). I put the data in a memo to Senator Domenici, hoping to convince him to oppose the deal as too expensive and a terrible precedent. I reminded him of his previous success in 1997 on shipbuilding, but this time I failed.

At a Defense Subcommittee markup of the FY 2002 Defense Appropriations bill, Senator Stevens announced he had cut a deal with Boeing, the Air Force, and CBO on how to lease-purchase the one hundred Boeing 767s. As soon as Stevens stopped talking, Domenici chimed in and warmly praised the deal. I was surprised and disappointed. As far as I knew, Stevens had never spoken to Domenici about the matter, and I expected, at worst, that Domenici would just keep his mouth shut and silently let the deal go through, but instead he warmly and loudly endorsed it.

After the meeting, I went back to the Budget Committee and stuck my head in the door of my immediate boss, Bill Hoagland. Dejected, I told him what Domenici had done. Like me, Hoagland was surprised Domenici had gone the extra mile to praise Stevens, but we both knew why: the subcommittee markup was not just on the tanker deal, it was on the entire 2002 DoD appropriations bill, and Domenici wanted to ensure that as much New Mexico pork was included in the bill as the system could bear. Domenici knew he would run again for re-election in 2002, and he did not want New Mexicans to think his advancing age had diminished in the least his ability to bring home the bacon.

Domenici seemed content for the nation to pay a few extra billions for leasing, rather than buying, the Boeing tankers so that the nation could also pay a few extra million for pork spending in New Mexico. Senator Domenici's laudable impulse for opposing expensive budget proposals was trumped by his eagerness to stuff more pork into New Mexico. Senator Stevens never had to say a word to him, other than "thanks."

It was a prime example of one of the most pernicious aspects of the pork system. Probably the least damage caused by the pork system is the wasted money.

Pork Ignorance Is Pork Bliss

Unfortunately, when Senator Domenici traded in good government for pork, the pork he was pushing did little to aid New Mexico.

When I started to work for him, visions of changing Domenici's mind about pork danced in my head. My office neighbor on the Budget Committee staff told me flatly, "Forget it." He explained Domenici voraciously pursued pork for New Mexico and considered it a pillar of his electoral success in the state. "If you ever see him eating a steak," my colleague told me of an experience with Domenici at a restaurant, describing how the senator permitted nothing to impede his inhaling the meat, "you'll know what I mean." Domenici gobbled up spending for New Mexico as aggressively as he devoured a good steak.

This told me I had to be smart if I was to slow down the Domenici pork operation. Just arguing for a sharper focus on defense spending that strengthened real defenses, not only the New Mexico economy, was clearly inadequate. I decided on what I thought was a surefire approach: with Domenici's permission, I requested a study from GAO to assess the impact of defense spending on the New Mexico economy. To make certain the study was done right, I steered the study request to some former colleagues in GAO who I knew would do a thorough and professional job.

A few months later, the study came up with some dramatic results. Most of the defense contracts for major weapons programs Senator Domenici was supporting on the grounds that their subcontracts significantly helped New Mexico in fact generated only tiny numbers of jobs in the state, some none at all. Rather than the hundreds of jobs Domenici assumed for systems like the C-17 and C-130 aircraft, for which Honeywell in Albuquerque held subcontracts, there were only a tiny number of jobs, usually less than twenty. In other cases, the money "awarded to New Mexico" simply passed through the subcontractor in the state for work actually performed in another state. Only the military bases in the state, of which there were four, generated enough jobs to have any meaningful economic impact in New Mexico.

Thinking that GAO's findings would result in Domenici's reducing his porking to just the items that had any real in-state impact, I arranged for the GAO team to brief the senator. He listened to the briefing, which—while typically dry—made the results clear, and then he asked a few questions and thanked the briefers. After the meeting when we were alone, he said to me, "I don't know what you want me to do with that information." Thinking he missed GAO's point, I restated their findings about which DoD spending generated New Mexico jobs and which did not, and I recommended to him that in the future he focus on just the spending that generated the most jobs. While I forget his exact words, he politely dismissed me from his office, conveying the message that it was not going to happen.

I had failed to understand an important point about Senator Domenici's political success in New Mexico: his reputation as "St. Pete" depended not just on his actually bringing home the bacon but also on the perception that he did so. If he significantly reduced the number of projects in his press releases, describing what he had done for New Mexico in defense appropriations bills, he would be undermining his hard-won reputation.

As I had been told many times by my first immediate boss on Capitol Hill in Senator Javits's office, Pete Lakeland, it does not matter what the facts are—it matters most what the judge *thinks* the facts are. In this case, the judge was the voters of New Mexico, and if they thought Domenici was reducing his pork operations, they would think he was losing his interest or his skill in bringing home the bacon. Moreover, it is likely that Senator Domenici believed the voters of New Mexico admired him because of his success with pork; he was not about to ask them to love him for some other reason.

My efforts to reduce the scope of the Domenici pork operation were an abject failure, but I had learned the benefits of the system for New Mexico amounted to very little trickle down, and in some cases no drops at all. I began to discuss with other staff the results from GAO's study in an effort to encourage others to learn what delusions they, like me, operated under. I do not think I got very far with them, and my former colleagues in GAO never received any requests from other senators' offices to assess the actual impact of defense spending in their states. Most staffers on Capitol Hill are much too busy chasing pork to understand it fully, or they just do not want to know.

Taking a Break from Pork

Senator Domenici's refusal to consider diminishing his pork operation was actually unique among the four senators I worked for. The other three taught me there were more palatable routes to senators' electoral success. Each, at some point, actively opposed pork in their own state, and they never regretted it.

Early in my career, when I worked for Senator Javits, he faced a dilemma involving the antiballistic missile (ABM) system the United States built in the 1970s. Javits believed ABM systems were a waste of money and were strategically destabilizing. (They could induce national leaders to think they were invulnerable under an ABM umbrella and therefore free to attack the enemy.) At President Nixon's recommendation, the United States had decided to build an ABM system called Safeguard. Javits remained opposed despite a General Electric plant in Syracuse, New York, having a major part of the work for the ABM system's radar. Representatives of GE lobbied me and, primarily, Javits to nonetheless support the system because of the money and jobs it meant for New York. He ultimately decided not to compromise his position and to continue to oppose the system. He instructed me to call the GE lobbyist we had been dealing with and tell him, as a courtesy, that when an upcoming amendment was offered in the Senate to eliminate funding for the Safeguard system, Javits would support the amendment. I remember the phone call; the GE lobbyist was utterly bewildered. He said something like, "Didn't Senator Javits remember that the Syracuse plant had the radar work and hundreds of GE employees were involved?" He did. "Didn't Senator Javits appreciate this meant millions of defense dollars for GE?" He did. The lobbyist had blandly assumed Javits would support the system, given GE's involvement, and discard his previous convictions. The senator's continued opposition to ABM simply did not compute. Dumbfounded, he concluded on the phone, "Well, okay" and hung up. I never heard from him again.

Although it is entirely possible that GE quietly took actions to inform its employees of Javits's non-support or complained off the record to the press or to Javits's future political opposition, I never heard or saw any evidence of it. No great rush of phone calls or letters came in from GE employees, no heaps of newspaper articles, no nasty editorials in the Syracuse newspapers, nothing. We expected all of it and looked for it but never saw any of it. As Javits's staffer handling defense issues, if there was a meaningful negative reaction out there I should have seen it, and I did not. While GE had a reputation that was no better and no worse than other defense contractors when it came to its political operations on Capitol Hill, the adverse and painful political consequences that Senator Javits and I expected from his decision to oppose the Safeguard ABM system turned out to be more ominous in our imaginations than in reality. We had been victims of the conventional wisdom that failing to support pork was tantamount to writing off chances for electoral success in the area where the pork was located, and certainly not worth the trouble.

It was an important lesson to learn: sticking to one's own convictions did not always have negative consequences.

When I worked for Sen. Nancy Kassebaum, as discussed, she made a name for herself as a "military reformer" speaking plainly about, and frequently in opposition to, her own party's defense program. One of the worst parts of that program—one that President Reagan emphasized in the 1980 presidential campaign—was the B-1 bomber. Once inaugurated, Reagan re-ensconced the B-1 as a new "improved" B model. By adding weight, less thrust, overly ambitious electronics, phony claims of a tactically significant reduction in radar cross section (i.e., "semi-stealthy-ness"), and, of course, great cost, the B model barked and woofed loudly. Senator Kassebaum's problem was that the Boeing plant in Wichita, Kansas, had a large piece of the avionics work, more than $1 billion worth. Boeing lobbied her hard and long. The company's CEO spoke with her about the aircraft more than once. Always polite, she ultimately told Boeing she would vote against the B-1B.

Boeing, like GE with Javits, did nothing adverse to Senator Kassebaum. In her case, she happened to be the chairman of the Civil Aviation Subcommittee of the Senate Commerce Committee, and as Boeing knew, if the company took any action to make painful her decision to oppose the B-1B, she was in a position to return the favor, in spades, to the nation's largest producer of civilian aircraft. Not only did Boeing want to avoid turning Senator Kassebaum into an enemy, it wanted to retain her as a friend, on both civilian and defense aviation issues. They took no action, such as attempting to inflame their workers and the local newspapers against her. Indeed, Boeing remained friendly to her, both on the surface and, as far as I could tell, under the table. Relations remained good. In future years, Senator Kassebaum and I worked with Boeing to advocate its cheaper, better 747 as an alternative to the Air Force's preferred option for a long-range, heavy cargo aircraft, the notorious Lockheed C-5. That effort failed, but it also demonstrated Boeing's need not to burn its bridges with Senator Kassebaum.

Senator Kassebaum also reaped an unanticipated benefit; sometime after she notified Boeing of her decision, she spoke publicly against the bomber. The Wichita newspaper noticed and, rather than castigating her for failing to slavishly support Boeing, it praised her for her independence. In short, her opposition to Kansas pork won her local kudos. Senator Kassebaum created political benefit for herself not by pursuing pork, but by opposing it!

There are five significant characteristics of the defense pork system in today's Congress.

First, it is a system controlled from beginning to end by military officers and civilian bureaucrats in the Department of Defense, with only slight modification from Congress. Pork is not something Congress forces on an unwilling Defense Department. It is spending that someone in DoD wanted to include in the original defense budget, but with the project failing to pass muster in the executive branch, the DoD sponsor, or his industry or university or contractor surrogate, uses the back door in Congress to breathe life into it. Even if the project is not initially the brainchild of someone in DoD, getting it successfully inserted into a defense bill on Capitol Hill requires a positive answer to the Appropriations Committee or Armed Services Committee from DoD.

In the rare cases where the project truly is a congressional creation and the military services do not want it, it would take only a public statement to that effect to give the project a quick death sentence. Senators and representatives are eager to curry favor with DoD and to present themselves as pro-defense to the electorate; a DoD official, especially one in uniform, calling useless a project someone in Congress is pushing, will usually cause the politician to drop it like a hot potato.

The senior, old bull appropriators who wave through the pork approved by DoD might reduce the amounts for miscreant senators, but these reductions are at the fringes of the process. In truth, the old bulls and all the others in Congress processing pork are little more than messenger boys for the DoD personnel who originate and approve the thousands of pork projects Congress adds to defense bills each year.

Second, the pork process makes everybody engaging in it happy: the DoD manager gets the spending he or she wants, the lobbyist earns a fee, the old bull appropriator poses as a dispenser of goodies, staffers play at power broker, and the recipient senators broadcast how effective they have been at bringing home the bacon, especially around election time. All that makes pork universally loved, almost.

There might be just one or two unhappy people—the secretary of defense has been circumvented by his own bureaucracy that wedges back into the budget all manner of projects the secretary thought he killed or that he was never shown. His and the president's budget is converted into an ever-expanding spending machine. Recent secretaries of defense, including the current one, seem to have no problem with this. They sit idly by as their own bureaucracy shreds their defense budget.

This process has both short- and long-term budget implications: items the secretary and president may have wanted in the budget—whether sensible or not—are shouldered aside, and herds of camels' noses shoved under the tent compromise future defense budgets. To exist, the pork system must be ever expanding; as it does so, it takes spending levels with it.

Third, the pork system undermines military effectiveness and good government. It raids the DoD budget of money needed for more important things, such as training, equipment maintenance, and spare parts. Sometimes the raids on readiness spending are direct and brazen; sometimes they are indirect and veiled. In either case, the effect is the same: military readiness is degraded. Even more important, the pork process deflects members of Congress from doing their job in a manner the voters have a right to expect: to remain in the good graces of the old bulls who can and do deny pork, members of Congress flinch at selecting good government when it means crossing members like Ted Stevens.

Fourth, Americans like to think our system of government is one that runs by laws, not men, and that keeps itself under control through a system of checks and balances. The pork system is a system where things happen because people want them to happen, and parliamentary rules and U.S. statutes, such as the Budget Act, are circumvented or ignored when they pose an impediment. It is also a system that avoids review by outside or objective parties. Meaningful checks and balances simply do not exist in this system.

Fifth, it is all getting worse, and no one is doing anything about it.

Preoccupation with pork is just one of the characteristics of the modern Congress and its involvement in national security. Another prominent element is the absence of a different activity—oversight.

III

How the System Operates, or Doesn't

7

Oversight: The Triumph of Appearances over Reality

While pork involves great amounts of time and energy on the part of both members and staff, it constitutes only a part of Congress's impact on national security. Another impact results from Congress not doing what it should.

I learned from the senators I worked for, especially Javits, that the most important thing I could do as a national security staffer was to help members understand what was going on; put more formally, such work in Congress is called oversight. For national security it means, for example, to find out what is really happening in the Defense Department behind the gloss of official testimony, the military services' pseudo-informative budget presentations, and officers' overproduced PowerPoint briefings on weapon systems. If I could get under the superficial fluff, my bosses would be able to ask the kind of questions at hearings that would prompt Defense Department witnesses to glance nervously back at their staff for help and promise to provide complete answers—just as soon as they found out themselves.

When I worked in the 1970s for Senator Javits, a member of the Senate Foreign Relations Committee, hearings with cabinet members were a big deal, especially if they involved the war in Vietnam. The secretary of state then, William Rogers, did not like to testify to that committee on that subject. He sometimes left hearings fuming because the committee told him things about the war it was not supposed to know. On one occasion as his entourage left, I overheard one of Rogers's deputies instruct a subordinate, "Find out how those bastards found that out."

With Senators Kassebaum and Pryor, I had a lot of help from friends in the Pentagon. Together, we told the public about many things the Pentagon wanted hidden, none of them classified and all of them about incompetent or venal behavior. Not only was it good government and politics, but also the press loved it.

By the opening of the new century, things had changed. On Thursday, 13 February 2003, I went to an oversight hearing the Senate Armed Services Committee (SASC) had with the Pentagon's leadership. Among Senate staff I spoke with that morning, rumors were rife that the war with Iraq would begin that coming weekend. I ran into a former colleague from the

Budget Committee in the Dirksen building basement, and she was concerned enough that she was making plans to leave the city at the end of the week, but was not sure where she would go. I offered her my weekend house in West Virginia and told her to call my wife to make arrangements. Luckily, she never had to call.

But, in such an atmosphere that day, you'd think an Armed Services Committee hearing with the secretary of defense would be extraordinary: senators seeking remediation for problems their staff found on the adequacy of preparations; informed, probing questions on the readiness of the combat units in the war theater; and discussion about the messages the administration sought to convey to the enemy and the world on the eve of conflict.

Here is what I observed.

Oversight—SASC Style

The hearing started at 9:35 AM and lasted two hours, fifty-three minutes. Twenty-one senators were there at some point, which was a good turnout, even for a secretary of defense. Clearly, the members knew it was a major hearing.

There were also forty-five staffers, many of them jockeying for a seat close to his or her boss among the insufficient chairs behind the members. The staff crowding got worse as the hearing progressed; the standing overflow jammed itself into the back corners of the elevated platform on which the senators were seated.[*]

Secretary of Defense Rumsfeld and the chairman of the joint chiefs, Gen. Richard Myers, testified for DoD, with a seemingly small DoD staff of seventeen behind them. In the press section were twenty-seven reporters. The public audience numbered about two hundred.

The committee chairman, Sen. John Warner (R-Va.), started the hearing declaring, "the troops deserve Congress's support [in the war,] and they will get it." Ignoring that DoD had not yet requested a single penny for transport, ammunition, or anything else to pay for the fighting, Warner turned quickly to the navy shipbuilding budget, which he said, "is increasing but not as much as we would like to see it." War might have been looming, and not a single penny had been requested by the president or provided by Congress to pay for it, but the shipyard back home in Newport News, Virginia, was elbowing its way to the head of the line.

Then the committee's senior Democrat, Carl Levin from Michigan, complained about being misinformed by the Republican White House

---

[*] Apparently, none of the staff was willing to submit to the ultimate humiliation: to sit with the audience, which would concede for all to see that one's member could somehow get through the hearing without the benefit of the staffer whispering into his or her ear.

regarding how much data the CIA had given the UN weapons inspectors in Iraq. A real issue, but these witnesses were from DoD, not the CIA or the White House.

Chairman Warner regained the microphone with a budget initiative, but it was not to pay for the war: it was the Armed Services Committee's budget for its own staff. Warner wanted the senators to okay it so he could send it to the full Senate for approval.

At 9:56, it was finally Rumsfeld's turn to talk; he read excerpts from his prepared, written statement for twenty-two minutes. During this time, most senators were not listening but were casually talking with each other or reading, likely going through their staffers' memos trying to figure out what questions to ask. Even though the memos had probably been available since the day before, as the senators I worked for all required, these senators seemed to be reading the memos for the first time. The giveaway was their periodic prompting of their staff to come talk with them and explain things.

After Rumsfeld finished reading, we got a taste of what questions those memos urged. First Warner asked General Myers: "Are U.S. armed forces ready to fight in Iraq, Korea, and Afghanistan, at the same time, if necessary?" Myers responded, "Absolutely."

That was it, the entirety of the inquiry into our military readiness to fight three separate wars simultaneously, if necessary. This fifteen-second query and response were not the precursor to a lively exchange; it was the totality of the hearing's probe into the—literally—life-and-death question of military readiness. Had Warner or the horde of staffers sitting behind him bothered to scratch the surface, they would have found real problems. Shortly after this hearing, the chief of staff of the Army, Gen. Eric Shinseki, sent a letter to Congress complaining that the U.S. Army was anything but absolutely ready. Army readiness accounts were already $3.2 billion short for base operations, ammunition, and training. I saw staffers bringing their bosses coffee, nodding to each other to say hello and tussling over chairs, but I saw none jumping up to tell any senator that General Myers's assurance needed probing.

When it was his turn to ask questions, Sen. Ted Kennedy (D-Mass.) wanted to know if the United States would use nuclear weapons in Iraq. Rumsfeld refused to say no, but neither Kennedy nor anyone else asked a follow-up question to Rumsfeld's provocative response. It was as if Kennedy, and his staff, had done no preparatory work to anticipate Rumsfeld's answer, didn't like—or comprehend—the response, and didn't want to mess around with the subject any more for fear that more discussion would generate more unwanted—or incomprehensible—answers. The lack of more inquiries after the initial ones between so many senators and Rumsfeld made me think the Armed Services Committee must have a rule against follow-up questions.

There also seems to be a rule that it is okay not to listen. At one point, Chairman Warner almost breathlessly made an announcement that he had just received a hand-delivered rush letter from the CIA stating that evidence of a North Korean missile with range to reach California was old information—nothing new as had been recently reported. Immediately after that, Sen. Daniel Akaka (D-Hawaii) had his turn to ask questions. He read off from a piece of paper a prepared question about a CIA revelation the day before that the North Koreans had a missile that could reach Hawaii. It was not clear whether he was simply not paying attention or had just realized that Hawaii was somewhere between Korea and California. After his staff explained the situation to him, Akaka moved on to his concerns about the Migratory Bird Act and Guam.

Later came the new senator from Arkansas, Democrat Mark Pryor. I was looking forward to his questions. As a senator, his father, David Pryor, had sometimes been a real tiger on oversight. The younger Pryor first read off two questions from Senator Byrd, who had by then left the hearing. Byrd's queries probed the missing budget request to pay for the war. Pryor got a non-answer from Rumsfeld and, without any follow-up, moved on to his own question: Wouldn't Secretary Rumsfeld agree that it would be terrible if Little Rock Air Force Base and Pine Bluff Arsenal in Arkansas were closed?

Rather than beat up on the junior senator, I should thank him. His focus on home state pork as the nation prepared to go to war said everything anyone needs to know about Senate Armed Services Committee oversight. Pryor was merely conforming to the priorities that Chairman Warner and innumerable other senators on that committee had already established.

As far as I could tell, the forty-five-plus staffers at the hearing had done nothing to help their bosses understand where soldiers on the eve of war needed help, almost nothing to help senators exercise control of the purse strings to pay for the war, and very little that had anything to do with examining serious national security issues in peacetime, let alone on the eve of war.

It is inappropriate to say that most of these staffers for members of the Senate Armed Services Committee were preoccupied with doing marginal things like getting coffee for their bosses, jostling for seats, or greeting each other. Most were simply doing nothing. Based on the questions their bosses were asking, that appears to be their job. They were doing it well.

The senators were not any better. Not paying attention, reading off questions with dated information, and nudging Rumsfeld about home state pork seemed to be their idea of how to prepare for war. The whole performance, including Rumsfeld's lack of interest in communicating anything of significance to the committee and getting away with it, was a demoralizing example of what passes for oversight in Congress at the opening of the twenty-first century. Like the new senator from North Carolina, Sen. Elizabeth Dole, who appeared in a brilliant orange dress with her hair coiffed with precision and who left the hearing without asking a single question, it was all for show.

Historians Beware

There is no telling what the Armed Services Committee's official transcript for this hearing might show. Before printing, staffers will have gone over it word by word. Each raw (verbatim) transcript is delivered to senators' staffs with an admonition to make only minor changes; the caution is routinely ignored. Non-sentences, clumsy grammatical constructions, embarrassing misstatements of fact, and very probably Senator Akaka's inelegantly read-off question will all be transformed to perfect English—if not silver-tongued rhetoric—as astute questions asked by carefully listening senators. The hearing in the official committee transcript, when it is printed, will very likely be something that casts the committee's members in a much more favorable light than what actually transpired in that hearing room that morning. Having rewritten many transcripts for my own senators—transcripts not just for committee hearings but for debates in the Senate chamber as well—I know the drill.

Historians use these official, printed committee hearings and the *Congressional Record* of House and Senate debates as a primary historical source. Lawyers even use them for court cases. They all should be more careful. Whole sections can be, and often are, heavily altered by staff, and there is no indication in the official text of what portions are staff rewritten and what was actually said at the hearing or in the floor debate. The *Congressional Record* and hearing transcripts have become yet another way members of Congress exercise a free hand to improve appearances.

Oversight—Appropriator Style

The Senate Armed Services Committee is hardly alone in its cursory attitude toward oversight and its preoccupation with appearances. From 1996 to 2002, I was assigned to staff Senator Domenici for hearings of the Defense Subcommittee of the Senate Appropriations Committee. From March to June of each year, the Defense Subcommittee would hold hearings to help it put together the Department of Defense appropriations bill. The subcommittee would hold a maximum of one hearing per week, and some weeks would go by with no hearing at all. Each of the three military services would get one hearing (the Marines were wrapped in with the Navy) to explain and justify their budgets, each costing about a hundred billion dollars. Other hearing sessions would be devoted to subjects like missile defense, the National Guard and Reserves, and the Defense Health Program. One might argue that one hearing, usually lasting just three hours (from 10:00 AM to 1:00 PM), is hardly enough to probe an entire military service, the highly controversial missile defense program, the $20 billion DoD health program, or the hundreds of thousands of soldiers in the Guard and Reserves. However, the subcommittee virtually never held more than one hearing per year on any of these areas during the time I worked for Senator Domenici. Some weeks the subcommittee would postpone a hearing and never reschedule it.

Attending one of these Defense Subcommittee hearings provides a quick answer for why just one, or none, is adequate to the subcommittee's purposes. Like the SASC, there is no meaningful oversight performed at these hearings, but unlike the Armed Services Committee, sometimes there is not even any effort to pretend oversight is on anybody's mind. When he was chairman, Senator Stevens would usually start things off with a question he read or summarized from a notebook in front of him. It would be something relevant to the jurisdiction of the day's hearing. Then, he would ask a question that directly or indirectly involved defense spending in Alaska. (Sometimes he would go immediately to the Alaska-related question.) Then, he passed the questioning to the top Democrat in attendance at the hearing, usually Senator Inouye.

No slouch for either pork or Senate courtesy, Senator Inouye would usually say something warm and cozy about his good friend and partner Senator Stevens and move to his own favorite subject area, Hawaii and defense spending there. And so it would go. With the questioning bouncing from Republican to Democrat and back again, the witness typically would be bombarded from both sides with questions about spending that was somehow related to the state of the senator doing the asking. When the member ran out of time, he or she would submit questions for the witness to answer later for the printed record of the hearing. These too usually addressed the benefit of the home state.

My own boss, Senator Domenici, was no exception. Each week, I would prepare a notebook for him for the hearing. In the front was a memo I had written trying to direct his attention to some serious issue: poor readiness of the military service testifying that week, failures in acquisition programs, lousy recruitment and retention numbers for that service, et cetera. Sometimes Senator Domenici would read these memos and the related questions, and on a few occasions, he would ask a question or two. Invariably, however, he would turn to what I always made the last tab in the hearing notebook. There, the defense staffer from Domenici's personal staff (I was on his Budget Committee payroll) had written out questions and statements about New Mexico pork. Domenici almost always asked these questions, and the ones that could not be asked due to lack of time were invariably submitted to the witness for written answers later. Immediately after the hearing, the senator's press secretary would call the New Mexico press to tell them what Domenici had asked and what answers he got. The subject matter of these phone calls was never oversight—it was always pork.

Early in my tenure with Senator Domenici, I tried to have some of my own non-pork questions, which Domenici had not asked at the hearing, submitted with the unasked pork questions for later written answers from the witnesses. I sent Domenici a memo urging him to permit the questions to be submitted and answered. The memo came back with a large "no" scrawled next to my question. Later in my time with Domenici, when I felt more secure in my relationship with him, I stopped asking him for permission to have these unasked questions submitted to witnesses; I simply went ahead on my own and did so. These questions attempted to probe failures in personnel, hardware, and readiness programs, and while the DoD witnesses were quite adept in writing, usually months later, long non- or one-sided answers, there was, from time to time, a tidbit of new and important information. When any such significant information surfaced, I would try to use it in a new memo to Domenici to pique his interest. I usually failed in that effort and would later give the information to a journalist or another staffer who I thought might ask some follow-up questions to develop the issue.

I had learned from hard experience with Domenici that I would only get a puzzled, sometimes perturbed, look if I told him I had found some sort of problem in the military services that might embarrass them by contradicting what they had told the public or Congress. I came to believe that Domenici's reasons for being uninterested in any real oversight of the military services were quite simple. He wanted to be a friend to DoD, and friends, at least what is called a friend in Congress, don't ask unwelcome questions and don't go looking beneath the well-polished surface.

Being a friend to DoD had two consequences Domenici ardently desired. First, it enhanced his reputation for being "pro-defense." It meant that generals and secretaries of military services would show up at public meetings with Domenici and say nice things about him, thereby helping Domenici score points with the electorate. Second, being a friend to DoD also, and more important to Domenici I believe, meant there was less impediment in DoD to the flow of pork for New Mexico.

Unwanted questions on things like the deficient range, payload, and cost performance of the F-18E/F, or the dumb personnel policies that degraded Army and Air Force retention and readiness, or why the Marines were misrepresenting the cost of the V-22 were not likely to engender DoD warmheartedness. They certainly would not encourage DoD bureaucrats and the services' milicrats to say "yes" when the appropriations committee staff asked them whether they wanted a spending project Senator Domenici had requested for New Mexico.

Domenici also had zero interest in lighting off Stevens's tinder-like temper. Just as Stevens reacted angrily against Eric Thorson's effort to conduct oversight on Air Force friendly fire accidents,* he was likely to resent any senator challenging well-honed DoD pretenses. Domenici certainly did not want an irritated Ted Stevens looking for ways to express his displeasure.

Pork and oversight simply do not go together in Congress. You can get one, but not both, and given a choice, pork just about always wins.

A Pie for Every Finger

The Armed Services Committees and the Defense Appropriations Subcommittees in the House and Senate are just part of the national security infrastructure in Congress that is supposed to perform oversight. In the Senate, there are three other committees that regularly deal with national security.

From the 1950s through the 1970s, the Senate Foreign Relations Committee was a prestigious committee and was sought after by both the press looking for news stories and the senators seeking to join. The nature of the times—the cold war and the war in Indochina—made Foreign Relations a natural for press coverage, and clever, activist chairmen, like J. William Fulbright and Frank Church, ensured that the committee was at the cutting edge of Congress's national security activities. However, after 1980 the Foreign Relations Committee entered a never-ending decline. The times still made international affairs a primary issue; however, the committee was chaired by senators who commanded little respect from the rest of the Senate, and, it seemed, the press. They included Sens. Charles Percy (R-Ill.) and Claiborne Pell (D-R.I.), whom few took seriously, and Jesse Helms (R-N.C.) and Joseph Biden (D-Del.), who were generally perceived to be consumed with political dogma or themselves, respectively. Foreign Relations Committee hearings became unattended, desultory affairs. The committee

---

* See chapter 1.

was often unable to pass its primary legislation, the foreign aid bill, through the Senate; other committees, especially the Armed Services Committee, bit off pieces of jurisdiction, and Foreign Relations often had to go hunting for new members when sitting senators either left for more attractive committees or retired from the Senate.

A relative newcomer to the Senate's national security apparatus is the Select Committee on Intelligence. It was established in the late 1970s after a special investigatory committee, chaired by the same Frank Church who later chaired Foreign Relations, uncovered scandals and abuses galore in the CIA and the rest of the intelligence community. The Intelligence Committee was set up to improve oversight of the CIA, the Defense Intelligence Agency (DIA), and other agencies that had previously been handled by the Armed Services Committee. Scandals, abuse, and major screw-ups have, of course, continued in the intelligence community, and it is unclear, at least to me, whether the creation of the Intelligence Committees (there is also one in the House) has made congressional oversight of the intelligence community better, worse, or any different.

Depending on how involved its chairmen and subcommittee chairmen want to be in national security issues, the Senate Government Affairs Committee can make itself an actor, sometimes a major one, on defense issues. For example, a bill to establish in DoD a new office to push for combat-realistic weapons testing originated in the Government Affairs Committee; David Pryor and William Roth (R-Del.), also of the committee, were the primary authors.*

However, defense-related work at the Government Affairs Committee has also seen a decline. When the Democrats took control of the Senate in 1987, Senator Pryor became a subcommittee chairman. The subcommittees that had previously handled defense issues there were already under the control of other, more senior Democrats, and the subcommittee that Pryor was given was the Post Office, Civil Service, and Federal Services Subcommittee. Pryor, nonetheless, wanted his subcommittee to get into defense issues and had the idea that the all-embracing term "Federal Services" in the subcommittee's title permitted him to stick his nose into international arms sales. After all, the State Department did write licenses to permit U.S. weapons manufacturers to export arms, and these licenses could, of course, be thought of as a "federal service." Thus, Pryor launched his new Post Office and Civil Service Subcommittee into this substantively and politically juicy area.† From there Pryor branched the subcommittee into

---

* Roth is described in chapter 1.

† Despite Pryor's seizing this piece of jurisdiction from the Senate Foreign Relations Committee, we heard not a peep of protest from Chairman Pell.

any defense subject he wanted, especially one of his favorites, weapons testing, and held hearings on that subject as well. One of these exercises resulted in uncovering widespread problems in the testing office Senator Pryor and others had started, and as a result the leadership of that office changed.

Pryor's forays into defense issues were so successful that when the Republicans took back control of the Senate in 1995, Sen. Thad Cochran (R-Miss.) changed the name of the Post Office, Civil Service, and Federal Services Subcommittee to the International Security, Proliferation, and Federal Services Subcommittee. Cochran's favorite subject matter was national missile defense, and he and a staffer, who was much consumed with the subject, transformed the subcommittee into a locus of advocacy for national missile defense.

Unimaginative readers will think the former Post Office and Civil Service Subcommittee a strange place for advocacy of national missile defense. Senators and staff with an agenda they want to pursue may be many things, but one thing they are not is unimaginative.

With the twenty-three senators on the Armed Services Committee, the nineteen on the Defense Appropriations Subcommittee, the nineteen on Foreign Relations, the seventeen on the Intelligence Committee, and the seventeen on Government Affairs, there are a total of ninety-five Senate committee seats available for members who want to dabble in national security affairs. There is a pie for every finger. Quantity in oversight does not, however, ensure quality.

Not Just Anecdotes

The anecdotes described here are only isolated examples. All one hundred senators are available for viewing from the public gallery above the Senate chamber when they vote. Then, there is an opportunity to evaluate how seriously senators weigh the issues. It is really quite revealing, but it is not particularly visible on the television broadcasts of Senate sessions, given how they control the cameras. It is worth an in-person visit.

During Senate consideration of an amendment or a bill, there are rarely more than just a few senators in the chamber, usually not more than half a dozen. The television cameras rarely show how empty the chamber almost always is. The small numbers of senators present but not talking during these debates are frequently waiting for their turn to talk. Once they have their chance and finish, they usually leave right away. Give and take between speakers does still occur, but it is far less frequent than it used to be. Most typically, the "debate" is nothing more than staff-prepared orations delivered seriatim.

In some cases, there will be no debate whatsoever; the Senate will vote on a measure immediately after it becomes the pending business. In one case, the staffer to the Military Construction Subcommittee proudly announced to me the subcommittee had made a new record; the $10 billion Military Construction bill was taken up, considered, and passed by the Senate in a grand total of about twenty seconds. In other cases, the debate will be limited to just two or three minutes for each side to make its case before the bill is passed by a voice vote.

If there is a roll call vote on any amendment or bill, bells ring in the Capitol building and the three Senate office buildings. One long ring tells senators not in the chamber a roll call vote has started. They start going to the Senate chamber to vote, but the traffic is desultory. They all know they really do not have to show up until they hear the bells ring five short times—this signals that five minutes remain until the roll call is shut down.* When they walk into the Senate chamber, senators are sometimes handed a small card by clerks standing at the door just inside the chamber, or they will walk over to a table in the "well" of the chamber, just in front of the dais where the presiding officer, usually a stand-in for the president pro tem, sits.† The notes handed to senators or placed on the desk in the well will be short descriptions of what is being voted on. For many, it is the first, and last, they learn of what they are about to vote on.

Democrats will have their description, and Republicans will have theirs. These descriptions are invariably a sentence or two, and the Democratic and Republican descriptions can sometimes be quite different. The staff of the leaders of the two parties will write the summaries, and when it is a partisan issue, they will include a strong bias in favor of how each leader wants his senators to vote. They often conclude with a recommendation, understood to be from the party leader: "Vote aye," or "Vote nay." After reading the description of the motion to be voted on and the party leader's recommendation—if he makes one—the member will frequently mill about in the well of the chamber. There, he or she may have a conversation with another member about the vote (a lot of lobbying goes on in that well); sometimes the conversation will be about business totally unrelated to the

---

* The five-minute warning frequently is extended as a senator lets it be known he or she is on their way but is downtown or otherwise unable to get there in five minutes. In most cases, the senator will be afforded that extra time; on occasion the five-minute warning has taken forty minutes or more.

† The president pro tem is the most senior member of the majority party. This person is a stand-in for the vice president and is number four in succession to the presidency. The vice president, who the Constitution makes the president of the Senate, is almost never in the chamber; he will preside only when a tie vote is expected at which point he is permitted to vote to break the tie. Being the majority party's most senior member, the president pro tem is sometimes not just old but frail in mind and body; the late Strom Thurmond, a strange choice for close to the top of the succession to the presidency, is an example.

vote (roll calls in the chamber are good opportunities for senators to track down others they need to talk to about any number of things). Sometimes, the conversation will be about dinner, tennis, the weather, or whatever subject comes to mind.

The vote on the $40 billion Warner "Tricare for Life" proposal, discussed in chapter 2, was not a partisan vote, and the party leaders did not attempt to command the votes of their senators. Being a vote where members were free to vote solely on the merits, one would expect the senators to want to know as much as possible. The written description actually made available read something like the following:* "Motion to declare National Defense Authorization Act Conference Report out of order under Section 602(b) of the Budget Act. Senator Bob Kerrey objects to the cost of the Warner provision to provide health care to over-65 military retirees."

That is all. Most senators would seek out no further information. While terse, the summary of the issue will tell the members all that most may feel they need to know. In the case above, they will understand that the issue is what the military retirees and Senator Warner want versus Sen. Robert Kerrey (D-Nebr.), who was objecting to the cost.

Once they make up their mind, the senators either tell the clerk how to record their vote, often with a thumb pointed up or down, or wait for their names to be called, whereupon they respond "aye," or "no." They will then talk some more with other senators or leave the chamber to go back to what they were doing before they came in.

A very few senators will not go straight to the well when they enter the chamber to vote; they will go to a row of benches in the back corner of the chamber where staff sit. The member—often one of the two senators from Arizona, McCain and Jon Kyl—will search out his or her own staff, and they will talk about the amendment. The staffer will identify what the amendment or motion is and will give two or three sentences of background and a recommendation. The member will often nod and walk away. On rare occasions, there will be a real discussion between the member and the staff. On even rarer occasions, the member will invite other staffers not otherwise busy to offer opinions or information.

In short, many votes in the Senate are given only very casual attention. Little of the substantive issues, let alone their full implications, will be articulated or probed. It is very often merely a question of the politics of the issue, rather than the substance: What is the party recommendation? What is the constituency involved? What is the "smart" thing to do? To vote based

---

* For better or worse, I know—I helped write it. The example provided here is a rough approximation based on memory and is basically hypothetical. These notecards are closely held and are never made available to the public.

on those considerations, a great deal of time-consuming information and discussion is not needed.

These casual and perfunctory votes are not just cast when the issue is unimportant. Sometimes the issue is supremely important, but the motions and amendments have been prepared in such a way by the Democrats or the Republicans to make a member's vote as automatic as the jerk of a knee. Each party will frequently try to frame a vote on an issue to advantage itself in elections: Republicans will attempt to force a vote on, for example, tax cuts, "live birth" abortion, or another issue that they can use in November to beat up the Democrats in ads and speeches. The Democrats will happily do the same with minimum wage, freedom to choose (abortion), or whatever else is in the party liturgy at the time. The issues are important and often complex, but the vote casting is virtually on automatic pilot.

There are some votes that members take seriously. Domenici's against health care for military retirees is one example. There are also votes of such obvious significance and controversy that virtually all members will take time and care to consider both sides, or at least to think through the implications. The members will discuss such votes with their staff and contemplate memoranda from them. They may discuss the vote with friends and informal advisers back home; they will almost certainly do so with other senators.

Such votes are, however, not common. There may be none during an entire two-year Congress, or there may be as many as half a dozen. When they occur, such as when the Senate considered war with Iraq in October 2002, the politics of the issue is as important to some as the substance and the effects. It can make for some rather strange and unhappy happenings (as will be discussed in chapters 13 and 14).

In the normal course of events, however, an observer in the public gallery above the Senate chamber will see perfunctory, hurried voting based on tiny amounts of information.

A Beehive of Single-Minded Activity

There is good reason why members often give short shrift to the amendments and motions they vote on in the Senate chamber. They are too busy to do otherwise.

A senator's daily schedule is a nightmare to behold. For all four senators I worked for, there was little variation. The day typically starts at 8:00 or 8:30 in the morning with a breakfast meeting and proceeds through the day at half-hour, or even fifteen-minute, intervals. The day might end around 7:00 or 8:00 PM after the last dinner or reception. That is, unless the Senate remains in session into the night. If the Senate is being run by a majority leader who makes the Senate pay a penalty for being dilatory by keeping it in session, the day may not end until quite late.

Some days, usually Tuesdays, Wednesdays, or Thursdays, a senator will be scheduled for two or more committee hearings simultaneously at 10:00 in the morning. Some senators (Domenici, for example) will usually try to go to each of these events, making some sort of appearance long enough to pose a question or two, often pre-written by staff. Other senators (Javits, for example) would often choose one that he felt most important or interesting, and stay at least as long as it seemed useful. In the case of Senator Kassebaum, I was asked sometimes to perform a routine to check out the attendance of other committee members and of the press and television cameras and phone the information back to the office; if the hearing was well attended, it might get the nod.

During one appointment, other appointments often double up. During a hearing in one of the Senate office buildings or a floor debate in the Senate chamber, other appointments will be ushered to a separate room, and the senator will meet the appointments when he or she is not otherwise fully occupied.

The grueling pace goes on as long as the Senate is in session, and when it adjourns for a holiday or a recess, the same pace takes place back in the home state.

Such a work tempo affords little opportunity for study or reflection, and the pace often produces a protagonist too fatigued at the end of the day to read carefully, if at all, the pile of papers the staff thrusts upon him or her each evening. Nevertheless, the members insist that the pace continue. The staff collaborates: multiple staffers urge meetings and events upon the senator as too important to miss. The collective result ensures that any narrow gap left in the senator's daily schedule is instantly filled. In most senators' offices, one of the most hectic jobs is that of appointment secretary.

All this activity has a point. The object of most meetings is outreach. Endless meetings are with the press (interviews with print journalists, radio talk show hosts, or television commentators), groups seeking some form of accommodation (defense contractors, university research centers, public interest groups), or voters (families and church or community groups). In each case, the strategic intent for the meeting is to put the word out about what a great job the member is doing or to accommodate the group so they will walk away impressed with the great job the senator is doing. A far smaller percentage of the meetings have the object of expanding the member's understanding of an issue or a problem, but such meetings often get crowded out as the day's schedule gets behind and the time available for such secondary activities is squeezed.

Oversight or Overlooking?

The Senate is a beehive of self-promotion. Senators run from one appointment to another. They hurriedly cast votes for which they give barely any substantive attention. It all becomes a grueling pace designed not to focus on, prepare for, and think about issues carefully but to convince enough people that the protagonist is doing a great job. One might think that serious contemplation of the issues and the demonstration of what a great job senators are doing are complementary objectives. Unfortunately, however, today's senators very clearly do not see it that way. With only rare exceptions, senators deny themselves and are denied by others (especially their own staff) the time to read detailed reports, speak seriously to experts, and think deeply about any given issue.

The Constitution tasks Congress with the responsibility to "raise and support the army" and "provide and maintain a navy." This "oversight" function should be one of the most important things the members do. Instead, they leave that work to someone else. Their staff? Hardly. They are too busy helping the member with what he or she deems most important—looking good—or doing nothing at all.

The good news is that Congress has created some agencies to perform their oversight work, and there is also the press to hold the politicians' feet to the fire. The bad news is about to follow.

8

Watchdogs, Lapdogs, and Distorted Lenses

Congress has built around itself an apparatus to conduct objective, professional oversight in the form of audits, investigations, cost estimates, and just about any research a member wants. There is also the press, which many regard as an essential bulwark against government abuse. These institutions do not perform consistently. It is only sometimes that they produce balanced, accurate work. When they perform poorly, it is sometimes because Congress wants them to and can influence their performance. Other times these institutions try hard to perform poorly.

The Congressional Research Agencies

In the early-twentieth century, Congress realized it needed professional help. In 1914 it established a Legislative Reference Bureau in the Library of Congress. The new bureau's mandate was to respond to policy questions from members, specifically work that required more time or expertise than congressional staff could provide. This bureau ultimately became the Congressional Research Service (CRS) in the Legislative Reorganization Act of 1970; in 2002 it had a professional and support staff just over seven hundred.[1]

Congress established the General Accounting Office (GAO) in the Budget and Accounting Act of 1921. It did so by transferring audit functions of the Comptroller of the Treasury to the new congressional agency. As with CRS, GAO accepts requests for research from members and committees. GAO's portfolio was initially financial audits, but it expanded to include program evaluations and investigations. (One thing Congress did not permit GAO to investigate until recently was Congress.[2]) GAO's staff grew to more than five thousand by the early 1990s.[3]

The last* major congressional research agency was the Congressional Budget Office, set up in the Congressional Budget and Impoundment Control Act of 1974 to provide to Congress nonpartisan budget analysis and estimates of the costs of bills.

---

* In 1972 Congress established the Office of Technology Assessment (OTA) to review the policy impact of scientific developments. OTA was short-lived; in 1995, when the Republicans took over Congress and made numerous organizational changes, OTA was abolished.

Each congressional agency has a separate domain and character. For example, only CRS will accept quick order research requests: when writing a memo or a speech, if I or any other Hill staff needed data not in our own files, we could call CRS and usually get a response in an hour or two, if not in minutes. CRS can also perform long-term research and produces background papers at its own instigation, as well as in response to requests. Many regard the quality of CRS work to be high, but it studiously refuses to make specific conclusions or recommendations. Doing so would alienate some faction in Congress, and some form of retaliation (a budget cut or a new politically biased director) could result. The biases of the researchers would, of course, frequently leak through, but rarely so clearly that a member would complain that his or her position was attacked.

CBO's work on estimating costs is ostensibly a straightforward matter, but cost estimates can become complex and politically loaded analytical tasks. Opponents of a measure may want costs not just exposed but exaggerated; proponents may want costs understated, if not ignored. Members of Congress and staff often apply pressure to influence CBO cost estimates. I have seen extremely nasty letters to CBO's director, threats to cut CBO's budget, and bullying behavior from staffers and members against analysts who were "not cooperating."

An egregious example I observed was an attempt in 1996 by the staff of Sens. Robert Dole (R-Kans.) and Thad Cochran (R-Miss.) to cow CBO analysts away from their estimate of the costs of a bill Senator Dole introduced to push national missile defense. A staffer for Senator Dole thought she was being clever by not specifying precisely what "architecture" her draft bill would require for a "limited" national missile defense. This, she boasted, would obviate any CBO estimate at all and make the proposed bill appear to be one where cost was not a prominent issue. She was wrong and failed to keep up with developments in CBO. Multiple proposals for a limited missile defense were available for CBO to assess, and the analysts simply reported a band of possible costs.

When CBO reported that Senator Dole's "Defend America Act," which was to be a centerpiece of the defense plank of his 1996 presidential campaign, could cost something between $31 billion to $60 billion,[4] it was staffers for Senators Dole and Cochran who went ballistic, not any real missiles. They demanded a meeting with CBO's analysts where they and other advocates of missile defense asked aggressive questions and repeatedly interrupted the CBO analysts as they explained their work. The CBO analysts, led by an extremely smart and tough manager, "Mick" Miller,[*]

---

[*] Mick was to die of cancer a few years later; he remained working at his job in CBO until shortly before his death.

remained calm and professional in front of congressional staffers who were neither.

The abusive staffers failed to produce any evidence to justify a change in CBO's cost estimate. It remained CBO's position and was widely reported by the press. The air, most of it hot, quickly went out of Senator Dole's effort to make national missile defense a major issue in the 1996 presidential campaign. It all was a good example of how poor congressional staff work can be: (1) avoid the facts; (2) use bullying tactics to attack anyone who has the facts; and (3) give the press a good reason to pay attention to what the staffers wanted them to ignore. With advisers like that it's no wonder Senator Dole's presidential campaign was such a non-starter.

GAO is the largest and perhaps most important congressional oversight agency. With thousands of auditors and evaluators, it produces hundreds of reports each year on virtually anything the executive branch does. The reports contain specific findings, conclusions, and recommendations, and it is standard practice for members to wave GAO "bluebooks" in the faces of their opponents as proof of the correctness of their views.

GAO also has an extraordinary reputation with the press, which routinely describes GAO as "Congress's watchdog" and handles the agency's findings as if they are the final word on an issue. Many journalists seem to believe GAO's work considers all of the data relevant to an issue and does so without any significant bias.

Unfortunately, GAO—where I worked for nine years—rarely even seeks out most of the data, and it almost never gets all of them. Findings and recommendations are frequently influenced by the political biases of GAO's researchers and especially its management, and reports are habitually limited by GAO's perception of what Congress and even the agency being investigated are willing to accept.

A case study is appropriate.

The Myths of Desert Storm *

The first war against Iraq, Operation Desert Storm, was in 1991. Five years later, in July 1996, GAO released a short report on that war's air campaign, and a year later a more detailed version of the same study was released. The story behind this study reveals everything you need to know about how the national security community, not just in Congress but also in greater Washington, D.C., operates.

---

* Major elements of the case study of GAO's work that follows were first published as a preface to a reprint of GAO's report, "Operation Desert Storm: Evaluation of the Air Campaign." This appeared in 2002 courtesy of Ross and Perry, of 216 G St., N.E., Washington, D.C. 20002, or at www.rossperry.com.

The study, which I helped to write with four colleagues in GAO, addressed the prevailing image of the first Gulf War air campaign: that of the spectacular success of "high-tech," "silver bullet" weapon systems. For example:

- F-117 "stealth" bombers were the unquestioned star of the war. To illustrate, as stated in an official Air Force report, in the first hours of the first night of the war, the F-117 "revolutionized warfare,"[5] for example, by flying into the teeth of Saddam Hussein's sophisticated integrated air defense system (IADS) and surgically dispatching it,[6] thereby opening up all of Iraq for conventional aircraft to attack with relative ease.[7] A "force multiplier" if ever there were one.

- F-111Fs "plinked" Saddam's tank force with laser-guided bombs (LGBs). This "spectacular success," along with the surgical elimination of bridges, command and control facilities, and many other military targets, was so effective that "one bomb, one target"[8] became a mantra characterizing the new "revolution in warfare."

- Tomahawk cruise missiles navigated over Baghdad's highways and unerringly found their way to pinpoint targets[9] in all forms of weather[10] against the heaviest defenses[11] and, according to estimates from the JCS, achieved a hit rate of 85 percent.[12]

It is all hogwash. None of it happened as described. The data my four GAO colleagues and I extracted from the Air Force, the Navy, and other DoD agencies documented these assertions to be utterly bogus. U.S. "silver bullets" performed well in the war, but not nearly as well as the world was told. Furthermore, low-tech weapons—B-52s, A-10s, and even "dumb" (unguided) bombs, which you rarely heard about—often performed as well and sometimes even better. To come to the descriptions of events and the conclusions many enthusiastically embraced before our report required a panoply of obfuscation, distortion, misinformation, and ignorance.

For example, regarding the F-117's "revolutionary" performance on the first night of the war against Iraq's IADS, consider the following:

- According to the Air Force's mission-by-mission and bomb-by-bomb records, the F-117s were tasked to fifteen Iraqi IADS targets on the first night of the war. F-117s aborted their attacks on four of these targets. Of the eleven attacked, two targets were simply missed. Nine were actually struck with LGBs. Defense Intelligence Agency battle damage assessments found two of those nine targets damaged sufficiently to require no more attacks; eight others were still functioning and required restrikes on later nights. One target could not be assessed. Of the fifteen air defense targets assigned to F-117s on the first night of the war, two (13 percent), maybe three (20 percent), were both hit and destroyed.

- F-117s were not the only aircraft attacking air defense targets on that first night. Air Force tasking data show that 167 other non-stealthy aircraft (including A-10s, F-4Gs, and F/A-18s) attacked eighteen air defense targets that same first night. Whatever was accomplished against the Iraqi air defense was the result of more than just a few "silver bullet" F-117s.

- Air Force intelligence assessed the effectiveness of the Iraqi IADS on a daily basis and reported its findings in daily intelligence summaries (DAISUMS). These stated that by day three the "evidence of degradation" of IADS was "beginning to show." By day five, the DAISUMS said, "In general, the Iraqi IADS is down but not out."[13]

F-117s demolished the Iraqi IADS in the first hours of the first night? Single-handed force multiplier? "Revolution in warfare?" Didn't happen. Well, at least we wiped out the Iraqi tank force with F-111Fs and LGBs ("tank plinking"), right?

For tank kills, good data were sparse. Of the 163 Iraqi tanks the Army's Foreign Science and Technology Center inspected on the battlefield after the war (a small and non-random sample that was not generalizable), only twenty-eight (17 percent) were assessed as having been hit from the air. The CIA looked more broadly at armor kills; its analysis concluded that the air campaign was potentially responsible for immobilizing 1,135 of 2,665 tanks (43 percent) in nine regular Iraqi armored or mechanized divisions after thirty-eight days of bombing. Against the key target set of the Republican Guard's three divisions in theater, the air campaign immobilized just 13 to 30 percent of the tanks.[14] Not quite the "spectacular success" the swamis of high tech asserted.

What about those pinpoint attacks by Tomahawks?

For starters, the Tomahawks did not "navigate down highways." Their guidance systems at the time were far more complex and vulnerable to foibles and countermeasures than the advocates let on. The Navy's Center for Naval Analyses wrote a multivolume review of Tomahawk's Desert Storm performance. DoD classified most of the report's results summarized in our GAO report, but not everything. DoD did permit a statement that about half of the Tomahawks that successfully got out of their launch tubes reached the target area. The other half were "no shows."[15]

There was more in our report; DoD's "all-weather" sensors and guidance systems were limited by anything but clear, dry air;[16] "stand-off" (long-range) systems required the operator to get close to have any clue what he was shooting at;[17] jammers failed to jam enemy radars, and a land-attack missile, known as "SLAM-ER," was so difficult to use the Navy virtually gave up on it.

Most disturbing (to some) were the report's findings regarding the relationship between the cost and performance of weapons. For years, DoD and the advocates of cost and complexity had nurtured the conventional wisdom that "high-tech" systems were, regrettably, more expensive, but the additional cost brought a major payoff in the form of incomparably better performance. We looked long and hard for generalizable evidence to confirm that well-entrenched conventional wisdom. We were unable to find it. While there were some performance measures where high-cost aircraft performed better (such as accuracy in limited circumstances), there were also areas where low-cost systems performed better (including payload and sortie rate). For most measures, however, there was no correlation between aircraft cost and performance (especially the important measures of targets destroyed and aircraft survivability). For munitions, the study found about as many advantages for low-cost dumb bombs as for high-cost guided munitions.[18]

DoD Strains to Preserve the Myths

In DoD some of the advocates of high tech knew they had a problem before GAO printed a single word. This is because when a defense-related report nears completion in GAO, managers frequently violate GAO regulations and instruct their staff to quietly send an early draft of the report to contacts in DoD. The purpose is to give DoD project managers and analysts an opportunity to tell GAO staff where GAO got the facts or analysis wrong and to tell GAO where and how to make changes. The process is oral and without documentation. In other words, GAO gives DoD an opportunity to instruct GAO to make factual and analytical changes in the report without documenting the newly asserted facts or analysis. This under-the-table editing process occurs before GAO formally approves a draft report and officially sends it to DoD for written "agency comments," which form an above-board part of the final GAO report.

The GAO unit where I worked, the Program Evaluation and Methodology Division (known in GAO as PEMD), refused to violate GAO procedures and follow the under-the-table practice, which was frequently done in GAO's National Security and International Affairs Division (NSIAD). The first time anyone in DoD saw our report was after senior GAO management approved it and sent it to DoD for formal agency comments. Staff in DoD were upset that they were being sent an official draft GAO report that they had never informally seen before and had no opportunity to quietly edit and, if necessary, alter.[*]

It got worse. Rather than just take good notes and fold when DoD told us what changes to make, our GAO team asked for documentation of any newly asserted facts during the official "agency comments" process. When DoD staff described a document as refuting our report, we had the temerity to ask for a copy of the report—not just excerpts, but the whole thing. This sometimes resulted in DoD staff accusing us of questioning their honor; they also complained to senior GAO managers that we were being a "problem." Despite DoD's aggressive tactics, nothing changed in our report when DoD was unable or unwilling to document its assertions.

Failure to get the changes it wanted in the report caused DoD to try another tactic: censorship. Our report was about 250 pages, but DoD classified massive amounts to such a degree that what finally passed the DoD classifiers' review was a mere 13 pages of vague summary with so little data to substantiate it that the report was not only hard to understand, it was hard to believe. That made it easy prey for pundits sympathetic to DoD's positions. That ploy was only temporarily successful.

One of the members of Congress who had requested the report was my former boss, Sen. David Pryor. When one of our team showed him the dramatic difference between the classified version of the report and what DoD had permitted to be released to the public, Pryor complained. He released a press statement that GAO's report had accused DoD and defense manufacturers of making claims that were "overstated, misleading, inconsistent with the best available data, or unverifiable,"[19] but DoD had classified just what those false statements were and how the data showed they were false. Employing his constitutional immunity,[†] Senator Pryor made clear to the press just what some of those misleading, inaccurate, or unverifiable passages were that DoD deemed so highly classified:[20] they were manufacturer newspaper ads; public statements by the secretary of the Air Force and other officials, and previously unclassified passages in the Air Force's public reports on the war.[21] In other words, DoD and others could make inaccurate

---

* When, for example, we met with DoD officials to formally start another study, a DoD official asked when he would be receiving his "under-the-table" copy of the draft study for his revisions. Another DoD official, who had worked with both GAO divisions on previous studies, explained with some embarrassment, "this isn't that division," and that DoD could expect no such favor from the GAO team that was present.

† Article I, Section 6, of the Constitution states " . . . for any speech or debate in either house, they [members of Congress] shall not be questioned in any other place." I learned in 1971 that this meant, among other things, that members—and only members—could make public classified information as part of official business and not be prosecuted. Sen. Mike Gravel (D-Ark.) had inserted the text of the highly controversial, and classified, "Pentagon Papers" into the text of a hearing transcript in order to inform the public about the origins of the Vietnam War. It is a power that can be used for ill or good, depending on the nature of the revelation; the only apparent consequence for members is political, not juridical.

statements to the public, but it was a threat to national security for GAO to point out what statements were misleading and what actually happened.

Once the hypocrisy of the Pentagon's position became clear, the building capitulated, and in 1997, GAO released a 235-page unclassified version of the report. While much remained classified, new details substantiated the very different picture of the performance of "high-tech silver bullets" and other favored weapon systems.

Public release of some of the facts did not prevent DoD from looking for other avenues to undo the report. "One bomb, one target" had been a Desert Storm–based mantra repeated by the advocates of guided weapons in and out of DoD. The mantra was widespread in advertisements by manufacturers of guided munitions, and DoD and academics frequently invoked it in articles.[22]

Our report looked closely at what it took in Desert Storm to destroy targets—something no other study had done across different types of munitions and different types of targets. We combined the available strike, target, and battle damage assessment data to tabulate the tonnages used against various point targets, area targets, and broad categories of targets.

"One bomb, one target" it was not. On average, across all targets, regardless of type, 11 tons of guided munitions and 44 tons of unguided munitions were needed to destroy a single target. Against specific types of targets, bridges, for example, where the Center for Naval Analyses assessed Navy strikes, it took, on average, 11.3 LGBs to make a bridge unusable by dropping a span of it into the water. Similarly, our own analysis of Air Force data found that it took, on average, 10.8 tons of guided munitions and 18.2 tons of unguided munitions to destroy a bridge.

Faced with this and other data, DoD folded again. Rather than attempt to find some small number of isolated cases where one bomb did destroy one target in just one try (a set of data that in Desert Storm would likely have been so limited as to prove the opposite), DoD reversed its field and asserted in a letter to GAO, "Nevertheless, no one has ever seriously attempted to argue that one-shot, one-kill is a realistic expectation for our platforms and weapons."[23] However, DoD did not exactly go out of its way with the press or the public to correct the mythology. Indeed, senior DoD officials simply continued to utter the baloney much as before. In one case, "one bomb, one target" became, "The accuracy of our precision-guided munitions is good enough when it takes only two or three weapons to destroy a target."[24] In another case, the mantra became "one target, one weapon."[25]

Mythology among the Press and Pundits

DoD's response to our report was failing badly. Too many articles and editorials appeared saying that DoD had played fast and loose with the facts. In fact, I had never seen as much press coverage for any GAO report on a defense subject. My incomplete files show twenty-two articles and nineteen editorials in major newspapers and defense journals. Most pursued the theme "'Smart' Weapons Were Overrated,"[26] "Debate Swirls Around F-117,"[27] and "GAO Study Takes Aim at Gulf War Weapons."[28] As the favorable articles and commentary poured out,* the advocates of complexity, cost, and conventional wisdom realized they had a problem.

The *Washington Post* was among the first to come to the rescue. It argued in an editorial that it was nothing new that someone in DoD had overstated the performance of guided munitions in the war,[29] a theme its own reporters had largely missed. To the *Post,* it was okay for the Pentagon to boast just so long as there was at least one good hit in one attempt during the overall campaign against a major target. The editorial did concede that the GAO study may have helped the United States learn some lessons, but it proceeded to complain that the report lacked the facts and was "weak on questions of context and comparison." While it is true that the *Post* had available to it only the early, short, classification-censored version of the report, it is also true that the *Post*'s editorial writers did not make a single inquiry to GAO or the report's authors to determine just what facts, context, and comparisons were behind the report.

The *Washington Times* also printed an op-ed commentary that would have benefited greatly from the author's reading of the report and/or a rudimentary discussion with the report team. This piece also showed no surprise at the news that "the Pentagon did overstate the effectiveness of its Gulf War performance."[30] In supporting its argument that high-tech systems were more important in winning the war than we had said, the author asserted that GAO ignored events, but if he had read the report carefully or asked the GAO authors about it he would have found that the report covered these events in excruciating detail. Specifically, the author cited the standard myths about the uniqueness of F-117 and Tomahawk operations over Baghdad, tank plinking, and the destruction of the Iraqi air defense system to try to argue that GAO had not analyzed high tech's biggest successes.

---

* Some of these favorable articles and commentary took considerable liberties with our report. One commentary bent the report into a reason to vote against Bob Dole for president. Another overgeneralized the report's finding on non-stealthy aircraft, and even the *New York Times* overstated at least one finding and said the report addressed issues it did not.

When this commentary appeared, I contacted the writer and pointed out that the examples of successful high-tech operations cited in his piece were both factually incorrect and exhaustively covered in our report. I offered a briefing on the unclassified contents. He declined the offer and seemed eager to end the conversation. Moral: you can lead a pundit to the data, but you cannot make him drink.

Perhaps the most Orwellian commentary on our report appeared in the *Washington Post* after its first editorial.[31] The author was a respected authority on the war based on his direction of another study. We had commissioned him in GAO to serve as one of six outside reviewers of the draft report; he should have known the report in detail. He said GAO concluded that "the F-117 stealth fighter . . . simply did not do very well." Not so, the report concluded that DoD and contractor descriptions of F-117 performance vastly overstated things, not that the aircraft did poorly.* The pundit also asserted that the "GAO further implies that the $58 billion . . . spent on precision guided munitions . . . is wasted or excessive." What we did do is point out the cost of these munitions compared to unguided munitions, and the performance advantages and limitations of both types.

What seemed to bother the commentator the most was that the report constantly attempted to articulate a balance about high-tech (complex, high cost) weapons and low-tech (simple, cheap) ones. The report stated prominently: "[T]he success of the sustained air campaign resulted from the availability of a mix of strike and support assets. Its substantial weight of effort was made possible, in significant part, by the variety and number of . . . platforms capable of delivering guided munitions such as the stealthy F-117, to high-sortie-rate attack aircraft such as the A-10."[32] Rather than arguing that money spent for guided munitions was "wasted," the report presented "recommendations [to] help ensure that high-cost munitions can be employed more efficiently at lower risk to pilots and aircraft and that the future mix of guided and unguided munitions is appropriate and cost-effective." [33]

It apparently troubled the commentator that GAO had pointed out that there were downsides to the cost and performance of high-tech weapons and that there were upsides to the cost and performance of low-tech weapons. The attempt at balance by GAO was taken as a slander. To cite both sides of the story was tantamount to being one-sided and was, in the

---

* For example, the report stated up front on page 2, "And although some claims for some advanced systems could not be verified, their performance in combat may well have been unprecedented." *Operation Desert Storm: Evaluation of the Air Campaign,* U.S. General Accounting Office, June 1997, GAO/NSIAD-97-134.

words of this commentator, "not merely incorrect but, if taken to heart, downright dangerous." Quite literally, to consider both sides of an issue was one-sided.

Welcome to Washington, D.C.

Congress Prefers the Myths

Except for Senator Pryor and three other members who had requested the report, Congress never showed any awareness that the GAO study existed.* Copies of it were sent to the relevant congressional committees (the House and Senate Armed Services Committees and the Defense Subcommittees of the House and Senate Appropriations Committees, among others), but no one called to ask any questions, or even to complain. Just as news articles and commentary for and against the study were hitting major newspapers, I contacted House and Senate staffers on these committees. Yes, they had read about the study in the newspapers. No, they had not read the study itself; they had no time to read a 235-page GAO report. I offered a briefing that would take as little as thirty minutes. They remained uninterested, every single one of them.

This was bizarre. A GAO report was contradicting huge portions of the conventional wisdom about the Gulf War. Moreover, the report was crammed with previously unrevealed data to prove its contentions; it was fuel for numerous articles in major newspapers, and it was fodder for feisty commentary for and against. Joining this debate, on either side, would be an opportunity for representatives and senators to attract much public exposure, which they usually craved, and they would learn a great deal. Not only were the congressional staffers not interested in a hearing to evaluate the study, they were not even interested in a short briefing! What on earth was going on? Two explanations are appropriate.

First, many staff in Congress's defense committees hold GAO in deep contempt. Given the large volume of GAO's work on defense issues, more than a hundred reports each year, it is surprising how seldom GAO testifies to the Armed Services Committees or the Defense Appropriations Subcommittees. In half a dozen years of working with the Senate's Defense Appropriations Subcommittee, I witnessed two hearings with GAO. In the Senate Armed Services Committee, GAO testifies more frequently, but not often. In 2000 GAO testified to that committee nine times. During that year, the Armed Services Committee held more than sixty hearings,[34] and GAO

---

* Congressman Andy Ireland (R-Fla.) and Sen. Tim Wirth (D-Colo.) originally requested the study, and Congressman Ireland and his staff evidenced interest in the study as it progressed. However, Ireland retired from Congress before the study was finished. Also, Congressman John Dingle (D-Mich.) joined as a later requester for the study, and his staff was given a briefing on the study's results.

produced 141 defense-related reports.[35] Just 15 percent of the time GAO was a useful witness, and only 6 percent of GAO reports were worthy of testimony to the committee. Not an impressive indicator of respect.

A second explanation for Congress's disinterest in the air campaign report is that it went against the general bias in Congress regarding weapon systems. For years, members of Congress have been hearing from DoD and advocates of high tech that there was a major payoff for expensive, complex weapons in the form of better performance. The myths emanating from Desert Storm about "silver bullets" and "one bomb, one target" reinforced that conventional wisdom and provided validation for profoundly held beliefs. Now, along comes an upstart GAO report that asks members of Congress to revise their thinking: that high-cost weapons did not perform immeasurably, or even measurably, better in many respects than low-cost ones.

Moreover, accepting—or even publicly listening to—the GAO report might also mean that the same senior generals, admirals, and top bureaucrats who had assured Congress of the righteousness of their views either did not know what they were talking about or, if they did, were misleading. Rather than engage this difficult, if not embarrassing, debate, it was a lot easier to ignore the whole thing.

Congress's Watchdog or DoD's Lapdog?

Despite the contempt of the defense committees in Congress for GAO and their studied ignorance of the Desert Storm air campaign report, many others in Congress and among the press adore GAO. When asked to look into something, GAO is sure to find something wrong. That makes good grist for press releases by politicians and news articles by journalists. Moreover, because it is GAO—the ever-reliable congressional watchdog—there is little need to double-check the facts or to explore fully the other side of the argument.

Not just among the congressional defense committees, but also in DoD and to some others, GAO is a joke. The thoroughness, reliability, and validity of our Desert Storm report were the exception, not the rule. Many times, GAO, especially its defense-related teams, gets only a part of the story. What I found inside GAO was a management-induced culture that encouraged incomplete research and truncated investigations and that shied away from challenging conventional wisdom.

When I worked at the agency from 1987 to 1996, most GAO managers asserted they wanted to maintain what they called a "positive relationship with the agency" being investigated. Among other things, this resulted in GAO personnel being denied the very data they needed to perform their research.

It was too aggressive to insist that a GAO project receive all the data its own researchers believed, or should have believed, they needed. Frequently then, as now, DoD withheld sections of a document, or the whole thing altogether—giving only an oral summary—and GAO management persistently refused to demand more.

This occurs despite GAO's having statutory authority to any and all DoD documents it deems necessary. Sadly, this authority is exercised only in the most rare of cases, and the division in GAO responsible for defense matters (NSIAD) and its successor organizations have almost never exercised it. PEMD, where I worked, exercised, or threatened to exercise, GAO's authority to obtain documents, and we usually got what we wanted.* However, when we used this authority, we did so over the strenuous objections of managers in NSIAD, who feared an impairment of their "positive relationship" with DoD.

The deeper you dig into GAO, especially on defense issues, the worse it gets. Despite a large and active training program, many GAO people—managers and staff alike—do not know how to do anything but the most elementary research. This can easily be checked by turning to the "Scope and Methodology" section of a GAO report. Most NSIAD reports will basically say, "we spoke to a bunch of officials and experts; we collected a bunch of documents; we went to a bunch of places; we began on this date, and we ended on this date."

How did GAO confirm it had collected all the available data on the subject? How did GAO work around limitations in the data? How did they cross-validate the data, especially what officials said with other forms of data? Did DoD deny access to any data, and what did GAO do about that? Why did the GAO authors select one form of data for one part of the study and another for a different part? When GAO interviewed personnel, were their superiors present? How were all the data analyzed? What are the strengths and weaknesses of that form of analysis in the context of this study? What were the overall limitations to the study? What is the generalizability of different parts of the study? If you do not see answers to these or other relevant questions, do not bother reading any more, unless you just want to collect anecdotal trivia.

The combination of a culture of being nice to the agency and the lack of sophisticated research techniques makes a lethal combination for the quality of many GAO studies on defense. It puts GAO at the mercy of DoD.

---

* Neither of these divisions currently exists in GAO. As discussed below, PEMD has been eliminated. NSIAD has been reorganized into two new "teams" ("Defense Capabilities and Management" and "Acquisition Sourcing Management"). However, nothing of significance has changed from the previous NSIAD way of doing things, according to individuals who have worked in both organizations.

Smart DoD officials will not stonewall GAO; they will cooperate, but only up to a point. They know that GAO will persist until it finds something negative to report. The smart DoD managers throw GAO a bone: that is, hand over enough information so that GAO's need for a report that offers some criticism is satisfied, but not so much that every element—both positive and negative—of an issue is fully probed.

PEMD was very different. The staff and managers were trained in evaluation and research techniques, but most important, the culture was different. We expected DoD officials to hand over all documents requested, and if they did not, we usually started the process to legally extract them. PEMD was not interested in nurturing a "positive relationship with the agency"; it was interested in documents and research, and acted accordingly.

The cultural differences between PEMD and NSIAD made for poisonous bureaucratic relations. This was clear at the very beginning of our Gulf War study. PEMD learned of an important Air Force database about almost every U.S. aircraft strike against an Iraqi target in the air campaign. PEMD also learned from DoD that GAO already had the database—in NSIAD. Our team went to the NSIAD manager who controlled the database; he told us it was his and another manager's "personal property," and, no, we could not have it. When we overcame that foolishness (it took several days), the same official tried to argue that the database was so complex and messy it was unusable. But, after months of hard work and various reliability and validity tests, our team made the information usable, and it became a key part of our report.

In addition to being obstructionist, senior managers in NSIAD were reluctant to permit any report that DoD had not tacitly endorsed. When the first draft of our report was finished in 1994, GAO procedures required that NSIAD managers also approve it. They were aghast. How could any of these things be true? DoD said the weapons were "all weather"; so what more was there to assess? If an Air Force study said the F-117 had an 80 percent hit rate, why would anyone want to challenge that? Half the Tomahawks missing their targets? That's not what their friends in the Navy said. They could not believe what they were reading. During one strained meeting, one frustrated NSIAD manager blurted out, "That's what the data say, but what does DoD say?"

An endless editing loop resulted. NSIAD would seek changes in the draft to grind the report's findings down to its comfort level, and sometimes to meaninglessness. PEMD was willing to edit the mode of expression but not the substance. After two years of bureaucratic agony, this ping-ponging back and forth resulted in a final report that retained its substance but was written and rewritten to accommodate bureaucratic, political, and cultural concerns. The result was stylistic mush organized in a haphazard fashion. NSIAD extracted its greatest editorial depredations in the parts of the report its management thought people might actually read. Thus, the "executive summary" is an overlong twenty-eight pages that said little of substance about the contents of the report. On the other hand, while they contain some pedantic and plodding portions, the appendixes of the report were, relatively speaking, left free of the tender mercies of GAO management's editorial talents.

Even though PEMD approved the draft report in 1994, the first (DoD-censored) version did not become public until 1996. After Senator Pryor cowed the DoD censors into submission, the more complete 235-page version came out in 1997.

PEMD may have won the battle over our report, but it lost the war. It had been fighting similar skirmishes not just with NSIAD but with virtually all other GAO divisions. The rest of GAO had tired of PEMD invading their turf and writing reports that challenged their wisdom and that of the agencies they sought to curry favor with. That PEMD could make its substantive arguments stick in bureaucratic fights was more than some senior GAO managers could bear.

The first blow arrived when Comptroller General Charles Bowsher forced into retirement PEMD's highly intelligent and assertive—but also extremely acerbic—division director, Eleanor Chelimsky. After she left, the rest was easy. In 1996 PEMD was formally abolished, and the rest of GAO absorbed its staff.[36] When the press made inquiries, budget cuts (imposed by the Republican Congress) were the stated cause. It was a convenient excuse, but it was also inaccurate.[37]

Thus, while the air war report did not result in any DoD programs being discontinued or revitalized, it did help chalk up one "kill": the only division in GAO capable of and willing to write the report.

Members of Congress live in a dream world concerning national security. It is a world of their own making where facts are ignored, and the opiate of bias flourishes. Wholly conjured appearances are everything; comprehending what is, has, or could happen counts for nothing. Many in Congress consider it important to keep things that way. If facts and quality analysis were unavoidable, it would be difficult not just to ignore reality but to distort it.

There are many ways they do that. Read on.

9

Beyond Nonfeasance:
The Utility of Distortion

Congress's contemporary behavior goes beyond nonconduct of oversight and nonpursuit of inconvenient facts and analysis. Members also work hard to distort reality. The activity is directed at the heart of Congress's constitutional authority, its power of the purse.

Some of the budgetary malfeasance originates in the Defense Department, but rather than reduce or kill it off when it reaches Congress in budget requests, the members welcome it and incorporate it in authorization and appropriations bills. Of course, deceptions also originate in Congress; most are designed to present false images of the defense budget—to make it look too big, or too small, to push an argument in a direction a member prefers. The effect is to present to the outside world the appearance of an earnest, data-based deliberation that is not, in fact, occurring. From all political sides (liberals, moderates, conservatives, Democrats, Republicans, and independents) members design presentation after presentation to mislead for the purpose of pushing a preselected agenda.

To demonstrate, it is useful to reverse-engineer some of the gimmicks.*

Decapitating Budget History

A common measure in Washington of whether you are "pro-" or "anti-" defense is how much money are you willing to spend on the Pentagon. For "pro-defense" types, more is always better; less, they claim, means things like Pearl Harbor in 1941 and Desert One in 1980, although in both 1941 and 1980 defense spending was, in fact, on a dramatic increase. Sometimes, especially after a major conflict (e.g., Korea, Vietnam, the cold war), even most big spenders will agree decreases are appropriate, but the domestic political environment can change and encourage some to exploit the situation.

In the late 1980s, the threat-engine of U.S. defense spending, the Soviet Union, collapsed. The first Bush administration's "Base Force Concept" and then President Clinton's "Bottom Up Review" mandated large and con-

---

* Several of the examples and data discussed in this chapter originally appeared in a chapter, authored by "Spartacus," of an anthology. See *Spirit, Blood, and Treasure: The American Cost of Battle in the 21st Century*, editor, Donald E. Vandergriff (Novato, Calif.: Presidio, 2001).

tinuing force structure and budget reductions to adjust to the reduced threat. These efforts went relatively smoothly in the beginning, but with Democrat Bill Clinton in the White House when the Republicans took control of Congress in 1994, the government became divided, and both sides tried to extract political advantage with cooked budget presentations.

Such an occurrence was on 5 March 1996. President Clinton's secretary of defense, Dr. William Perry, was testifying to the Senate Armed Services Committee to present the fiscal year 1997 defense budget. A key part of his presentation was the administration's weapons procurement program; Secretary Perry described how he had done the best he could—"we have hung on, sort of by our fingernails"—to slow the continuing decline started by the first Bush administration, and much desired increases were just around the corner.[1] The chart he presented looked like the figure below.

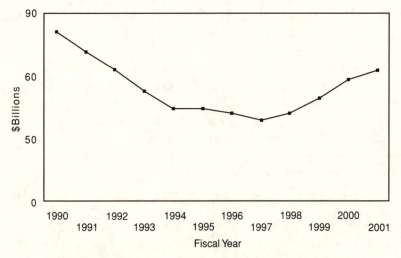

DOD Procurement Program ($ in billions)
Department of Defense Authorization for Appropriations for Fiscal Year 1997 and the Future Years Defense Program, Hearings before the Committee on Armed Services, U.S. Senate, 104th Cong., 2nd sess. on S. 1745, Part 1, 5, 6, 12, 13, 14, 19, 21, 26, 28 March, 16 April 1996, p. 36.

Not so, protested Sen. William Cohen (R-Maine), one of the established stars of the Armed Services Committee. "[I]t would seem to me that the decline in procurement is a lot deeper than what is projected" on Secretary Perry's chart.[2] Senator Cohen showed a different chart, looking like figure 2, which he described as "a much more accurate reflection of exactly how deeply we have cut into the procurement accounts than the one that is presented today."[3]

Tough words, and they were backed up by facts. Comparing the charts, it was obvious the procurement decline involved five more years than Secretary

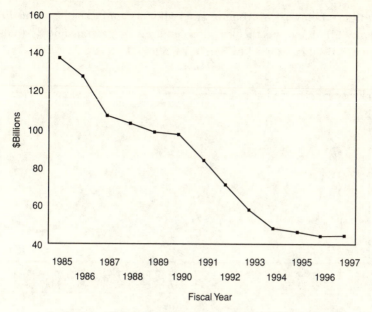

Senator Cohen's Procurement History ($ in billions)

Perry had shown, and the slope of the decline was steeper. According to Senator Cohen, the procurement budget had suffered far larger losses, and when the Clinton plan executed its increases, it was still feeble compared to recent history.

Clearly, Cohen caught Perry cutting out several years to understate the decline, and the forthright Senator Cohen was setting the record straight. Right?

In fact, not just Secretary Perry but also Senator Cohen—a future secretary of defense—was using several gimmicks to adjust appearances. The two were using different types of dollars. Perry was using "current" dollars: that is, the same number of dollars actually appropriated by Congress in each fiscal year. Because of inflation, the purchasing power of the earlier dollars was greater, so fewer could buy more. This reduced the apparent difference between 1990 and 1997, and it lessened the slope of the decline on the graph. Senator Cohen used "constant" dollars—a DoD price index adjusts the purchasing power of dollars in different fiscal years to make them equal, thus maximizing the differences between the high in 1985 and the low in 1997. Each was using a technical difference in the dollars presented to adjust the visual presentation.

Not just Secretary of Defense Perry, but also Senator Cohen was decapitating history to assist appearances. Senator Cohen's "much more accurate reflection" may have shown a little more history, but it was still selective.

The figure below shows the entire (1948–89) cold war history of the procurement budget, plus the years immediately thereafter. The figure is in "constant" dollars, as used by Senator Cohen.

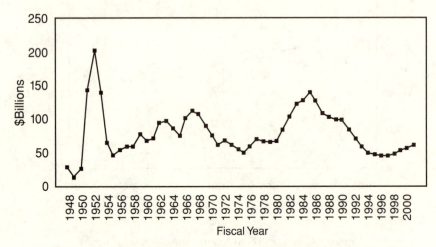

DoD Procurement: Cold War and Beyond: Berlin Blockade to Present
(FY 2001 constant dollars, $ in billions)
National Defense Budget Estimates for FY 2001, Office of Under Secretary of Defense
(Comptroller), March 2000, pp. 110–15.

A number of distortions in Senator Cohen's "much more accurate reflection" are apparent.

First, the base of his comparison, the year 1985, was abnormally high, thereby making the Clinton procurement budget seem lower than it would appear relative to a longer view of history. Even though the Soviet Union, and the major conventional and nuclear threat it posed, had disappeared, the Clinton procurement budgets were at roughly the same level as during the administrations of Republican President Ford in 1975 and Republican President Eisenhower in 1954–55, neither of whom were particularly anti-defense. Thus, in terms of money spent on procurement in relation to the size of the military threat to the United States, a longer view of history shows President Clinton's procurement budgets to be more robust and to match at least two past cold war Republican presidents—a comparison the Republican Cohen was certainly not eager to disclose.

Both Cohen and Perry were pushing an agenda. Cohen, however, had the political skill to come off as the more factual, direct critic, but putting his data in a broader context shows he was doctoring appearances at least as much as Perry. Cohen's pretense at accuracy and his indignation at Perry's presentation were pure charade.

The tricks Cohen and Perry used became standard devices to play to the supposition that a bigger budget meant a better defense. The 1985 Ronald Reagan peacetime high for defense spending was a favorite Republican "base" to compare Clinton administration defense spending. Pro-defense Democratic presentations were likely to show less of the past and to project big healthy increases in the future. Little did they know that even the biggest of those projected increases were poor country cousins to the defense budget explosion the second Bush administration was to sponsor.

Decapitating Entire Budgets

When they wanted to reduce the defense budget, liberal Democratic senators played a variation of the same incomplete-data game. During the Senate debate on the fiscal year 1997 budget resolution, Sen. Dale Bumpers (D-Ark.) offered an amendment to permit moving money from defense to civilian spending. He wanted to remove the "firewalls" in the 1997 congressional budget resolution that prohibited any such transfers. He stated, "No matter how bloated the defense budget may be, it [the congressional budget resolution] says you cannot take a penny out of defense for any other purpose, no matter what the emergency is."[4] He supported his argument with a figure like the one below to show how defense spending compared to "domestic."[5]

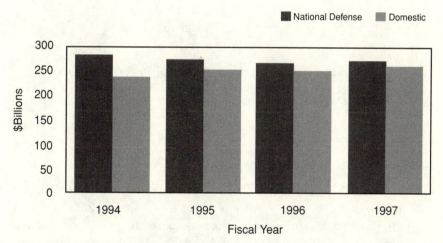

Defense and Domestic Spending, 1994–97 ($ in billions, current dollars)
Data from *Historical Tables*, Budget of the United States Government, Fiscal Year 2001, p. 117.

Senator Bumpers was asserting that defense had a bigger share of the federal spending pie than domestic expenditures, especially since 1994, when the Republicans had taken over Congress. He was presenting less than a half of the relevant data. He showed only the "discretionary" budget (i.e., the portion supported by annual appropriations). He did not show the "mandatory" budget, which included the largest non-defense programs, (i.e., "entitlement" programs, such as Social Security, Medicare, and Medicaid). The whole story would have looked like the figure below.

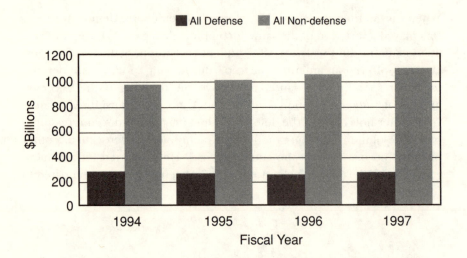

Defense Spending Compared to Civilian Spending
($ in billions, current dollars)
Data from *Historical Tables,* Budget of the United States Government,
Fiscal Year 2001, p. 117.

Showing all civilian spending certainly changed the picture. Not only was defense a much smaller portion of the total, but in addition, civilian spending had been growing somewhat, compared to a relatively stagnant defense budget. These inconvenient data were, of course, not displayed.

DoD Budget Gimmicks—More Is Less, and Less Is More

Misleading numbers are not the preserve of only senators and secretaries of defense, and the showplace is not just Capitol Hill. The Pentagon's senior staff is no slouch for cooking the numbers, but, again, it takes the skills of Capitol Hill veterans to make the deceptions especially bedazzling.

After he became secretary of defense, Senator Cohen appointed a former Hill staffer as comptroller of the Defense Department. While it is unclear whether the impetus for the gimmicks was his own or others, that ex-staffer presented to Congress an impressive array of budget gimmicks in the fiscal year 2000 DoD budget. The gimmicks were complex, and they had to be. They sought to achieve two contradictory objectives: first, to make the increases in the defense budget seem larger than they actually were and, second, to make them seem smaller than they actually were. Specifically, the administration wanted to appear to some to be pro-defense, which meant showing large increases, but also it wanted to show others how prudent it was: it did not want to be seen punching through a budget limit, called a "discretionary spending cap," on defense that it and Congress had adopted in 1997.

The DoD comptroller and Secretary Cohen widely advertised their FY 2000 DoD budget as a major $12.6 billion increase: a dollar change that was then big enough to sell as pro-defense in Washington terminology.[6] However, the numbers did not add up. The 2000 budget request for national defense was $280.8 billion. The amount Congress had appropriated for FY 1999 was $279.4 billion. That is a difference of only $1.4 billion. How could anyone call it a $12.6 billion increase?

First, the increase used a changed base of comparison: it did not compare the 2000 budget to that of 1999; instead, it compared to the previous year's defunct plan for 2000. In 1999 the administration planned to spend $276.7 in 2000 on defense, a lower "baseline" than the $279.4 billion appropriated by Congress for 1999. However, the difference between the new 2000 budget and the old 2000 budget plan was only $4.1 billion. We still do not have a $12.6 billion increase.

The second step was to call a decrease an increase. This was done in the Military Construction part of the DoD budget where programs costing $5.4 billion were funded with only $2.3 billion. The budget deferred the remaining $3.1 billion of these costs to the next fiscal year, 2001. Using impressive linguistic gymnastics, the comptroller termed this deferral of $3.1 billion to 2001 an "increase" in 2000.

Next was to ask for a savings that was not actually requested. Specifically, the budget submission asked for $1.6 billion in "rescissions" (i.e., cuts in past year programs and moving the money to 2000). However, just where to cut past programs was never identified and submitted to Congress. Nevertheless, the 2000 budget was credited with the additional $1.6 billion in transfers.

The final device was to exploit the inaccuracy of earlier economic projections. Because the economy had been healthier than economists had expected, inflation had been growing slower than projected, foreign currency exchange rates for DoD expenses overseas had turned out to be more favorable than anticipated, and fuel prices were less than what DoD had programmed. These three factors added up to a "savings" of $3.8 billion, and the money was plowed back into the new defense budget. In fact, because the addition actually increased the purchasing power of dollars—not adding new dollars—the "added" $3.8 billion did not change the total dollar amount in the new budget by a single unit. Due to factors well beyond the control of the Defense Department, its budget had more purchasing power without changing a single number.

Thus, you get a $12.6 billion "increase": $4.1 billion in real money added to a defunct baseline; a reduction of $3.1 billion that is called an increase, $1.6 billion in nonexistent savings, and a $3.8 billion adjustment in buying power that did not change the dollar total. The nominal sum is, indeed, $12.6 billion, and President Clinton and his secretary of defense could all pose as "pro" defense.

The tricks took care of the problem of making the budget seem bigger than it actually was, but on other political fronts the same team had to make it seem smaller than it actually was. The 2000 national defense budget request of $280.8 billion was well above the spending level specified by the 1997 budget agreement between President Clinton and Congress. That agreement had projected just $274.3 billion for national defense. Clinton's defense budget was exceeding that by $6.5 billion.

The administration went to work. First, it discounted from the defense budget savings from past years in non-defense programs (specifically "entitlement" programs, such as Social Security, Medicare, and Medicaid). This was a violation of OMB counting rules that specifically prohibited using old apples to offset new oranges. Those rules were thrown out the window. Unfortunately, that device was not large enough, so the team decided to twist other rules. A $5.6 billion increase for higher military pensions would no longer count in the defense budget. The ruses were included in the 2000 budget presentation materials, buried deep among other mind-numbing budget trivia. Former Senator Cohen and the Clinton administration were able to permit the Clinton administration to claim a $12.6 billion defense increase that, in fact, did *not* exist, while at the same time asserting that an increase over the previous budget agreement that *did* exist, did not exist.

Feeling confused? Good! That is exactly how the authors of the gimmicks want you to feel.

Weapons Costs—Caveat Emptor

Senior military officers and the services also play the budget numbers cooking game.

When Americans buy an automobile, the cost of the car includes things other than the cost of the steel, wiring, plastic, and other materials the car is made of and the labor costs to fabricate the car. We also pay for overhead, such as the salary and commission of the sales staff, other dealership operating costs, and the costs of overhead back at the plant (foremen, corporate managers, advertising, health care, and more). Because the manufacturer and the dealer embed these costs in what we pay (even after bargaining), the manufacturer and the dealer can pay for their expenses. If they are not paid for everything, they lose money. If they get a little extra, they make a profit. That's capitalism. That's how it works.

The Defense Department has a different approach. We will look at two examples: the V-22 "tilt-rotor" transport for the Marines and the Air Force's new "stealth" fighter, the F-22.

On 11 April 2000, DoD held a news briefing for reporters on the crash of a V-22 on 8 April in which all nineteen Marines on board were killed. At the start of the briefing, the main speaker, Marine Corps Lt. Gen. Fred McCorkle, made a sobering tribute to the dead Marines and how "Marines really take personally the loss of life of any [of] our Marines."[7] However, by the end of the briefing, the tone had changed; General McCorkle was cracking jokes[8] with the press and insisting on the accuracy[9] of misleading cost figures for the V-22.

Stating, "I run aviation for the Marine Corps"[10] (and [McCorkle] was clearly the authority), he refuted as "an inaccurate representation" reporters' questions about the V-22's unit cost being $80 million per copy.[11] The reporters made it clear they were asking for a "layman['s]" figure for the "price tag" of the aircraft.[12] They were obviously asking for a cost figure Americans would understand. The general was equally clear; he insisted the price of the V-22 was $39.9 million. He added, "I understand now that that is going to increase to, like, 41.7 or something million dollars."[13]

The most definitive statement of weapon system cost sent to Congress is DoD's "Selected Acquisition Report" (SAR). The then-latest V-22 SAR was declassified and cleared for publication by the Navy on 28 March 2000.[14] It showed the total cost (in "current" dollars—i.e., the past, present, and future dollars actually appropriated by Congress) to be $38.1 billion for a total fleet of 458 V-22s.[15] That math ($38.1 billion divided by 458) makes the unit cost $83.2 million per copy. How could General McCorkle derive a figure between $39.9 and $41.7 million per copy?

We can retrace the steps the general seems to have taken in the SAR, which presents program costs several different ways. One part of the SAR shows only the "procurement" (fabrication, or production) costs; that is, $30.9 billion in "current" dollars, a figure that ignores the costs to develop, test, and modify the V-22 to the point where it was to be ready for production.[16] For 458 units, the procurement cost came to $67.4 million per copy. Not close to the general's number; we need to keep looking.

The SAR uses what it calls "base year dollars" (dollars valued in the year the specific program was started). The V-22's "base year" was 1986. In 1986 base year dollars, the V-22 production is listed at $19.3 billion for 458;[17] that math comes to $42.2 million per copy. Finally, we get close to General McCorkle's V-22 "layman's price tag." We had to: (1) pretend that the research and testing to develop the V-22 ($7.2 billion) had nothing to do with the cost of the program, and (2) use obsolete, fourteen-year-old dollars.[18]

In addition, that price tag does not even include other overhead costs, such as General McCorkle's salary, salary and health care costs for DoD civilian and military people working on the program, DoD oversight in various offices of the secretary of defense, and so on.

Marine generals are not the only ones to play these games. A 1999 trip to the Air Force's official Web site yielded a page on "AF separates F-22 facts from myths" regarding its fighter for the new millennium, the F-22. This page asserted "an average aircraft 'sticker price' . . . of less than $85 million."[19] Reverse engineering this dollar figure reveals the same twice-cooked method as the Marine's V-22. The Air Force F-22's SAR reveals a base year dollar (in this case, 1990) cost just for procurement of $27.1 billion for 333 production aircraft; that gives us an $81.4 million per copy cost. Add the money for the F-22's research and development (without which it would not exist), and we get $48.3 billion; for 333 copies we get $145.1 million per aircraft. Put the obsolete 1990 dollars into the ones Congress actually appropriates, and we get $61.9 billion, which means a unit cost of $186 million per F-22. The Air Force "fact" sheet told us "less than $85 million." As with the V-22, the officially advertised unit cost was less than half the actual total unit cost.*

Note also in the Air Force fact sheet they call their $85 million price a "sticker price." When you next buy a car, tell the salesperson that you want to go by official U.S. Air Force definitions of sticker price and would they please deduct from the sticker price all development, testing, and other overhead costs to design, engineer, sell, and deliver the car.

---

* In addition, since that 1999 calculation, the actual cost of the F-22 started to exceed $200 million because of cost overruns.

These games have a purpose. Even at the incomplete, obsolete dollar cost levels, these programs are expensive. The deceptions help to put the public and congressional perception of the costs at as low a level as possible. This is especially helpful if the system under discussion is controversial. That was certainly true of the V-22 when General McCorkle held his briefing. Nineteen Marines had just died in one. It was prudent Pentagon politics to add no cost controversy to the human tragedy at hand. In the case of the Air Force's F-22, the system and its cost had been controversial for years. That was demonstrated by the simple fact that the Air Force had to have a "facts separated from myths" fact sheet.

Apologists for General McCorkle and the Air Force would protest that they were merely measuring the costs of the V-22 and F-22 as DoD normally does. They were, indeed, giving what in DoD parlance is the "flyaway" cost of the aircraft (i.e., the direct fabrication costs only), which happened to be in the program's "normal" base year dollars. However, recall that in both cases the subject at hand was the layperson's price tag or the sticker price, not some narrow technical version of unit cost. Had there been a desire to be complete and accurate, it would have been simple to give the costs in both versions. However, that would have revealed the narrowness of the technical version.

Non-Emergency Emergency Spending

After weapon systems with inappropriately low price tags are wedged into the DoD budget, their inevitable real costs inexorably add up. Not willing either to sort out the needed systems from the unneeded or to insist on measures to actually reduce the unit costs, Congress makes room for the ballooning expenses by adding money on top. One perennial favorite of the appropriations committees, "emergency" spending, helps quite a bit.

The Balanced Budget and Emergency Deficit Control Act of 1990 provided that limits on appropriations, "spending caps," can be lifted for emergencies.[20] The theory was that deficit reduction should not impede the legitimate need to address unforeseen disasters, such as unanticipated conflicts, damage from extraordinary weather, oil embargoes, and so forth. In 1991 OMB suggested criteria for the new form of spending to keep things under control: emergencies and spending for them should be "vital," "sudden," "unforeseen," and "temporary." Congress decided to keep things simple. It adopted no criteria, except that for defense spending both Congress and the president have to designate the proposed expenditure as "emergency."[21]

Congress's use of emergency spending evolved into a pattern. In 1991 it used the emergency mechanism to pay for Operation Desert Storm— expenses that would certainly qualify for OMB's criteria of vital, sudden, unforeseen, and not permanent. However, in later years—with only a few exceptions—emergency spending became a mechanism to pay for additional routine defense expenses. For example, about $5 billion of the $19.7 billion of emergency defense spending in 1999 paid for the cost of the U.S. air war over Yugoslavia (Operation Allied Force), which would seem to meet the 1991 OMB/Desert Storm criteria. But, the remaining $14 billion in "emergencies" bought, among other things, a pay raise for military personnel ($1.8 billion) that did not even commence until the following fiscal year; additional cruise missiles, JDAM satellite guided bombs, and Predator reconnaissance drones ($684 million); additional spare parts, depot maintenance, recruiting, training, base operations, and personnel programs ($2.4 billion); missile defense research ($800 million); and classified intelligence activities (more than $1 billion). Congress was simply adding to regular defense spending and was using the "emergency" designation to circumvent the limits on 1999 appropriations.

For fiscal year 2000, there was no unforeseen war, and most objects of the emergency spending had nothing to do with combat readiness, which had been used in 1999 to justify part of the emergency designation. Fiscal year 2000 recipients included F-15 cost overruns, M-1 tank modifications, CH-46 helicopter engines, U-2 aircraft sensors and simulators, Patriot missile modifications, and support for the Olympics in Utah. The overall bill containing this and other spending was controversial enough for Senator McCain to march down to the Senate floor and give yet another speech about "unnecessary, unwanted, unauthorized, unmitigated pork."[22] The bill also included emergency spending for six unrequested C-130J aircraft for the U.S. Coast Guard for $468 million. Because they were included as a non-defense "emergency," they were subject to a budgetary point of order, if any senator wanted to challenge them. (In such a case, the proponents of the C-130s would have needed a sixty-vote "super-majority" to retain the aircraft.) However, as usual, no senator made the point of order, and President Clinton signed the bill into law on 13 July 2000.

Things evolved still further for fiscal year 2001. Just a few weeks after it passed the emergency add-ons for 2000, Congress passed the 2001 DoD Appropriations bill, which included still more emergency spending for 2000. This included $529 million for depot maintenance and other "readiness" items, but it also included a $1.1 billion fund with permission for the secretary of defense to transfer any portion to virtually any program he wanted. In other words, Congress was apparently aware of nothing to justify an emergency designation, so it gave the secretary of defense the authority to spend the money as he saw fit. Things like this $1.1 billion account used to be called "slush funds," and in the past, Appropriations Committees assiduously hunted them down in presidential budget requests and killed them. In today's environment, it is the Appropriations Committee creating the slush fund and handing it over to the executive branch to use as it sees fit.

In 2003 there was the legitimate emergency of paying for the opening stages of the second war against Iraq, but when the costs for the 2003 fighting were not as high as Congress and the president had funded, Congress started to play with the "extra" money. The chairmen of the House and Senate Appropriations Committees, Congressman C. W. "Bill" Young (R-Fla.) and Sen. Ted Stevens, simply transferred $3 billion "extra" emergency DoD dollars to non-defense programs, including education, veterans benefits, and other popular, ongoing, non-emergency social programs.

The Ultimate Budget-Cooker

The biggest gimmicks are not directed at the inside baseball of obscure budget rules. These big-time gimmicks appear to be supported by solid history and sweet reason and are presented over and over again to the press and public to make permanent their misunderstanding of the defense budget.

One such device is the argument that DoD does not receive its fair share of gross domestic product (GDP). This argument will point out that the percent of GDP spent for defense in any given year (spending in 2003 was 3.3 percent) compares unfavorably to past years. A convenient year to compare is 1941, the year of the Pearl Harbor disaster. Defense's percent of GDP that year was 5.6;[23] ergo—they want you to think—at any lower percentage, we are exquisitely vulnerable to sneak attack. These presentations might also point out that during the cold war, the United States typically averaged 5, 6, or 7 percent of GDP on defense—or more. Surely, the advocates argue, we can afford more than 3 percent.

An important corollary is to argue that we should make just a small adjustment and increase defense spending to only 4 or 4.5 percent; it helps to make the whole thing sound reasonable.

These arguments were popular toward the end of the Clinton administration as the pressure to increase the defense budget gathered, but they really took off in the George W. Bush administration: with the defense budget exploding, those who wanted to spend still more needed to seem reasonable.

Even though it was used over and over by the George W. Bush administration defense budget advocates, and frequently regurgitated by the press, the percent of GDP argument is specious in the extreme. It assumes there is a logical connection between the size of the national economy and the size of the defense budget, and defense is entitled to some particular "share." In other words, as the economy grows, so should the defense budget. What, one might ask, is the connection between the size of the national economy and the size of the defense budget? Is not the defense budget supposed to have a size proportionate to the threat, rather than to the level of domestic prosperity? Why should the defense budget grow with the economy, especially when the threat has diminished, as it apparently had before September 11, 2001?

During the cold war, experts constantly explained that defense budgets should be threat based, that against the Soviet Union we needed a national defense of a certain size to deter and, if necessary, fight that opponent—all logical arguments. However, when the Soviet Union evaporated, the upward pressure it applied to the defense budget was gone. It was then that the "share of GDP" argument began to take center stage.

Although September 11 made it undeniable that there was a new threat, the nature of that threat did not automatically justify a huge budget. Certainly high costs were understandable for homeland security and fighting the conflicts in Afghanistan and Iraq, but even those were not budget drivers like the old Soviet Union. Afghanistan's defense budget was tiny; Iraq's was larger, but at $1.3 billion for 2002, it was still just 0.03 percent of the U.S. defense budget.[24] Something more was needed to justify spending that was 43 percent of worldwide military spending.[25] The "fair share" of GDP argument filled the bill.

Early in the George W. Bush administration, Deputy Secretary of Defense Paul Wolfowitz began to regularly argue in favor of an increase in defense spending from 3 percent to just 3.5 percent. How modest, just a half of a percentage point. But, with the defense budget at about $300 billion per year, going from 3 percent of GDP to just 3.5 percent meant an increase of about $50 billion. Surely, Wolfowitz thought, that would be plenty to pay for all programs his administration would want to add to the budget. However, after September 11, the defense budget zoomed up to $400 billion for fiscal year 2004, not counting the costs of the conflicts in Afghanistan and Iraq, which pushed it up another $87 billion. Not to worry, the gigantic budget increases can be made to seem modest: after a historically unprecedented $187 billion increase, it can be argued defense has gone up less than 2 percent. The increase was "only" from 3 percent of GDP to something under 5 percent.

The percentage of GDP argument can also be a double-edged sword. In years when the economy is growing and the defense budget is also growing, but less so—that is, when the defense budget is growing in absolute terms but by a smaller percentage of the faster-growing economy—this measure shows "decline." This can also mean that if the economy were to become stagnant or to shrink, and if defense spending were to shrink, but less, this measure would show "growth." The absence of a serious analytical relationship between the size of the national economy and the size of the defense budget shows just how misleading the measurement truly is. Indeed, advocates of the measure could "grow" the defense share of GDP up to 6 percent or even 10 percent of GDP just by getting the economy to shrink enough. Under the logic of these advocates, this would be good news.

The Effect of It All

The result of these and many other games is budget chaos. It is not just figurative, but literal and documented in a series of reports of the Inspector General of the Department of Defense (DoD IG). Year after year, the DoD IG has found the military services to be such a financial management shambles that each service is literally unauditable. Other parts of the DoD infrastructure were at least auditable, but they failed to pass. The IG found billions of underestimates and overestimates of assets, accounts, bills due, and bills paid.[26]

An even more distressing IG report found $2.3 *trillion* in adjustments to DoD's books that were unsupported by adequate audit trails and were a potentially fraudulent attempt to make the books add up. These adjustments were made in just one year (1999), and it can only have been the auditor's understatement when the IG said, "Internal controls were not adequate to ensure that resources were properly managed and accounted for, that DoD complied with applicable laws and regulations, and that the financial statements were free of material misstatements."[27] Congress and DoD have done little about it. There were some congressional press releases decrying what the DoD IG found; there were also some hearings.

Afterwards, things remained the same. No senior official in responsibility was seriously reprimanded, let alone replaced; no important new legislation was introduced, passed, and signed into law; potential fraud amounting to trillions of dollars was not seen as a cause to disrupt business as usual. No significant reaction occurred in DoD either. The department's comptroller did declare in 2000 "efforts to reform the [financial management] process are harmed by the political process" (i.e., the very same political process he engaged in when adjusting appearances of the 2000 budget [see above]).[28] He also recommended, in a figurative throwing up of the hands in abdication, that the Defense Department should hire private sector accounting firms to untangle the mess and reform its financial management systems.

In 2001 there was a new DoD comptroller under the Bush administration. Under duress from Sen. Charles Grassley (R-Iowa) and Senator Byrd, the new comptroller appointed a deputy to focus on DoD's financial management, but by 2003 little progress had been made. In that year the DoD IG reported: "(1) DoD financial management systems do not substantively comply with Federal financial management systems requirements, generally accepted accounting principles, and the U.S. Government Standard Ledger at the transaction level and (2) DoD financial management and feeder systems cannot currently provide adequate evidence to support various material amounts on the financial statements."[29]

In plain English, DoD's books remained such a mess that they could not be audited; the auditors could still not even begin. Still, nothing else changed; no one was held accountable for the continuing failure; no one was called onto the carpet by the Armed Services or Appropriations Committees to offer more apologies or make more promises; no one lost his or her job; and no one dared suggest that DoD should receive a single penny less until it made some measurable progress toward what is a commonplace level of competence in the rest of government and in private business—knowing where its money is, how much is being paid for what, whose invoices have been paid, whose have not, who has been overpaid or underpaid, and who is robbing the cash register. In DoD all of these elements are mostly unknown.

Exceptions to the rule, Senators Byrd and Grassley have repeatedly asked DoD witnesses about the issue, complained about DoD's financial incompetence, commissioned GAO and DoD IG studies to uncover still more of it, and from time to time have offered amendments to defense bills intended to improve things. When offered, these amendments usually pass and become law, but ultimately nothing changes.

One gets the impression that a senator like Charles Grassley, who in the past expressed outrage about the chaos in DoD's financial books, has grown numb after years of persistent DoD ineptitude and recalcitrance. In 2002 I listened to Senator Grassley complain to the deputy secretary of defense and the DoD comptroller about their lack of progress toward financial integrity. The senator came to a Senate Budget Committee hearing, read off his complaints from a prepared statement when it was his turn to ask questions, and listened to the response. It was the usual, "We're trying; we're sure what we're doing will work this time." Shortly afterwards, Grassley nodded to his staffer, as if to say, "Was that okay?" and then left the hearing.

I had the strong impression that the fire was out in Grassley's belly. His staffer passionately disagrees, but what I saw was a senator simply going through the motions. With DoD entering its third decade of IG reports certifying that the department's books are so hopeless they cannot be audited, one wonders when the members of Congress who state they are concerned about the mess will run out of patience.

Only a little facetiously, Congress's exercise of the "power of the purse" can be summarized in three ways: (1) exploiting budget rules to add spending; (2) pretending to be frugal while adding spending; and (3) approving DoD gimmicks to add spending. The persistent theme stems from the universal thinking that more spending is always better. If Congress, at the pinnacle of constitutional budgetary authority, behaves thus, why should anyone in the rest of government act any differently? It is very hard to point an accusing finger at the Defense Department when the ones charged with the ultimate responsibility are leading the way in the wrong direction.

For the most part, the staff in Congress do not reduce the problem, they expand it. They are next.

10

The Engine of Congressional Good and Evil: The Staff

A t the start of the twenty-first century, there are 30,593 of them.[1] To write the Constitution, there was only one. The additional 30,592 have not matched the U.S. Constitution with their work, but they have accompanied, if not caused, a fundamental change in the nature of Congress, and how it does, and does not do, its work. "They" are the congressional staff. I was one of them for thirty-one years.

We come in all forms. At the turn of the twenty-first century, 11,488 were "personal staff" working directly for the 435 House and 100 Senate members handling scheduling, mail, press, casework,* all the legislative issues Congress deals with, including, of course, pork. The "committee staff" comprised 2,177 others working for the forty-four committees of the House and Senate, handling the issues and processing the bills under the jurisdiction of the committees, including, of course, pork. An additional 4,254 worked for Congress's support agencies, GAO, CRS, and CBO, doing research and analysis requested, and often ignored, by committees and members. There were 1,251 Capitol Hill police officers, 2,012 maintenance and facility personnel in the Office of the Architect of the Capitol, and 1,964 clerks, elevator operators, stenographers, computer specialists, barbers, hairdressers, manicurists, bank tellers, cooks, cafeteria workers, cashiers, and janitors working for various offices, such as the secretary of the Senate, the clerk of the House, and the sergeants at arms of both the House and Senate.[2]

The ones of interest here are the personal and committee staff working for members of Congress. Among them, there are good, bad, and mediocre ones; they are even more diverse than the 535 members of Congress for whom they work. While many are supposed to be the members' link to constituents, the executive branch, the private sector, and much else, they have, in fact, helped members of Congress lose touch with reality. While many of them perform research and provide advice, many do not act as a

---

* Casework consists of attempting to solve problems constituents have with the federal government, such as receiving overdue Social Security checks, lessening jet noise at the local airport or Air Force base, and thousands of other issues.

check or a balance on members' thinking or actions; instead, many open the door to less and less restraint by members. In general, the result is members who are individually and collectively focused on themselves and a huge congressional bureaucracy that, overall, serves to reinforce the members' partisanship and self-preoccupation.

How it came to be this way starts at the U.S. Constitutional Convention and proceeds—first slowly, then in a rush—to the vast expansion of the congressional staff in the late-twentieth century. Contrary to what Capitol Hill experts in the Washington, D.C., think tanks say, few of whom ever worked on Capitol Hill, the reason for the expansion had less to do with the growing complexity of modern life than it did with power struggles with the executive branch and members' personal agendas. Aggregation of staff became synonymous with power in Washington and status on Capitol Hill. In the later stages of the staffs' growth, Congress applied itself to making them less professional.

A brief history on how it became thus.

The Good Staffer

At the Constitutional Convention in 1787, the framers did their own thinking. They had to; they had no one else to do it for them. The convention hired just one staffer, and all he was supposed to do was take notes.

An officer in the revolutionary army, an aide to continental delegations to France and Holland to negotiate war loans, an assistant secretary of war under the Articles of Confederation, and a man with many contacts among revolutionary leaders, William Jackson was a highly qualified candidate to serve as the Constitutional Convention's official recording secretary. To win the job, he beat out nepotism in the form of Benjamin Franklin's grandson.[3] His employers frequently described him as self-effacing and unobtrusive, ever faithful, and yet highly professional and competent. Jackson was the "quintessential civil servant" and "established a model of professional behavior for succeeding government employees."[4]

As what we could call the first staff employee for the American national legislature, Jackson had the historically monumental job of recording—and making official with his signature—the discussions and debates that were the Constitutional Convention. Jackson may have been too good a staffer. After the convention, he was instructed to protect the secrecy of the closed-door deliberations because the founding fathers feared the details of their discussions, if publicly known, might hinder the Constitution's adoption by the states. They told Jackson to destroy all his notes and records, except for an official journal,[5] which was not particularly illuminating.[6] Imagine the gold mine for today's historians and constitutional scholars if

Jackson had taken it upon himself to disregard his instructions and seques-ter all his records for posterity. Such records to complement the existing notes of James Madison could have been historically priceless. Although it is a trait most modern congressional staff shun, disobeying the boss may be a surer sign of a "quintessential civil servant" than simple obedience.

Small Beginnings

The growth of the congressional staff from the obedient Jackson to the cur-rent horde was slow in coming. The House of Representatives hired the first post–Constitutional Convention congressional staffer, a clerk, on 1 April 1789.[7] Several weeks later, the Senate, which met only in secret session in its early years, hired a staff of six, including a doorkeeper (to keep the public and the press out), a secretary (not Jackson, he moved on to work as President Washington's personal secretary), two clerks, and a chaplain.[8]

For its first sixty-six years, Congress hired no full-time staff to work di-rectly for members or committees. Any member who wanted a personal assistant for himself did so at his own expense, or he used his own family members.[9] Committees and members who wanted substantive policy infor-mation or advice usually relied on executive branch personnel or outsid-ers.[10] In some special cases, they had access to temporary staff hired by the clerk of the House or the secretary of the Senate.[11]

In 1855 the House and Senate began to hire permanent committee staff, but only for the chairmen of two committees:[12] the House Ways and Means and the Senate Finance Committees, Congress's two tax-writing com-mittees.[13] The staffers were termed "clerks" even though they performed duties well beyond those of scribes: they drafted legislation and provided information and advice to the members. For decades thereafter, the num-ber of committees and chairmen with staff slowly expanded, but the total number remained under one hundred.[14]

Personal Staff

In 1884 individual senators who did not chair committees gained one "cleri-cal" staff to work directly for them. These were the first personal staffers hired at federal expense. In the early 1890s, the House followed suit and granted each of its members a clerk.[15] Typical responsibilities of these House and Senate personal staff were to act as secretaries handling correspon-dence and scheduling and to provide information and advice to the extent desired by their individual member.

In 1910 the staff allotment for senators was increased to two—then to three in 1914, five in 1940, and eight in 1947. Meanwhile, the House al-lotment for personal staff grew to two in 1919, to three in 1940, and to six in 1945.[16] As this personal staff grew, duties specialized. Some were left in charge of scheduling and the personal activities of the member; some would handle casework; some provided advice on bills and became known as legislative assistants.

And, as the staff grew, so did the workload. The more constituents realized they could get information and help from a member of Congress, or from the more accessible staff, the more they called and wrote in to do so. The availability of legislative assistants also made more numerous and more complex bills and amendments possible.

As the staff grew, it needed office space. In 1909 the first official House and Senate office buildings, now known as the Cannon and Russell buildings, respectively, opened. Each had hundreds of rooms to accommodate members and their staff. Some of these rooms had elaborate marble fireplaces for the member's personal office, but other rooms were simpler, although certainly not spartan. High ceilings, heavy mahogany moldings and doors, marble trim, and granite floors are abundant, even in rooms for opening and sorting mail. One can easily imagine a member of Congress in a congressional hearing gruffly berating the head of a cabinet agency for building such an elaborate and expensive edifice to house agency staff.

Over time, the Cannon and Russell buildings became inadequate. The House and Senate both added two more office buildings. Each of these four buildings were, again, fancy and expensive according to the construction methods of their time. The most modern House office building, the Rayburn building built in the 1960s, was reputed after its construction to be the most expensive building per square foot ever built by mankind. That is, until the Senate built its newest accommodation, the Hart building, which was even more costly.[17]

In 1948 the Senate ceased authorizing a specific number of staff for each member and simply gave each office a pot of money for payroll expenses. In 1951 the payroll accounts were organized into five different size categories, depending on the population of a senator's state. California and New York had the largest staff payroll pots, and Alaska, Montana, and other low-population states had the smallest. Over time, all the money pots grew, proportionately, to permit more staff for all. When I started work in 1971 for Senator Javits from New York, his personal staff was approximately thirty people. In the House, where there was little numerical variation in the population of members' districts, all personal staffs expanded to twelve by 1966 and reached eighteen in 1975. In 1979 the House further authorized an additional four part-timers for all members.[18]

The growth continued throughout the 1970s and into the early 1990s. Rather than simply expand their own personal office payrolls, members used various technical artifices to acquire more staff. Senators who were on committees that failed to give them committee staffers were allotted up to three new people. Some committees, such as the House and Senate Budget committees, gave members "associate staff." These staff handled the issues under the jurisdiction of the committee in question, but they did so just for an individual member.[19]

Another change adopted in the 1990s was to permit members to combine their previously separate accounts for staff payroll, travel and office expenses, and the franking (free mail) privilege.[20] This permitted members significantly more flexibility in the management of their own offices. They could, if they chose, use money previously devoted just to mail or travel to pay for more staff, or vice versa. This was more flexibility than they were willing to grant most federal agencies, where Congress built high walls between accounts for different purposes, and office management "slush funds" were verboten.

Committee Staff

After the House and Senate established committee staffs for the two tax committees in the mid-nineteenth century, members tended to create committees for obscure purposes to obtain the staff and Capitol building office space assigned to them, or they added staff to preexisting committees. By 1913 there were sixty-one committees in the House and seventy-four in the Senate. Many, if not all, had staff assigned, but Congress did not record the numbers. Many committees neither held meetings nor reported bills; they were simply staff and office space sinecures. For example, the Senate Committee on Revolutionary Claims remained in existence until 1921.

Committee staff expansion in the 1930s included the modern Senate's first racial integration. In 1937 the Senate Finance Committee hired the first African-American recorded by the Senate Historical Office. He was Mr. Jesse Nichols, and he worked as the committee's documents clerk and librarian until 1971.[21]

The Legislative Reorganization Act of 1946 initiated a period of major committee staff growth. It eliminated superfluous House and Senate committees and reorganized them into their modern array. The superfluous committees and the staff positions they afforded members for what amounted to personal staffers were all eliminated. (Likely, many of those staff transferred to the expanding personal staffs of the time or were simply rehired by the newly reorganized committees.) Each new committee was permitted ten staff, consisting of four clerks and six "professionals."[22] This was the first time any staff were designated anything but clerk,[23] reflecting not so much growing responsibilities as an admission by members that these people had been playing a significant role in legislation and other congressional activities for decades. In addition, the Legislative Reorganization Act also authorized additional "investigative" staff on an as-needed basis.

The Democratic chairman of the House Appropriations Committee, Clarence Cannon, objected to what he believed to be excessive levels of staffing permitted by the Legislative Reorganization Act of 1946.* As a result, the new rules exempted the Appropriations Committees in both the House and Senate from these staffing authorizations.[24] To this day, many of the top professionals on those committees are still termed "clerks." However, under subsequent appropriations committee chairmen, the exemption originally intended as an economy became license for growth. By 2002 the Senate Appropriations Committee had far outstripped all the other Senate committees with a staff budget exceeding $10 million, at least double most other committees.[25] The House Appropriations Committee was not far behind.

In all cases, staff were to be hired not just by the chairman but by a vote of all the members of a committee. The staff were obligated to work for the entire committee. The intent was that they would be without political affiliation or bias. Furthermore, committee staff were to work only on committee products, such as bills, reports, and hearings. Any personal, let alone campaign, work for individual senators was strictly prohibited. By the time of my arrival in the Senate staff in 1971, these strictures were observed in some committees, but in most cases, as discussed below, one or all of them were either formally changed, circumvented, or simply ignored.

The Legislative Reorganization Act of 1946 did not address how many subcommittees each committee could have. Uncontrolled, these rapidly proliferated, thereby creating the opportunity for subcommittee chairmen to justify and hire still more staff.[26] The growth of committee, and subcommittee, staff paralleled that of personal staffs in the 1950s through the 1980s.

In 1974 another "Legislative Reorganization Act" expanded the baseline staff allotment for committees from ten to thirty and removed in most cases the distinction between "professional" and "investigative" staff.[27] Expansion beyond thirty was to be permitted when it was justified to the Rules Committee in the Senate and the Administration Committee in the House. There came yet another expansion during the "Post-Watergate Reforms" of 1975. Then, subcommittee and personal staffs expanded yet again, but the staffs for the clerk of the House, the sergeant at arms of the Senate, the parliamentarians, and other offices were reduced. Thus, while total legislative

---

* The Cannon office building on the House side of the Capitol complex is not named after this congressman. Instead, it is named after "Uncle Joe" Cannon, who was a Republican speaker of the House in the late-nineteenth century renowned for his authoritarian control of the body.

branch appropriations remained stable, the personal and committee staffs—the ones most directly connected to members—grew.

The figure below shows the growth of combined personal and committee staff in the House and Senate from the first Congress in 1790 to the turn of the twenty-first century. The growth, especially since World War II, has been remarkable. From 1946 to 2000, legislative branch appropriations for staff grew 4,498 percent while the consumer price index grew 783 percent.[28]

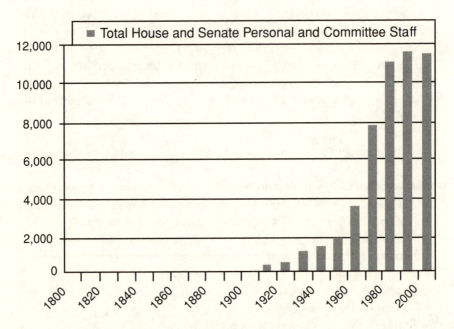

Approximate Senate and House Total Personal and Committee
(Professional) Staff, 1790–2000
Norman J. Ornstein, Thomas E. Mann, and Michael J. Malbin,
Vital Statistics on Congress: 2001–2002 (Washington, D.C.: AEI Press, 2002).

Details and Fellows

After the public expansion of staff via legislative reorganization acts, committee rationalizations, and subcommittee proliferations ceased, members found a subterranean way to expand their staffs. After I left GAO in 1996, my first year with the Senate Budget Committee was as a "detail." A "detail" is an assignment to a federal employee to work for a member or committee of Congress for a specified period (often six to twelve months) while remaining on the payroll of the original agency. The intended purpose is to give an employee firsthand experience with Congress to widen his or her horizons and better assist the agency after the detail returns. In my case, however, I was not looking for a parole from GAO; I was looking for permanent escape. Rampant careerism in senior GAO management and complex and senseless bureaucratic procedures had drained me of patience with the agency.

After I received an offer for a detail from the Senate Budget Committee, I told my GAO superiors, including the comptroller general, it was my intention to leave GAO and not return, but the agency agreed to pay my salary during the detail nonetheless. That way, what was normally a training opportunity for GAO employees became, in my case, a trial period paid by GAO for the Budget Committee to assess whether it wanted to take me on for the longer term. GAO was willing to pay for this because its relations with Senator Domenici, the chairman of the committee and an advocate of budget reductions for GAO, were quite poor. The agency hoped that I could help improve them.

When I arrived at the Budget Committee, I learned that details and fellows had proliferated all over congressional staffs. They came from an unending list of private organizations—a search on the Internet reveals congressional fellow programs in the American Meteorological Society, the Institute of Electrical Electronics Engineers, the American Welding Society, the Institute of Navigation, the American Society of Human Genetics, the American Society of Mechanical Engineers, and many others. In addition, some fellows come from defense manufacturers, such as Northrop-Grumman, sometimes through a clearinghouse operation, in one case run by the Brookings Institution. Some come from organizations created by Congress to honor past members, including Carl Albert, John Stennis, and my old boss Jacob Javits. Some come from CBO. Some come from government agencies, such as the Department of Energy, or from subentities, such as the Los Alamos National Laboratory. The largest number I encountered, however, were from DoD. Active-duty military officers and civilian officials were assigned to many of the members of the House and Senate Armed Services Committees and the Defense and Military Construction Subcommittees of the House and Senate Appropriations Committees.

In 1996, because no one knew how many DoD fellows worked in Congress, Sen. Charles Grassley asked the DoD inspector general to find out. The DoD IG report found one hundred working for members and committees that conducted DoD oversight, but the IG also reported that it was not sure it had located all of them in the rest of Congress.[29] After the report, I was told by a colleague that one military fellow, an officer working for the Senate Appropriations Committee, objected to a follow-on report the DoD IG said it would release on what duties and responsibilities the fellows were performing in Congress. The Appropriations Committee recommended a $3 million reduction in the IG's next budget,[30] and the follow-up report never appeared. Just what the military fellows were doing for the Appropriations Committee was apparently something the military fellows and the Appropriations Committee did not want the public to know about.

In some cases, the members relying on these details and fellows for professional advice may be getting a bit more than they bargained for. The ones I encountered were as varied as the congressional staff. Some were highly professional and offered every appearance of being objective and well informed. Some were out for themselves and made it clear they considered their fellowship either a vacation or an opportunity for immediate career advancement. Still others were out for bigger game. A Marine officer assigned to a member of the Defense Subcommittee in the Senate Appropriations Committee explained that to me. He was there, he said, to learn about how the Senate worked so that when he returned to the Pentagon he could help run the Marines' congressional liaison office—its lobbying shop. In addition, he mentioned almost casually, he could make known to the senator what positions the Marines had on various defense issues, and if there arose any problem between the Marines and the senator, he could alert his superior officers and help get the problem worked out.

What a great deal!—for the Marines. Not only does the Corps get an officer schooled in the ways of Congress so the Corps can better lobby it in the future, but while the officer is in the senator's office, if the senator develops any wayward views on controversies affecting the Marine Corps, the military fellow can get the commandant on the phone with the senator to set him straight. If, for example, the senator might be thinking about voting for an amendment by Sen. Russ Feingold to improve testing on the Corps's premier aircraft aspiration, the V-22, the fellow would be emplaced in the senator's office to know about it and mobilize the commandant to solve the "problem."

The more I looked around, the more I saw exactly that type of thing happen. When monitoring the Senate's debate on the Department of Defense Authorization bill, I frequently saw military fellows talking to senators advising them how to vote on amendments and even writing amendments favored, if not originated, by the military service they were a part of. I personally observed military fellows advocating to their sponsor senators amendments that increased insurance and retirement benefits for military personnel, potentially including themselves. One particularly egregious case was an amendment offered, successfully, by Sen. Michael Crapo (R-Idaho) to permit retired military officers to "double dip": that is, to collect both any military pension they earned plus any salary for employment on Capitol Hill. Doing so had previously been considered an abuse, but the Armed Services Committee had several retired officers in its employ who would benefit. A military fellow could also benefit should he or she choose to retire and continue with any senator who elected to employ them, which, as the DoD IG report made clear, occurred in several cases.[31]

After the 1997 DoD IG report, there were minor changes. The Senate Rules Committee began to collect information about detailees from government agencies, but it released the information only every two years, buried in a larger and obscure report about Senate expenditures. In addition, it addressed only committees, not personal staffs. To learn about details and fellows on senators' personal staffs there is no report, biannual or otherwise. There are, however, records maintained by the Senate Ethics Committee, and they are supposed to be open to the public for inspection. In researching this chapter, I called both the Senate Rules and Ethics committees to review their reports and files. After I made the purpose of my phone calls clear, I could never get them returned.

In 2001, according to information a former colleague in the House extracted, there were 227 DoD fellows in the House and Senate. In 2003, however, the numbers fell to 171; the fellows were banned from the committees that performed oversight of DoD. Secretary of Defense Donald Rumsfeld complained that fellows had "told the committees too much" about what was going on in the Pentagon.[32] The members of the DoD oversight committees simply circumvented Rumsfeld's ban by putting most of the fellows on their personal staffs.

Congressional details and fellows have become a way for members to augment their staffs at no budgetary expense to themselves. Depending on the nature of the individual detail or fellow, these "free staffers" can be a benefit providing real expertise to a member, or they can be a danger in the form of an individual pursuing a personal or agency agenda.

Staff and Partisanship Grow

As I worked in Congress, I began to find the institution more and more partisan and inwardly focused. The way Congress expanded its own staff during this period both reflected and augmented those tendencies. An important milestone was the Legislative Reorganization Act of 1970. It recognized the unworkability of both Democrats and Republicans relying on the same "bipartisan" staff the Legislative Reorganization Act of 1946 had created.

I witnessed just how unworkable the 1946 act was. Even after the changes effected by the 1970 act, the Senate Foreign Relations Committee (where

Senator Javits was a member) was still operating on the "bipartisan" staff principle. In truth, the "bipartisan" staff worked for the chairman of the committee, J. William Fulbright (D-Ark.). His staffers were mostly competent and professional, and the committee observed the legal formality that a majority of all senators on the committee select them. However, the more liberal Democrats on the committee, such as George McGovern of South Dakota, and the more conservative Republicans, such as Hugh Scott of Pennsylvania, simply relied on their own personal staff for foreign policy advice, not committee staff. Even in the case of Republican Javits, who had high respect for Democrat Fulbright across the party divide and who had more in common (substantively) with Fulbright than he had with many Republicans, it was an illusion to think that staffers who had their primary allegiance to Chairman Fulbright could satisfy Javits's requirements.

For example, when the Foreign Relations Committee reported out the 1972 version of the War Powers Act to the full Senate, Chairman Fulbright's staff drafted a committee report describing the bill, its purpose, and background and sent it to Javits, the primary committee author of the bill, for his consent. Javits's primary staffer for the issue, my immediate boss, Pete Lakeland, reviewed the draft report and found it unacceptable. It did not adequately address the need for the legislation, its constitutional legitimacy, or the exhaustive process the committee went through to arrive at the final bill text. It also gave excessive attention to some idiosyncratic ideas that Chairman Fulbright had on related issues. Lakeland rewrote the entire report, and only with Javits's insistence did Fulbright and his staff accept the rewrite. Even though Javits and Fulbright had much in common on an issue such as war powers, they also had much they did not agree about. For both to rely on the same staff was simply a nonstarter.

Recognizing this kind of problem, the Legislative Reorganization Act of 1970 entitled the minority party of any committee to demand that one-third of the professional staff payroll be devoted to a staff for the minority party only.[33] This establishment of majority and minority committee staffs certainly eliminated the problem of a nominally "bipartisan" staff that did not adequately reflect the views of all committee members. However, the change exacerbated a more serious problem. Committee staffs in Congress, that is the staffs that many regard as the most professional and substantively knowledgeable on Capitol Hill, have now become highly partisan. Majority and minority committee staffs frequently now go out of their way to withhold information from each other, lay plans to undermine the work of the other, and side for or against legislation depending far more on political affiliation than on the merits of the argument. In the past, there was at least an attempt to be bipartisan and to offer to any committee member who asked information and advice. In the modern, more partisan era, committee staffers would always be polite to members from the other party, and usually their staff, but information and advice unaffected by political biases from across the party divide are rare.

The Effect: Politics Trump Facts and Ethics

When I worked for the Senate Budget Committee in the late 1990s, I routinely encountered partisanship among committee staff. When I wrote analyses of President Clinton's defense budgets for the Republican staff of the Budget Committee, I was permitted considerable latitude in describing in official committee documents the gimmicks and inadequacies of Clinton defense budgets. After the 2000 elections when Republicans took control of the White House and the Pentagon, very little changed in defense budgets before September 11, 2001, but the way I described the problems in budget committee documents certainly changed. Where previously my analysis of inadequate spending for military readiness was harsh and unforgiving, the criticisms of the Bush defense budget were muted, when they survived at all.

Moreover, there was role reversal between the Republican and Democratic staffs on issues like budget gimmicks. The new regime of Donald Rumsfeld in the Pentagon switched to budget ruses that attempted to make the defense budget appear smaller, rather than larger, as usually, but not always, favored by the Clinton administration. The new regime's favorite tactic was measuring defense spending as a percentage of GDP, which we have already discussed and which made the defense budget appear not only small but to be shrinking when it was actually growing. Although we were both disgruntled about it, the Republican chief of staff at the Budget Committee, Bill Hoagland, and I knew that Senator Domenici and the other Republicans on the Budget Committee would have little toleration for their committee staff trashing such gimmicks with the contempt they deserved in committee documents. We did add some explanations and questions about the Rumsfeld gimmicks in materials we prepared for Republican senators at Budget Committee hearings on the defense budget, but, unsurprisingly, none of our senators asked them. When it came to exposing gimmicks in the Bush defense budget in official committee documents, we were required to essentially keep silent and to figuratively hold our noses.

We sometimes actively used in congressional budget resolutions other gimmicks for which we scornfully trashed Democrats when they used them. Having bad-mouthed during the Clinton years the White House's misrepresentation of costs of military programs and policies by using "cooked" expenditure rates, we quietly used those same scoring practices during the Bush years. For FY 2002 we adopted OMB's optimistic budget scoring rather than the more realistic estimates of our own CBO. Doing so made current budget surpluses appear larger, future budget deficits seem smaller, and huge tax cuts and big defense spending increases seem painless and affordable. Of course, the Democrats played their part by loudly criticizing the very same practices they defended under the Clinton administration. For both sides, reliable facts and objective analysis drove the argument only when the politics made them acceptable.

Less Defense, More Politics

These problems notwithstanding, the Senate Budget Committee was an oasis of reasonableness compared to other committees. Our staff director urged fact-based analysis and a moderate tone whenever we thought we could get away with it. I was frequently able to cooperate with the staffer on the Budget Committee who handled defense down the hallway for the Democrats by sharing information and our professional views on smart and stupid things both the Clinton and Bush Pentagons did (as long as we both kept reasonably quiet about it). However, on the Senate Armed Services Committee, party loyalty and politics appeared to affect substantive staff work to a far greater degree. Relations between the majority and minority staff on Armed Services were usually poisonous. When the Senate was debating defense bills, the staff benches in the two back corners of the Senate chamber would be filled with defense staffers from the Armed Services Committee. Republican staff sat, ironically, in the left rear corner of the chamber; the Democratic staffers sat on the right. To talk across party lines, one had to walk across the rear of the chamber in plain view. I considered it quite normal to talk to a colleague on the other side and, from time to time, got up, walked over, and consulted. Very few others did, and virtually none on a frequent basis. More than once, I received quizzical, if not disapproving, looks from both Republican and Democratic staffers when I talked or worked with Democratic staffers in the Senate chamber.

My consulting with Democratic staffers gave Republican staffers the excuse to accuse me of working for the other party. One occasion occurred when the Republican chairman of the Armed Services Committee, Senator Warner, offered the amendment to increase spending by more than $40 billion on the Defense Department's health program for military retirees. Because of the extraordinary expense of the amendment, it violated the Budget Act and was, therefore, subject to a point of order in the Senate and, by extension, some serious procedural hurdles. As the Budget Committee staffer monitoring the matter in the Senate chamber, I was asked by the

Senate parliamentarian to consult with him on whether the amendment did, indeed, violate the Budget Act. He and I agreed on the facts of the matter, and he ruled the amendment to violate the Budget Act. The chief of the Republican staff of the Armed Services Committee was hovering close to this conversation, making himself obvious and eavesdropping. Knowing his outlook on things, I interpreted his behavior as an attempt to intimidate my advice to the parliamentarian.

As I turned to walk away from my consultation with the parliamentarian, the Republican chief of staff looked at me coldly and remarked that I was "working for the Democrats." I started to give him a factual response to inform him how his senator's amendment had violated the budget rules, but he turned stiffly and walked away. His clear and obvious message was that by relying on the facts of the matter, I was being disloyal. When I returned to my seat among other Republican Armed Services Committee staffers in the back of the Senate chamber, I was greeted with silent stares into the distance from his staff. Later, I was informed by one of them that I had "caused a real problem," implying that I would hear more about it in the future. As on previous occasions, the implied threat was empty, but it did demonstrate their values and tactics. To them, partisanship was clearly a more important guide than the facts, and bullying tactics were an accepted part of the game.

While I encountered partisanship from Democratic staffers as well, the smart ones toned it down with me. They knew that they could make more hay, and maybe fifty-one votes—a majority— if they could convince a few Republicans to join their propositions. Sometimes the propositions were pure partisanship, and they were not even pretending to look for Republican support. Other times the staffers would make an approach to solicit the support of the senator I worked for, but their offer was one-sided and seemed more like a proposition to add Republican window dressing to a partisan idea. However, there were also many cases where their efforts, to my way of thinking, seemed genuine and had merit, and I tried to enlist my boss's support.

I had a very mixed record with the various senators I worked for on such bipartisan propositions. It almost never bothered Javits to work with Democrats; often he preferred them to aggressively conservative, obsessively partisan Republicans, such as Jesse Helms of North Carolina. Senator Kassebaum would work with some Democrats but not with others, and her willingness to work with any varied, depending on the subject matter and other political considerations (such as whether her relations with the Reagan White House were at a high or low ebb). Senator Domenici was the most difficult to convince to cross party lines. While he worked with certain Democrats on some social issues, he rarely seemed comfortable doing so on defense issues.

Although it was natural for the liberal Javits to cross party lines in the 1970s more often than the somewhat conservative Domenici in the 1990s, there was more behind the increased partisanship I observed in the Senate than the different outlooks of Javits and Domenici. The speeches were becoming more strident and shrill, and the parliamentary tactics were becoming more directed at either grasping for some short-term immediate advantage, such as blocking what the other party wanted to do, or generating a vote on an issue that would help one party at the expense of the other in the next election. The two parties were not trying to consider or debate an issue on its merits; they were simply trying to foil each other for political gain.

The expanded staff was behind much of this heightened partisanship. As the staff grew in size in the 1970s and 1980s, it also became more partisan for the simple reason that the members wanted it that way. In turn, the increasingly partisan staff egged on their members with biased evidence and advice on how to advance one side at the expense of the other. The entire institution threw itself into a deteriorating vicious cycle. The Senate chamber was becoming little more than a noisy viper pit in which to fight political wars. The congressional staff was clearly a part of this deterioration.

The partisanship grew as the staff numbers increased, and it grew when the staff numbers declined.

Cutting Staff Augments Partisanship

After the voters gave the Republicans control of both houses of Congress in the 1994 elections, several changes in congressional staffing occurred. Declaring the need for economy on Capitol Hill, the Republicans significantly reduced total legislative branch staffing from 26,837 in 1993 to 23,604 in 1999, a reduction of 3,233, or 12 percent. Where the cuts occurred is revealing; they were not proportionate or across the board. The 11,538 personal staffers of House and Senate members (the single largest component of legislative branch staffing) were basically left uncut: between 1993 and 1999, there was a grand total reduction of just 50 positions. Committee staff was, on the other hand, reduced significantly from 3,141 to 2,177, a reduction of 964 positions or 31 percent. Staffing in Congress's support agencies—GAO, CRS, CBO, and the Office of Technology Assessment (OTA)—was reduced from 6,166 to 4,210, a reduction of 1,956 or 32 percent. OTA was abolished entirely, and GAO was reduced by 1,683 positions, thus absorbing 52 percent of the total Capitol Hill staff cuts.[34] Thus, under the banner of economy, Congress decided to reduce its more expert committee staff and the more objective and independent research staff in its own support agencies. Congress retained the more partisan, and less professional, personal staff.

It was a perfectly logical continuation of the staffing principles Congress, both Republicans and Democrats, had been following.

The Effect of Party Purges

In the 1970s there was a substantial liberal wing in the Republican party and a substantial conservative wing in the Democratic party. The liberal Republican senators, such as Javits, Clifford Case of New Jersey, and Mark Hatfield of Oregon, loosely organized themselves in a "Wednesday Group" of about a dozen moderate to liberal Republicans. The conservative southern Democrats, such as John Stennis of Mississippi and Herman Talmadge of Georgia, had no commensurate public organization, but they remained an ideologically cohesive group who frequently talked among themselves and voted together.

In both cases, the minority wings of the parties tempered the more extreme ideology and behavior of the majority. If, for example, the Republicans wanted to stand united on an issue, they had to accommodate the liberals in the Wednesday Group to bring them along. Failure to do so could result in their defection to the Democrats on key substantive votes. The same was true for the Democrats.

In the late 1970s and 1980s, the two parties became less diverse. Republicans purged their party of most liberals. Ideological, right-wing Republican senators, led by Jesse Helms of North Carolina and activists on his personal staff, supported more ideologically akin challengers against the liberal Republicans, such as Javits and Case, in pre-election primaries to select party candidates. With a more generally conservative party base doing the voting in party primaries, these challenges against the party's minority, liberal wing were frequently successful. In the Democratic party, southern conservatives became a literally dying breed and were replaced by increasingly liberal candidates selected in that party's primaries. These more liberal Democrats in the South increasingly lost to ideologically conservative Republicans in general elections, and several of the remaining conservative southern Democrats (such as Phil Gramm of Texas and Richard Shelby of Alabama) simply defected to the Republican party to survive. No longer needing to accommodate substantial minorities of nonconforming liberals and conservatives, both parties became more ideologically homogeneous.

Staffing paralleled the evolution among members. More uniformly conservative and liberal senators and representatives naturally selected for their personal staffs advisers with whom they were ideologically compatible. On the minority and majority committee staffs, the same thing happened. Republican staff became more and more uniformly conservative, and the Democratic staff became more thoroughly liberal. The uniformity brought with it a lack of toleration for nonconcurring opinions, and the breach between the two ideologically pure camps left few, if any, bridges for working together.

As someone who dissented from true-blue Republican party positions on issues like the size of the defense budget, and from party dogma, such as the need, cost, and efficacy of a national missile defense, I found myself increasingly out of place among fellow Republican staffers. In addition, as someone who also failed to agree that a worthwhile end in itself was to re-elect Democrats, I remained highly suspect among many Democratic staffers as well.

The Senate, where I worked, was becoming an increasingly unfriendly place unless the information and advice provided was directly convertible to partisan advantage for one's party and re-election for one's member. Not only was objective, professional analysis from a place like GAO—when the agency permitted it—being ignored, but more and more it was becoming risky for staff inside Congress to tell members things they did not want to hear. Of course, there were congressional regulations that prohibited staff from engaging in political activities and protected the integrity and objectivity of their work, but by now the reader surely knows how assiduously today's members want those rules followed.

Next stop, daily staff life on Capitol Hill.

11

Hill Life and Death

[T]hey can make no law which will not have its full operation on themselves and their friends, as well as on the great mass of the society. This has always been deemed one of the strongest bonds by which human policy can connect the rulers and the people together. It creates between them that communion of interest, and sympathy of sentiments, of which few governments have furnished examples; but without which every government degenerates into tyranny. . . . If this spirit shall ever be so far debased, as to tolerate a law not obligatory on the legislature, as well as on the people, the people will be prepared to tolerate any thing but liberty.[1]

The above is an excerpt from James Madison in Federalist Paper Number 57 assuring the public that Congress would never treat itself as a special or privileged caste. Congress has discarded that concept, utterly and totally. For decades, Congress has exempted itself from laws it enacted and deemed acceptable for the general population and even the rest of government. These exemptions result from and exacerbate an already high level of arrogance and pomposity. Sadly, there is almost nothing the self-designated aristocracy on Capitol Hill cannot affect in our daily lives. Just how special members of Congress think themselves is most vividly shown by how they run Capitol Hill itself.

Appearances and Reality in Hill Staffing

We can trace Congress's official self-designation as a special caste to the Civil Service Act of 1883. Instead of observing the various safeguards it imposed on the executive branch to impede arbitrariness, favoritism, nepotism, and patronage in hiring and firing, Congress simply exempted itself from this and subsequent Civil Service Acts. Unlike the executive branch where review boards, paperwork, safeguards, and complex and time-consuming bureaucratic procedures predominate in hiring and firing staff, on Capitol Hill you can be hired or fired on the spot, with or without cause.

If a member of Congress likes the cut of your jib even at a social gathering, he or she can tell you to go to the Senate or House Disbursing Office at the start of the next pay period to be sworn in to join their personal staff.

If there is no room on the payroll, the member can fire on the spot any of his or her employees to make room for you. If the member feels generous, the fired employee will get a couple of weeks' notice, but nothing requires that. When I started work for Senator Javits, I was told, as a piece of friendly advice, that the job opening I filled existed because my predecessor lost her job by making errors in travel plans for Senator Javits's wife. The advice alerted me to several things: ostensibly hired as a research assistant for Javits's work on the Foreign Relations Committee, I clearly would be asked to do things that under Civil Service rules would surely be questionable, such as making travel arrangements for his wife. Moreover, if I screwed them up, I would be toast. Senator Javits could hire and fire for any reason he, and he alone, deemed sufficient.

When they started work in Senator Domenici's personal offices, a chief of staff and a legislative director immediately fired staffers who had been with the senator for years. The actions came with little or no explanation, let alone warning, and were nonnegotiable; the targets had no right of appeal, except to the senator himself, and he did not make himself available.

Congressional hiring and firing rules have both good and bad effects. Sloth is rare on Capitol Hill. If something is not getting done, it is because the boss wants it that way, not because the staff is lazy. When I went to GAO, which operated under executive branch, Civil Service rules, I was horrified at the slow pace of work. Most secretaries spent their afternoons watching soap operas; every one, not just the secretaries, took a full hour for lunch; at the end of the day many watched clocks closely, and by 5:00 PM the building was near empty. There were some professionals at GAO committed to getting the work done and well, but they were struggling upstream against a river of oatmeal.

On the other hand, the absence of bureaucratic protections on Capitol Hill has its clear downside. The arbitrary hiring and firing rules create a staff that is constantly trying to please the boss. If he or she wants sharp intellect, critical advice, and lots of professional experience, the member gets it. If the member wants the opposite—poorly trained, ideologically biased, apple polishers—they can, and do, get that. Indeed, members who value and protect staff who disagree with them or who open new intellectual vistas are rare commodities on Capitol Hill. It is a system where members get what they want, not necessarily what they need, and it is a system where unwanted data or advice, and their originators, can be dealt with efficiently and effectively whenever a member wishes.

To achieve the bliss of a hardworking staff devoted to what the member wants, the self-exemption from Civil Service rules was just the beginning. Congress also exempted itself from the Freedom of Information Act to deny the press and the public access to its own private records;[2] from the National Labor Relations Act of 1947 to prevent job actions by staff,[3] and from the Occupational Safety and Health Act of 1970 to prevent workplace safety complaints.[4] As we already know, Congress also gave GAO authority to audit any agency of the federal government, except Congress.

In other cases, Congress permitted only limited applicability of laws to itself. Portions of the 1964 Civil Rights Act, the Equal Employment Opportunity Act of 1972, and the Occupational Safety and Health Act of 1970, among others, were applied to Congress but without the enforcement mechanisms each act contained for the executive branch and the private sector.[5]

All that appeared to change in 1995. When the Republicans mandated staffing economies (which protected personal staff at the expense of others), they also legislated substantive reforms. With support from many Democrats, Congress enacted the Congressional Accountability Act, which made eleven previously exempted workplace laws apply to Congress. The act also established a new congressional office with a five-member board to enforce the new application of workplace rules.[6] The act established counseling, mediation, formal complaint with discovery and subpoenas, and, finally, judicial review for congressional employees with complaints against their employers.

It all looked impressive, but there were just a few problems. In 2002, after six years of operation, the Office of Compliance established to enforce the Congressional Accountability Act was asked by more than thirty thousand Capitol Hill employees to mediate in just 102 instances, a rate of 0.003 percent. Of those, 36 cases were settled in mediation; the complaining employee dropped 25 of their complaints; 13 moved to the formal complaint stage, and 5 resulted in a civil suit. The rest were still pending at the end of the year.[7] None of the actions that reached the final, public stages involved a member of Congress; they were actions against various administrative offices, such as the architect of the Capitol, the Capitol Police, and the Senate sergeant at arms.[8]

Logic would lead one to believe that when a staffer lodged a complaint against a member, he or she somehow accommodated the complainant, thereby removing the potential for public embarrassment. That does not appear to be the case. The Office of Compliance reported that frequently after employees informed their employers that they had contacted the Office of Compliance—a step the reformed process requires for complaints to move beyond counseling—the employing office started to harass the employee.[9] Under the Whistleblower Protection Act, such harassment is a punishable act in executive branch agencies, but not in Congress.[10] Congress conveniently retained its self-exemption from the Whistleblower Protection Act, and reserved for itself the right to harass its own whistleblowers. In other words, under the new—reformed—regime, an employee has a right to protest actions by a Capitol Hill employer, but in doing so the employee makes him/herself vulnerable to harassment for which there is no remedy. The Office of Compliance understood exactly what was going on and complained to Congress in its annual report: "Without effective enforcement against intimidation and reprisal [under the Whistleblower Protection Act], the promise of the [Congressional Accountability Act] that 'Congressional employees will have the civil rights and social legislation that ensure fair treatment of workers in the private sector' is rendered illusory."[11] The Office of Compliance requested an amendment to the original law removing the whistleblower exemption but was ignored for its pains. Congress held not even a hearing on the matter.[12] To do so would, of course, make the charade noticeable and might alert the somnambulating press.

In addition, Congress today simply ignores the statutory requirement that whenever it legislates a new workplace protection for the private sector or the executive branch, it must explain whether Congress is exempted and why.[13] Of course, the staff of the Office of Compliance could complain about this to the press, but that would constitute whistleblowing, and they clearly know how much protection they have in that situation.

An example of post-reform attitudes occurred in the fall of 2002. Then, Democrats in the Senate were arguing with the Bush administration over the employee rights and protections for workers in the new Department of Homeland Security. President Bush was arguing for essentially the freedom of action that senators afforded themselves: the right to hire and fire promptly, the flexibility to pay employees by merit determined by supervisors, not longevity, and the freedom to transfer employees rapidly according to changing needs. Bush threatened to veto the legislation if he did not receive this direct control over the Homeland Security Agency's employees. The Democrats argued strenuously for the same civil service rules for the new agency as prevailed in other cabinet agencies. Senate Democratic Leader Tom Daschle argued: "This is basically a question of accountability and making sure we never go back to the politics of a federal workforce we saw in the bad old days. . . . I don't want to see someone fired because they're a Republican or a Democrat."[14]

Those "bad old days" are alive and well on Capitol Hill. When Senator Daschle pleaded for standard employment rights for the workers in the new Department of Homeland Security, his own staff's statutory rights were, as described by Congress's Office of Compliance, "illusory."

The Result: Staff Life on Capitol Hill Today

The unencumbered control a member of Congress legally retains over his or her employees translates into some unwritten rules of congressional staffing. Based on my experiences, I offer the following observations about staff life and work on Capitol Hill.

Most staffers work hard. The ease with which members can fire unproductive employees and the loyalty most staff feel, or learn to feel, for the member usually result in highly motivated staffers who will cooperate with demands for long and hard work. Depending on one's responsibilities, the day is frequently longer than the normal 9:00 AM to 6:00 PM day—without overtime pay, of course. A member's chief of staff, their personal secretary, the press secretary, the legislative director, and whichever legislative assistant is responsible for the subject matter causing a late night will typically stay in the office as long as the member stays. Because so many members are workaholics, that can be a long time. A few will stay after the boss goes home.

When the Senate is run by a majority leader who does not mind keeping the Senate at work after dinner (such as Senators Dole and Frist), the work day can often extend well past bedtime or, on rare occasions, most of the night. In fact, my staff director at the Senate Budget Committee kept a sleeping bag behind the couch in his office.

When it is time to go home, no matter how late, there remains one person who is still not finished: the member. Virtually every Hill staff generates paperwork (memos, must-read newspaper articles, draft bills and speeches, important letters, and more) for the member to go through virtually every work night and on the weekends. Some members will not just read, but digest and scrawl notes over every piece of this paperwork. Javits did, virtually without fail. Others will look at almost none of it: in Senator Pryor's office we called his in-box "the black hole." Most will try to get through it all: Senator Kassebaum would eventually (within a few days); Senator Domenici would sooner or later get through some "homework," but not all. In each office where I worked, the hardest working person was almost always the member. That was even true of Senator Pryor, who almost never did his "homework." He simply preferred to communicate in person.

Whatever hours you may be working on a given day, lunch is often at your desk. The cafeteria is usually pretty full, but take a closer look; many of the people there will be younger interns, junior staff, or visitors. Many of the over-30 types will take their sandwiches back upstairs.

During slack periods, such as the weeklong recesses Congress takes for federal holidays, the month of August, and the period after Congress finishes its annual business (usually late October) until January, most offices will go on short hours, which means 9:00 to 5:00, or sometimes 10:00 to 4:00. Lunch will usually be for as long as it takes, and the restaurants close to the Senate and House office buildings will often be quite busy on good weather days. During these recesses, the members remain busy in the state or district, and it is the turn of the staff there to work longer hours.

Most Hill staff are smart, but not necessarily competent. Most members of Congress are pretty smart; the less-smart ones don't survive. They try to select as smart a staff force as they can, but there is a corollary: smart does not mean well informed or of sound judgment. Congressional staff are sometimes astoundingly misinformed about the substantive areas assigned to them. Some only start out poorly informed and they learn; some do not.

A memorable example was a staffer who worked for Sen. John Stennis (D-Miss.) on both the Armed Services and Appropriations Committees for several decades. He was a defense specialist and was widely respected on Capitol Hill. He was elevated to become Stennis's chief of staff on the Defense Appropriations Subcommittee. Over the years, he surely learned a lot of details about defense and the Pentagon, and he was clearly an intelligent individual.

In the early 1980s, there was a controversy over whether the Navy's new Aegis cruiser and its sophisticated air defense system had been realistically tested. To refute criticism, the Navy held a series of tests at which the Aegis system performed spectacularly, shooting down ten of eleven target presentations. Clearly, the critics, including myself, were wrong.

Shortly thereafter, a colleague got word that the tests were rigged: the captain and crew had been told in advance what direction, speed, and altitude the target drones would be operating—a tremendous advantage for the radar-based Aegis system and some of its specific operating characteristics. In reaction, Stennis's staffer said directly to me that he had looked into the allegations, and there was nothing to them: the Aegis system was every bit as good as the Navy was saying.

A few years later, after the matter was over, but not forgotten, I was at the Navy's operational testing headquarters in Norfolk, Virginia, working on a GAO study of the very same Aegis system. Interviewing a Navy test official, I brought up the issue of those same tests. I commented that they were interesting because their results were so much better than any other Aegis tests before or since. I had heard that there was an audiotape of the cruiser's command center during the tests and asked to listen to it. Reluctantly, the official agreed. The next day he brought the tape, and we listened to it. Much of it was jargon, difficult to hear, or both. The part of the tests when the Aegis radar missed locating a target came up. I heard someone say something with a different tone than most of the tape but could not quite make it out. I asked the officer running the tape machine to back it up and replay it at a louder volume; I clearly could hear the voice say, "There's one more 'high diver' out there." I had known that the one target missed was, indeed, a high-altitude diving target and was immediately alerted to something being very wrong. I asked the official in the room whose voice that was. He responded unhappily, "The captain's."

The jig was up. No one on the ship's crew was supposed to know what the target presentations were to be. Someone had tipped off the captain, and on the tape he was coaching his crew about a target they had not seen but he knew was out there; he even knew when and roughly where to look. It was clear evidence that the tests were not on the up and up and, also, that the assurance Stennis's staffer had given me was wrong.

I was not prepared to think Stennis's staffer had willingly misled me, but it was abundantly clear that he had done nothing effective to establish the accuracy of the test-rigging accusations we had heard about. Given the way I had seen the staff of the Armed Services Committee and Defense Appropriations Subcommittee work for years and years, I suspected that all he had done to check was to call his contacts in the Navy and ask them if the accusation was true. They, presumably, said it was not, and that was that.

With investigatory techniques like that it's a wonder the staff of the Senate's primary defense oversight committees ever find out anything the Pentagon doesn't want them to know. Rather, it is a perfectly good explanation for why they never do.

Some staff are overpaid; some are not. The pay for individual staffers is what members want it to be. There is a typical hierarchy of Hill staff jobs; they start at receptionist and go through legislative assistant up to chief of staff, also known as administrative assistant ("AA") on personal staffs. Members pay whatever they care to for each individual at each level. House members typically pay less and hire younger, less experienced staff than do most senators. Senators mostly try to acquire experienced people with advanced degrees or some experience at higher individual cost. When House or Senate members run out of funds from their personal office payroll, they might hire others on a committee payroll and require these committee staffers to spend some or most of their time doing personal staff work, such as working on pork projects, writing speeches, editing press releases, or handling constituent mail.

Some members offer frequent, liberal pay raises above inflation. Others act as if it is a huge favor just to keep your salary level with inflation. Performing at what I thought was the same level in different senators' offices, I encountered both the generous and the penurious types.

Hill staff pay is a matter of public record. Each Senate staffer's pay appears in a semiannual report, the *Report of the Secretary of the Senate,* in two thick volumes. The exposition is not reader-friendly, but it can be interesting. Secretaries make more in some offices than legislative assistants do in others. Subject area analysts on committee staff can make more than chiefs of staff on personal staffs. It is all up to the member who is in charge, and in my experience it pretty much boils down to, what does the member think of you and what you do for him or her? There is just one pay threshold that is never broken: no staffer may make more than any member.

Unique staff selection criteria. When walking through the House and Senate office buildings, one quickly notices a difference between Capitol Hill staff and workers in executive branch agencies. Hill staff, both male and female, are generally younger, more physically fit, and more physically attractive than most agency workers. Being selected mostly through in-person interviews, after the resumes are culled, rather than through a mostly paperwork process, members and chiefs of staff have the opportunity to let personal preferences, such as physical appearance, creep into their selection process. Sometimes it does not just creep. Senator Lott's staff, whom I frequently saw in the Senate chamber when he was Republican Leader, were typically like him: tall, slim, hair well coiffed, and decent looking, both male and female.

Perks and "Primary Directives." One of the perks for defense and foreign policy staff is travel. DoD organizes frequent trips for staff groups to military bases, manufacturing facilities, and battlefields in the United States and abroad. DoD pays for all travel, accommodations, and meals. U.S. and foreign think tanks and foreign governments, the latter usually through some sort of front to conform to the porous congressional ethics rules on travel, also invite most defense and foreign policy staffers on foreign trips. I was able to travel to Israel, Japan, South Korea, Taiwan, Germany, Belgium, Russia, Latvia, Lithuania, and Hungary at the invitation, and cost, of such organizations. I also traveled to approximately twenty different defense facilities inside the United States.

A few staff consider these trips a lark and a major shopping opportunity. Others take them seriously, try to ask meaningful questions at meetings, and take serious notes. The chief of staff at the Budget Committee permitted his staff to go on such trips only if we wrote a detailed report on the trip. The next trip would not be approved until the report for the last trip was on his desk.

It was this trip report requirement that started my own writing career. Before going to defense facilities, I tried to learn from contacts in DoD and through reading what the relevant issues were for that facility. Trying to take good notes and collect materials on the trip, I would write a detailed and, I thought, meaningful report upon return. The first time I did this, my report addressed significant military readiness problems I found at the Army's National Training Center at Fort Irwin, California. Bill Hoagland agreed with me that my report uncovered some significant and troubling issues. At my suggestion, he agreed that after he and I edited the report, I should e-mail a copy to a friend in DoD, Chuck Spinney.

With my permission, Chuck e-mailed the report to various contacts of his own, including reporters. A reporter I had known for several years, Rowan Scarboro, at the *Washington Times* picked it up and wrote a front page story. As DoD busied itself denying the information my report revealed, Senator Domenici blew up. Bill Hoagland and I made the mistake of leaving our names on the report, and both I and the Budget Committee, which Domenici chaired, were cited as the source in the news story. Although the report was a major embarrassment to the Clinton Pentagon, which made Hoagland and me think Domenici would be pleased, he was, in fact, livid. Luckily for me, Domenici called Hoagland first to express his anger at me. Hoagland calmed him down, and the next day when I saw Domenici, I told him "it would not happen again." Domenici grumbled, but we moved on.

Hoagland's and my speculation about what angered Domenici and what happened next says much about how members think and staff work on Capitol Hill. We thought two things probably irritated Domenici: first, the front page *Washington Times* article never mentioned Domenici's name, thereby breaking a primary—but unwritten—directive of Hill staff work: except for an elite few, staffers' names are never to appear in the newspapers—all credit and public amplification shall go to the member, and only the member. Another "primary directive," certainly in Domenici's empire, was to do nothing to impede pork for New Mexico. Embarrassing DoD by revealing serious problems just might cause some senior officer or bureaucrat to take revenge on Domenici by reducing DoD spending in New Mexico. Or, Hoagland thought further, even if that was not likely, Domenici might think it likely.

Hoagland warned me not to let this happen again. It did not, but at the same time, it did. I continued to take trips to DoD facilities, to write trip reports on serious problems, and they were all reported in newspapers and defense journals. However, learning from my mistakes, I made sure the stories never mentioned my name or the Budget Committee. After each trip, I would write the report and send it to Hoagland, as his staff rules required. In the cover memo, I would make it clear I intended to send the report to others via e-mail. I normally did this through Chuck Spinney, who would resend it to hundreds of others. Hoagland would always tell me to "be careful," and he and I always agreed it was my neck if something went wrong and my name or the Budget Committee were mentioned.

The press cooperated. At first, the reports were simply attributed to an anonymous "congressional staffer." Later, I began to use the pseudonym "Spartacus." Things continued smoothly in this vein for about four years. Later, it did blow up, and I resigned under pressure,* but it does demonstrate that there can be several different levels to staff work on Capitol Hill. While there are risks to circumventing Hill staff "primary directives," it is possible to tell the public, and through it the member, things the member does not want to hear.

Opportunities for national policymaking and fetching coffee. The work for the professional staff in members' offices and on committee staffs varies from the sublime to the ridiculous. On my very first day as a research assistant for Senator Javits, my immediate boss, Pete Lakeland, showed me two fat loose-leaf notebooks. Thudding them on my desk, he said, "You better learn about this." They were files on the early drafts of the War Powers Act, one of the most important pieces of national security legislation that Congress would consider over the three decades I worked there. My role on that bill at the start of my career was that of only a research assistant, but I did have the opportunity to perform research on war powers issues, write memos and speeches about them, observe and sometimes participate in meetings and discussions with senators and historians, and help push through the legislative process a bill that would impact national security policy for decades to come. It was a heady experience for a twenty-something year old.

At the end of my Hill career in the late 1990s, on Wednesdays during the late winter and spring, the Defense Subcommittee of the Senate Appropriations Committee would have hearings on the defense budget. Beyond writing background memos on relevant defense issues for Senator Domenici, I quickly learned that part of my job for that weekly hearing was to get him coffee. Advised that I would need to do so by a colleague ("and make sure it's decaffeinated"), I was at first put off by such a gofer task. However, I learned to squelch my ego and be a little smarter about it. Rather than wait for Domenici to ask me at the hearing to go get it (at my own expense, of course),

---

* See the preface.

I would routinely bring it before the hearing started. He would invariably come late, being busy elsewhere. When I gave it to him when he came in, he seemed to genuinely appreciate its being there without his asking me. He even, on rare occasions, offered to pay for it. Knowing I was on a roll, I, of course, oh-so generously declined.

Aside from the aggravation and ego swallowing Domenici's coffee was for a fifty-something staffer near the end of his career, I believe it improved our relationship. It seemed to be part of his accepting me as someone loyal to him, and it proved to be something he did not forget.

At the end of my time with Domenici, when I was in trouble with him because of the essay "Spartacus" had written after September 11, I asked to meet with Domenici to explain what I had done and why. As he brought me into his office for what I expected to be an extremely unpleasant—indeed terminal—meeting, he said to me something like, "After all that coffee you got for me, maybe it's time for me to get you some." I declined, but much of the stress I felt about the meeting drained away. Small previous favors had made a lasting impression, and I understood that no matter how angry Domenici may have been with me, he was willing to recall something he felt was positive in our relationship and indicative of my past loyalty to him. What could have been a very rough "trip to the woodpile," if not a shouting match, turned out to be, instead, a reasoned explanation and discussion. The coffee did not prevent him from deciding to get rid of me, but it made our last meeting a lot more tolerable; it was a worthwhile investment.

Personal services and the consequences. Between fetching coffee and working to enact legislation that helps a nation decide to make war or peace, there is a lot of other congressional staff activity in between. At the low end of the scale, there are many personal service activities that staff perform for members. Each member has a personal secretary, who helps run not just the member's professional life, but his or her personal life as well. Making doctor's appointments, getting the dry cleaning, driving the member from home to work, and walking the dog are typical things the personal secretary will do, or ask another staff member, often an intern, to do for them. That may be typical for a president or CEO of a private company, but in Congress, it has consequences beyond personal servants paid at taxpayer expense.

Members become accustomed to the special personal treatment they get from their own staff. They also become divorced from the common pitfalls of American life the rest of us experience. I vividly remember watching Sen. Robert Dole (R-Kans.) opposing President Clinton's health care plan in 1993. Clinton's plan probably was as complex and unworkable as Dole was alleging, but Dole kept on referring to the existing system as "the best health-care system in the world." In one speech on the floor of the Senate, he literally used that phrase as a mantra and repeated it over and over again.

My wife had recently been through the long-term nightmare of a few hundred thousand dollars of doctor, lab, and hospital bills and a battle with the HMO bureaucracy in that health-care system for our newborn son. Any normal American knows the problems: the labyrinthian prerecorded telephone directions, the endless waits on hold, the only sometimes helpful attitude of the HMO workers, the crazy rules, the return of bills that everyone thought had been paid, and more.

Here was Bob Dole calling this fiendish torture "the best health-care system in the world." Of course, he had never been in its multiple torture chambers. He surely had lots of health issues from his serious and surely painful World War II injuries, but later in his life, as a senator, he also had a staff to wade through the health-care bureaucracy for him. He seemed simply out of touch and to have no clue how stupid and uninformed he sounded to a normal victim of "the best health-care system in the world." If he were the smart politician many give him credit for, he would have offered a reasonable alternative to Clinton's high-cost, complex ideas. However, he was interested only in the short-term tactical gain of bashing Clinton's proposal, and we all remain a victim today of the tender mercies of the system Senator Dole praised so highly.

Saying no to the Boss. Beyond the issues of education, experience, physical characteristics, and other hiring and firing criteria, members have varying degrees of willingness to hire staff who will disagree with them, give them information that contradicts long-held beliefs, and warn them when they are cutting ethical corners.

I received what was, to me, excellent training from Senator Javits. He expected his staff to disagree with him when we believed he was in error. He did not particularly welcome it, but he took it at the factual, intellectual planes at which we offered it. I often described my working for him as spending "half our time talking him out of ideas."

With Javits, however, there was one major caution: woe to any staffer who did not have the facts and logic to back up his or her argument. Javits was smart and abrasive. He had no patience for half-baked arguments and uncertain facts. To take him on, one had to brace oneself for a serious argument, but an argument based on the merits of the matter, not who was the boss and who was not. Javits held in most contempt any yes-persons who had the misfortune to make it on to his staff. They and any who could not back up their arguments quickly found themselves in what we called "the deep freeze," and if you did not get yourself out of the deep freeze quickly, the only door that would ultimately open for you was the exit.

Senator Kassebaum welcomed legitimate discussion of issues and would listen to new or contradictory information and advice, but only up to a point. She would always remain polite, but she seemed to have a personal quota for new information and argumentation. Senators Pryor and Domenici were more reticent. I could never figure out exactly how Senator Pryor was reacting to many of the things I told him, which probably explains why I worked for him for only two years. Sometimes Senator Domenici would simply not react to written or spoken information I gave him that contradicted some of his long-held notions about defense. This was probably his way of signaling me to shut up, but I did not always take the hint.

In one or two cases, after the evidence in memos and articles I sent him began to pile up, Domenici started at least to ask some questions of DoD witnesses at hearings. One such subject was the low military readiness of many DoD units, despite the assurances of the JCS to the contrary. Another was the proposition that politically popular across-the-board pay raises for all military personnel were an ineffective and too expensive way to try to address military recruitment and retention problems. Ultimately, Domenici seemed to accept and fully understand the information I was giving him, but when it came time to cast a vote consistent with that information, in most—but not all—cases he cast the vote that was politically easy but also wrong or counterproductive according to the information he had seemed to accept as reliable.

Staffers of some other senators would look at me as if I had several screws loose when I suggested that they give their boss unwanted news or disagree with them. The Republican staff on the Senate Armed Services Committee seemed to consider it particularly unthinkable to disagree with their chairman, Senator Warner. While Warner had a reputation for gentlemanly behavior, other members were reputed to throw typewriters at their staff (John Culver [D-Iowa]) or screaming fits (Bella Abzug [D-N.Y.]) when their staff did not please them. Beyond being just obnoxious and arrogant, these members were, in effect, training their staff. They were making it clear they wanted to keep things simple, if not simple-minded: give me what I say I want, and everybody will be happy. Culver lasted just one Senate term. Abzug became a national figure in the women's movement and various politically liberal causes. Unfortunately, pigheadedness does not always result in ignominy.

Swiss cheese ethics rules. The Senate and House ethics rules prohibit personal or committee staffers on the federal payroll from performing re-election campaign activities, including distributing campaign materials, calling constituents to get out the vote, researching the politics of the opponent, and writing campaign speeches. The prohibition is routinely circumvented. The rules do not prohibit staffers doing campaign activities on their own time, including vacation time. It is just amazing how many federally paid Hill staffers go on vacation in the weeks before a primary or an election.

In some offices, staffers are not pressured to exploit this loophole; in some they are. While I worked for Senator Domenici, several staffers traveled on vacation time and at their own expense from Washington to New Mexico to work for Senator Domenici's re-election. I never felt pressured to do so, and never felt I suffered in any way from my decision not to.

In other cases, staffers are pointedly asked to provide services on their own time, and the inference is clear that failure to volunteer will not be appreciated. In September 1980, Senator Javits was defeated in the Republican primary by a town supervisor from Long Island, Alfonse D'Amato. The senator decided he would run for re-election on a separate party ticket, but to do so, he had to file thousands of signatures from registered New York voters. Javits did not have the campaign personnel needed to verify the signatures his campaign staff collected in the short time available, so his senior staff requested volunteers from the personal and committee staff who worked for him to travel to New York City and perform the work. Nobody had to go, but nobody wanted to say no to the senator in a time his senior staff described as desperate political need. A skeleton staff was left in the Washington office as the vast majority of Javits's Senate employees showed up in Manhattan for the task at hand. We spent a day and a night verifying petition signatures against lists of registered voters, but we were unable to verify enough signatures in time to meet the New York State deadline. It turned out to be a wasted effort, and Javits ran on the existing Liberal Party ticket in a campaign that failed badly in the November 1980 elections. It was an example of the kind of loyalty a senator can call on from his staff to jump through loopholes in the Senate's forgiving ethics rules and help him out in an election.

Who does the thinking on Capitol Hill? An unavoidable consequence of the thousands of staffers on committee and personal staffs working for just a few hundred members is the huge number of issues brought to the members' attention. All staff want to get the boss's attention, and a good way to do so is to come up with some brilliant idea for a legislative initiative. As a result, a member will introduce hundreds of bills and amendments in a single term.

Staffers will usually, but not always, have a decent knowledge of the content and rationale for the legislation, but it is just about impossible for a member to have intellectual command of it all.

The intensity of the workload appears in each member's personal schedule. It will usually be broken into fifteen-minute pieces through the workday, and the shift in subject matter from one meeting to the next can take the member from nuclear weapons, to food stamps, to trade law, to a sit down with the local Cub Scouts. Moreover, the level of detail addressed will likely take the member into obscure corners of the subject: not just nuclear weapons will be addressed, but how the Missile Defense Agency fudged the latest test with unrealistic decoys; not just food stamps but how the Department of Agriculture changed the rules to the disadvantage of part of the member's district.

The specialized staff can keep track of this stuff, but only a superhuman member can. The smartest one I worked for, Javits, would usually not need to be reminded of the basics and many of the details of an issue. When another senator made an argument he had not heard, Javits would turn to me with a look in his eye of, "You didn't tell me about this, and you better have an answer." When I was lucky, I did; when I did not, he had the brains to conjure a reasonable one up.

Lesser mortals are easily overwhelmed. When she was arguing for her amendment to require women to register for the military draft, Senator Kassebaum gave me a look of sheer terror when Javits sent me over to her in the Senate chamber to ask her how her amendment dealt with orthodox Jewish women. When he testified to the Foreign Relations Committee on the military threat to the United States posed by Cuba, Sen. Steven Sims (R-Idaho) had to turn around so often to ask his staff for the answer to any but the most simpleminded question that he had the entire staff of the committee snickering. Senator Domenici would sometimes, but not always, ask to be reminded just what his bill accomplished or what points he should make at a press conference as he walked to the Senate chamber to debate his own legislation or to a room to tell a crowd of journalists about it.

Members who fail to know or remember everything are neither stupid nor lazy; they are overwhelmed. Staff eager to make an impression or to have an impact drag the members into issues and a level of detail that is impossible for them to command. When there are ten, twenty, or forty staffers doing this, the member cannot possibly be well informed about all of it. Usually, he or she will learn a mantra to recite when speaking to an initiative; it will sound good to the general population, but should anyone knowledgeable start asking questions, the black pit of ignorance and misinformation can often be found lurking just below the thin veneer.

In other cases, when members trust them, staff are permitted to run off on their own, doing things in the member's name that the member has not approved and may never even know about. The staffer who deserves this trust will validate what he or she has done with the member and pull back, if necessary. However, not all staff deserve the trust they are given. Senator Lott's staffer running amok with the Navy by crudely demanding more shipbuilding for the Pascagoula shipyard might be a case in point; it is hard to imagine a senator consenting to the methods used.

One characteristic of such a system is a proclivity for minor issues. The minutiae the Senate endorses are mind numbing. Aside from the hundreds of small, obscure pork projects, the Senate added the following items to the 2002 defense authorization bill: permission for female military personnel not to wear scarves in Saudi Arabia, "to authorize the Secretary of Defense to accept foreign gifts and donations for the Western Hemisphere Institute for Security Cooperation, and to require the Secretary's annual report on the Institute to include the annual report of the Board of Visitors for the Institute,"[15] and to prohibit "the use of any funds to relocate the headquarters of the United States Army, South, from Fort Buchanan, Puerto Rico, to a location in the continental United States."[16]

A result is bills that have grown from just a few pages—or at most a few dozen—to hundreds of pages. They contain thousands of decisions on minor issues and scores on major ones. The members virtually never take the time to read, let alone comprehend, what is before them. Neither do most staff. When these bills are presented to the Senate for final approval, the text of the bill and the conference committee report to explain it are often unavailable or available only in the form of one copy for all one hundred senators and a few thousand staff to read. Most staff will ask for and receive an oral summary from the authoring committee staff of a few key issues that the member is particularly interested in and, of course, the fate of the member's various pork requests. The best-informed members will have received an oral summary, or perhaps a hasty memo, of whatever their own staff chooses to tell them, perhaps only half a dozen items about a bill addressing thousands of issues. That content is filtered twice by staff: from the committee staff to the member's staff, and from the member's staff to the member. When the member votes, he or she may have knowledge of only small parts of a defense bill and little of what the member has been told may be the complete story on even those limited issues.

In the 1990s some members began to realize that staff were doing too much. Rep. John Kasich (R-Ohio) told a congressional reform commission: "It is real easy to [rely] on staff, so we get ourselves in a position where we don't do hands-on things ourselves and you've got staff negotiating all this."[17]

That commission and the rest of Congress ultimately decided to do nothing about it.

With staff there to write the bills, the amendments, the speeches explaining them, and the press releases after the legislation passes, the member is confronted with a tremendous temptation to become mentally lazy and let the staff do his or her thinking. All the member really has to do is make sure whatever he or she is led to do is advantageous for re-election—a much simpler and more practicable test than comprehension of the specifics. The member can rely on their more trusted senior staff to weed out the good ideas from the bad, or rather the good ideas that sound good from the bad ideas that sound good. Indeed, all the member really has to do is be able to read the stuff out loud in a convincing manner and remember enough lines to get through an interview with a journalist who is not an expert on the subject either.

By its size and the proliferation of its work product, the staff has become an only partially supervised arm of the federal government that controls much of what Congress does. Ironically, this occurs in a system where the members have a unique level of control over the staff. Except for ensuring that staff work is conducive to re-election, much of the staff's work is not just unsupervised by the members, it is unread.

Toward the end of his Senate career, Sen. Alan Simpson (R-Wyo.) said of congressional staff, including his own, "You cannot live with them and you cannot live without them." [18] With a grand total of approximately thirty thousand at the turn of the twenty-first century—a bureaucracy larger than the departments of Energy, Labor, Housing, or State[19]— it is questionable whether the congressional bureaucracy, especially the element members value most—the personal and committee staff—should be preserved.

Defenders of the existing system, such as think tank prognosticators on Congress, explain elegantly that the explosion of staffers in modern times was "needed to deal with the complexity of the modern world." [20] While the world has certainly grown more complex, there is much more to the explosion of the congressional staff than that. If modern complexity were the issue, one would expect Congress to be expanding its expert staffs on committees and the congressional research agencies. Instead, the staff has grown most in members' personal offices where they are immediately available to accomplish whatever bidding the member wishes. The bigger and more active the personal staff, the more pork, more legislative accomplishments, more speeches, more help to constituents with problems, more mailings to the voters, more press releases—all focused on enhancing the member's profile in Washington, D.C., and back home. The ethics rules say personal staff are not to work for a member's re-election campaign, but they rarely work, in a fundamental sense, on anything else. In addition, committee staffs are now frequently dragged into the same preoccupation.

The members dare not reduce the gigantic staff cohort for fear that they bring home less bacon, pass fewer bills, and give fewer high-sounding speeches. To fall back means to lose one's reputation for effectiveness, and the next step might be involuntary retirement. In short, the congressional staff has become a perpetual legislative and political motion machine focused on members' perpetuity.

The machine is blind and dumb: the staff produces ever more product, and most members, being human, learn only little of the details, the implications, and the effects. However, they feel compelled to constantly demand more, and in a system designed to keep the members happy, they get what they asked for.

This support system has three layers of problems. At the first level, what Madison assured the public in Federalist Paper Number 57 would not happen—a system where the legislature elevates itself above the public—has in fact happened. Congress has put itself in a self-designated caste separate from the public and even the rest of government. It passes laws for the general public's employment, health, and safety that it deems insufficient or bothersome for itself.

At the second level, the nation's national security goes unattended. As Congress shrinks its more expert committee and support agency staff to protect and expand the more politicized personal staff and then proceeds to demand that all forms of staff direct themselves at each member's short-term aggrandizement, there is not only less opportunity for the constitutionally vital responsibility of oversight, there is also less interest.

At the third level, Congress has granted itself a staffing system over which it exercises the most arbitrary authority anywhere in American government, indeed society, but Congress then proceeds to permit the staffing system to operate without controls over the legislation Congress enacts for national security. Indeed, it may be inappropriate to say that there is not control because that might imply Congress's self-knowledge of the condition and that level of responsibility do not exist.

Such a system has consequences. It can, and has, committed the nation to a course of action the consequences of which Congress does not appreciate, indeed does not even probe, when the commitment is made. Such a situation currently exists, at the time of this writing, in the second American war against and occupation of Iraq. It is not a question of being for or against this war, it is a question of attempting to probe the reasons for the conflict and the potential consequences at the start: activities that the majority of Congress carefully decided to avoid in October 2002 when it authorized war against Iraq and decided instead to behave in a manner consistent only with short-term political self-preservation.

Significantly, Congress did so despite a preexisting legislative framework specifically designed to enable it to probe important questions before charging headlong into war. That framework was put together in a time when at least a few members of Congress thought and behaved differently and attempted to restore a balance in the federal government's national security apparatus that had been eliminated.

The story of how Congress permitted itself to be herded into a war it did not try to understand begins with the efforts made in earlier times to ensure that that too would not happen.

IV

THE RIGHT AND WRONG WAY TO GO TO WAR

12

Politicians at Their Best

The question of going to war against another nation is the most important national security decision a government can make. The consequences are more important than adding pork, and when members permit themselves to be poorly informed and selfishly motivated, the decision-making process can show Congress at its worst. Conversely, when the members inform themselves and decide to take political risks, it can show them at their best.

It was the first and last political demonstration I ever attended. On 30 April 1970, President Richard Nixon had announced on television a U.S. "incursion" into Cambodia to attempt to find and destroy "COSVN" (Central Office for South Vietnam), which was believed to be a command and control center essential to the communist insurgency in South Vietnam. The action came shortly after a U.S.–encouraged coup had replaced neutral Cambodian Prince Sihanouk with a military regime compliant to the United States. What many called an invasion, not an "incursion," of a neutral country had stirred up the opposition to the war in the United States to new heights. I attended the demonstration because I thought Nixon's action was stupid: everything I learned about the region from my studies as a graduate student of East Asian history and from a thesis I had written about guerrilla warfare told me that this hunt for a command center in Cambodia was irrelevant, at best, to the core issues of the war. I believed then, as now, the Nixon administration fundamentally misunderstood the nature of the guerrilla conflict and was only embroiling America deeper in a misguided effort to use conventional means against an unconventional, guerrilla enemy. Worse, they were giving only lip service to the social and political reform needed to transform the corrupt and inept South Vietnamese government, its mostly demoralized armed forces, and its disjointed society.

As I walked toward the antiwar speaker's podium on the Mall in the center of Washington, I became more and more aware that, while I thoroughly disagreed with Nixon, I had zero in common with the self-absorbed antiwar radicals that were running the demonstration. After listening to a few shrill speeches, I went back to my apartment and resumed my academic life at the University of Maryland.

Origination of War Powers Act

While I lapsed back into scholastic irrelevance, unknown to me,[*] members of Senator Javits's staff were busy trying to address the issues that prompted much of the controversy over the invasion of Cambodia and the Vietnam War itself. Shortly after the invasion, four of Javits's staffers met in the Monocle restaurant near the Senate office buildings on Capitol Hill. They talked over their problems with U.S. war policy in Cambodia and Vietnam and ended up roughly outlining on a paper napkin a first attempt to address the war in a generic manner. Javits's staffers sought to inject Congress into the decision-making process by invoking its "power of the purse" to cut off funds for wars it disagreed with. In the words of one of the participants in the meeting, "It wasn't such a big deal," but it was a start.[1]

When the staffers took their idea to Javits, he liked it but also wanted to know the views of his foreign policy adviser, who was not at the luncheon. He was Pete Lakeland, a former Foreign Service officer, who had left the State Department in 1967 in disagreement with President Lyndon Johnson's Vietnam War policies. Lakeland had been working on his own proposal. He believed that the funding process, which would involve the parochial-minded Appropriations Committee, was the wrong way to go. Instead, he argued the issue went to the question of who under the Constitution held the authority to take the United States to war: Congress or the president.

Javits agreed that the constitutional issue was key and approved an effort to consult experts and write new legislation. The bill that resulted, S. 3964, was introduced on 15 June 1970. It had just one public supporter, Sen. Robert Dole (R-Kans.), who happened to be in the Senate chamber when Javits introduced the bill. Dole listened to Javits's speech about the legislation, walked over to him in the Senate chamber, and asked to be added as a "cosponsor," thereby publicly indicating his strong, personal endorsement of the bill.[†]

Javits's introduction of this novel legislation started a minor cottage industry in the Senate as several members and staff wrote their own versions

---

[*] I started working for Javits in November 1971, more than a year after these events. The details discussed here are based on the comments made to me by the staff participants in Javits's office after I came to work for him and later in 2002 and 2003, when this book was written.

[†] Dole had a long and twisted relationship with war powers legislation. When Dole subsequently became chairman of the Republican National Committee, he withdrew his cosponsorship of the war powers bill and voted against it. Later, after President Nixon dumped him as RNC chairman, Dole asked to be put back on as a cosponsor of the bill and told Javits it was the right thing to do. Later again, when Republican party ideology and allegiance to Republican Presidents Ford and Reagan argued against the inconvenience the War Powers Act sought to impose on presidents, Dole switched his public views yet again.

of the same sort of bill. Sen. Robert Taft Jr. (R-Ohio) introduced one version on 27 January 1971; Sen. Thomas Eagleton (D-Mo.) followed on 1 March 1971; Sen. Lloyd Bentsen Jr. (D-Tex.) on 15 May 1971; and, most surprising of all, Sen. John Stennis, a dean of southern conservative Democrats, the chairman of the Senate Armed Services Committee, and a supporter of the Indochina War, presented his own version on 11 May 1971.* Each of the bills in one way or another attempted to define when and how presidents could go to war and to interject Congress in the decision-making process.

Just what did these upstart senators think they were trying to do? Who were they to invade the president's constitutional powers as commander in chief? Every American knows from high school civics that the Constitution says Congress declares war, but that is just a formality, and an obsolete one at that. In the late-twentieth century, only presidents could be relied on to act quickly and decisively to protect America and its worldwide interests from the Soviet Union and its puppets. What idiot would want to involve Congress on questions of national survival? It is indecisive, partisan, parochial, and petty. It is certainly not equipped, as the presidency is, to properly study and understand questions of international security and to lead the United States in the life-and-death game of nations at war—or even at peacetime. To think any member of Congress should be a decision maker in these questions is not only antiquarian but also stupid and dangerous.

Javits and his like-minded Senate colleagues didn't think so, but where did they get off thinking they had any legitimate business mucking around in this area? To find out, it is necessary to look into three questions: (1) What does the Constitution actually say about the authority to take the United States into war, declared or not? (2) What did the authors of the Constitution mean with the words they used? and (3) If Congress was given a major role on questions of war or peace in 1787, does that make any sense for the modern age?

What Did They Write in 1787?

A simple regurgitation of the relevant portions of the Constitution is useful and may surprise some. Article 1, Section 8, enumerates the war powers explicitly delegated to Congress; they are to

- "Provide for the common defense" (clause [cl.] 1);
- "Define and punish piracies and felonies committed on the high seas" (cl. 10);

---

* After consulting more experts, Javits revised his own bill and reintroduced it as S. 731 in February 1971.

- "Declare war, grant letters of marque and reprisal,* and make rules concerning captures on land and water" (cl. 11);
- "Raise and support armies" (cl. 12);
- "Provide and maintain a navy" (cl. 13);
- "Make rules for the government and regulation of the land and naval forces" (cl. 14);
- "Provide for calling forth the militia to execute the laws of the Union, suppress insurrections and repel invasions" (cl. 15);
- "Provide for organizing, arming, and disciplining the militia and for governing such part of them as may be employed in the service of the United States" (cl. 16); and
- "Make all laws which shall be necessary and proper for carrying into execution the foregoing powers, and all other powers vested by this Constitution in the government of the United States, or in any Department or officer thereof." (cl. 18)

The wording for the president's war powers is, by comparison, sparse. Article 2 says

- "The executive power shall be vested in a President of the United States of America" (section 1); and
- "The President shall be Commander in Chief of the army and navy of the United States, and of the militia of the several states, when called into the actual service of the United States." (section 2)

We know from the history books that the Constitution sought to overcome the weaknesses of the Articles of Confederation that left the state legislatures in charge of just about everything, an idea that proved a dismal failure for a national government. Ergo, the authority intended by the Constitution's authors with the words "executive power" and "commander in chief" outweigh the authorities given to Congress on the question of war, right?

What Did They Say They Meant?

The men who wrote the Constitution, and whom we should remember as not just revolutionaries but also as politicians, did not see it that way. First, they

---

* While dictionaries shed some light on "letters of marque and reprisal," the following from a *New York Times* op-ed piece is more helpful: "We no longer charter private boat owners to prey on enemy shipping. Yet letters of marque and reprisal are the closest 18th-century analogue to the methods of retaliation that might be used in the low-intensity conflicts that the War Powers Act sought to regulate. The fact that the framers withheld even this minimal power from the president shows their reservations about unrestrained executive war-making." See "Who Declares a War?" by Jack Rakove, *New York Times*, 4 August 2002, Section 4, p. 13.

gave the new national legislature, Congress, many of the powers previously left with the state legislatures. Some of the centralization of power was directed at Congress, not just the presidency.

In their political writings in *The Federalist* and elsewhere to convince the state legislatures and the public to support the new Constitution, the framers explained quite clearly which branch was to have what power relating to the question of war. One key explanation involved the proceedings of 17 August 1787, when the constitutional convention amended the draft document with a "cryptic but momentous debate," changing Congress's power to "make war" to "declare war."[2] The alteration was offered by James Madison of Virginia and seconded by Eldridge Gerry of Massachusetts. Madison's notes (which—in the absence of official recorder Jackson's minutes that he obediently destroyed—historians describe as a basic source for understanding the convention) explained the change saying, "leaving to the Executive the power to repel sudden attacks."[3] Cosponsor Gerry argued against a concurrent proposition from Pierce Butler of South Carolina "for vesting the power in the President." Gerry said he "never expected to hear in a republic a motion to empower the Executive alone to declare war."[4] George Mason of Virginia supported Gerry and Madison, saying he "was against giving the power to the Executive, because [he is] not [safely] to be trusted with it." Rufus King of Massachusetts concurred, arguing that "make" needed modification because it might be misunderstood that Congress, not the Executive, was being empowered to "conduct" the war, which should be left to the president.[5] The Convention did not pursue the Butler suggestion to empower the president with the authority to declare war, and it widely supported and approved Madison's.[6]

Later, Madison wrote to Thomas Jefferson in Paris explaining the document as altered by his amendment: "The constitution supposes, what the history of all Govts demonstrates, that the Ex. is the branch of power most interested in war, & most prone to it. It has accordingly with studied care, vested the question of war in the Legisl."[7] While not an on-the-scene author of the Constitution but certainly an authority, Jefferson himself lauded the transfer of the power to go to war "from the executive to the Legislative body, from those who are to spend to those who are to pay."[8]

Madison also explained in a letter to James Monroe that he sought to recognize the president's power to repel sudden attacks, i.e., to "enter on a war, undeclared by Congress . . . when a state of war has 'been actually' produced by the conduct of another power."[9] The authority to repel sudden attacks without receiving prior authority from Congress also implies the authority to forestall an attack that is being formed. Modern scholars recognize this authority; one of the preeminent authorities when Congress considered war powers legislation was Professor Alexander Bickel of Yale; he said in 1971:

> The 'sudden attack' concept of the framers of the Constitution denotes a power to act in emergencies in order to guard against the threat of attack, as well as against the attack itself, when the threat arises, for example, in such circumstances as those of the Cuban missile crisis of 1962. So long as it is understood that this is a reactive, not a self-starting affirmative power, I have no trouble agreeing that it is vested in the President by the Constitution, that it provides flexibility, and that Congress cannot take it away.[10]

In other words, presidents were not required to dumbly wait for the first blow to fall if they knew one was coming; they can strike first, but only if it is to fend off an oncoming blow. Note, however, that this power does not embrace the power to strike when an actual attack is not imminent, impending, or being formed.

Among the original framers, even the arch proponent of the presidency, Alexander Hamilton, allowed no doubt where the power to go to war lay. In *The Federalist,* Number 69, he wrote, "The president will have only the occasional command of such part of the militia of the nation, as by legislative provision may be called into the actual service of the union."[11] And, more explicitly: "The president is to be commander in chief of the army and navy of the United States. In this respect his authority would be nominally the same with that of the king of Great Britain, but in substance much inferior to it. It would amount to nothing more than the supreme command and direction of the military and naval forces, as first general and admiral of the confederacy; while that of the British king extends to the *declaring* of war, and to the *raising* and *regulating* of fleets and armies; all which, by the constitution under consideration, would appertain to the legislature."[12]

Indeed, the term "commander in chief" had a specific meaning to the framers. When George Washington was appointed "commander in chief" during the Revolution, the Continental Congress gave him a specific delegation. It read: "And, you are to regulate your conduct in every respect by the rules and discipline of war (as herewith given you) and punctually to observe and follow such orders and directions from time to time as you shall receive from this or a future Congress of the said United Colonies or a committee of Congress for that purpose appointed."[13]

The sparse words "commander in chief" in Article 2 of the Constitution do not trump the power granted to Congress to be the source in the American government of the decision to go to war—except to "repel sudden attacks" and to forestall, even preempt, an imminent one. Clearly, also, once a war is commenced, the president was to execute command of military operations, not Congress.

Legalizing Bank Robbery

Despite the words in the Constitution and their meaning as explained by the authors, modern presidents and their lawyers have spun a doctrine of inflated "inherent powers" from the "commander in chief" phrase. The rationale starts with the more than 150 times presidents have used force against foreign threats with no congressional declaration of war, starting with John Adams's undeclared war at sea against France in 1798.[14] Counterposed against this long list of presidentially initiated hostilities are just five instances of congressionally declared wars. Their point is that declarations of war are not practical, especially in the modern age when wars are either too short or small to formally declare, or too time sensitive. President Ronald Reagan's 1983 invasion of Grenada is an example of the former; the nuclear exchange with the Soviet Union that, happily, never occurred is the penultimate example of the latter. Who would want Congress mucking about in either? In some cases, waiting for Congress to declare war would be an inappropriate waste of time; in others, it would be disastrous. Declaring war has become a modern irrelevancy. Congress's job is to keep out of the way, provide the president political support and money when he wants it, and generally play second fiddle. In short, the president's more practical powers as commander in chief fill in where Congress's obsolete 1787 delegation to declare war fails to protect the United States.

In 1970 Nixon's secretary of state, William Rogers, told Congress what this meant: "As commander in chief, the president has the sole authority to command our Armed Forces, whether they are within or outside the United States. And, although reasonable men may differ as to the circumstances in which he should do so, the president has the constitutional power to send U.S. military forces abroad without specific congressional approval."[15]

Any decision that could lead to war was solely the president's. Reasonable men might think him wrong, but he and he alone had the authority.

This "imperial presidency" was not just a Nixonian doctrine; it had become full-blown well before him, and its origins were bipartisan. Some saw it blossoming with Harry Truman's use of U.S. armed forces in the Korean War with no congressional authorization, and it was certainly alive and well during John Kennedy's initiation of U.S. involvement in the Indochina War and Lyndon Johnson's huge expansion of it.

Even if the imperial presidency was not a Nixonian contrivance, it did peak during his term. On 13 March 1973, I listened in a House of Representatives hearing room as the State Department's legal adviser, Charles Brower, was testifying to the House Foreign Affairs Committee. Rep. Jonathan Bingham (D-N.Y.) asked, "What are the limits to the president's authority to take the United States into hostilities?" Brower responded: " . . . no one can precisely define what the limits are . . . the Constitution is a pretty old document. . . . If I were trying to enumerate them, I would only be proving the wisdom of the proposition that I have been presenting this afternoon; namely, that it cannot be done."[16]

It was a breathtaking assertion; the constitutional reach of the president's power to go to war, originally described by Madison, Jefferson, Hamilton, and others as nonexistent, except for repelling "sudden attacks," had grown—without the text being amended—to become not just undefined in its expanse, but indefinable.

It's a concept called the "doctrine of adaptation by usage": if a power is exercised frequently enough, the authority to do so is first manifest and then unfettered.[17] Put more simply, it assumes that frequency of a previously proscribed activity, such as robbing banks, makes the activity not just legal but something that must not be impaired. Willie Sutton, the man who when asked why he robbed banks responded, "Because that's where the money is," would be delighted. Especially when used to turn the Constitution on its head to give a power to an entity that was expressly denied it, the doctrine permitting presidentially initiated war under any circumstances was then, and is now, preposterous. Presidents and their lawyers always strive to sheath it eloquently—to make it sound erudite and a simple exercise of sweet reason—but with inspection, the sow's ear hairs can be found punching through the thin veneer of the fake silk purse.

Constitutional, Perhaps, But Do We Have to Be Stupid?

Having Congress in charge of decisions to go to war is not a comforting prospect. Its gaffes and blunders, even war mongering, are legion: rushing into the War of 1812 and the Spanish-American War,[18] rejecting the Treaty of Versailles after World War I, maintaining isolationism in the face of fascist Germany and Japan in the 1930s, McCarthyism in the 1950s, and urging preemptive attacks on Cuba during the 1962 missile crisis are just a few examples.

Javits's foreign policy adviser, Pete Lakeland, agreed: "When I worked up on [Capitol] Hill I was asked many times if I thought it was a good thing for Congress to muck around in foreign policy. My answer then, as now, was 'no.' Congress seldom acts in this field with the grace, elegance, or the precision which our citizens probably have a right to expect."[19]

But, he continued, ". . . [T]here is only one thing worse that I can think of than having the Congress muck around in foreign policy, and that would be for the Congress to discontinue its involvement in foreign policy leaving us to the tender mercies of executive branch bungling and megalomania."[20]

Indeed, while Congress has often blustered and dithered on national security issues, presidents have had their own blunders, many of them gigantic and bloody: the Bay of Pigs invasion of Cuba, deceiving the nation about the Gulf of Tonkin incident that was used as a pretext to start in earnest the war in Indochina, the meddling in detailed military questions during that same war, the U.S. diplomatic hostage crisis with Iran and the bungled rescue attempt in 1980, the Marines' deployment to Beirut in 1982 and their rushed exodus after more than two hundred were killed in an attack on their barracks, and the military occupation of Haiti in 1994 to install a brand new dictator, Jean-Bertrand Aristide, come to mind. The current war and occupation in Iraq is another viable candidate.

Moreover, many of the presidential blunders do not just result from honest mistakes or imperfect intelligence. Congressmen are not the only politicians in America to raise a wet finger to the political winds or to put themselves and their political comfort first on questions of national security. The autobiographies of senior White House officials frequently refer to what Lakeland described as more "in-fighting and confusion within the executive branch than there is on [Capitol] Hill, and blatant, domestic, presidential politics [that] certainly emanates from the White House and colors every major foreign policy decision."[21] In his memoirs on the Reagan presidency, Secretary of State Alexander Haig agreed: "the Samsons of populism and petty ambition" in the White House were "almost always present" encumbering his foreign policy agenda, and " [t]he impulse to view the Presidency as a public relations opportunity and to regard government as a campaign for reelection . . . [that] distorts balance, frustrates consistency, and destroys credibility."[22]

Since then, we have witnessed President Bill Clinton, who was widely believed to have timed his attacks on terrorist facilities in Sudan and Afghanistan in 1998 to ease his domestic political situation during the Monica Lewinsky/impeachment scandal. Further, as we shall discuss later, it is very probable that President George W. Bush asked Congress for its support to go to war against Iraq before, not after, the 2002 elections to deny Democrats the opportunity to draw voters' attention to the state of the economy and other domestic issues that the Democrats thought would favor them in the 2002 elections.

We have not one branch of government that pollutes its national security decisions with politics and selfish considerations, but two.

The authors of the Constitution did not intend for us to have a Hobson's choice between two undesirables to make decisions on war or peace. As described by multiple constitutional scholars, the framers intended, instead, that "[i]f there is any aspect of our Constitution where powers and responsibilities are divided but shared, it is certainly here in what is termed the *war powers*."[23] Or, "Unique among world powers, the United States' system for participation in international relations is constitutionally bifurcated to divide authority between Congress and the president."[24]

Neither the president's nor Congress's power is absolute. Only Congress has the power to authorize new conflicts, whether "declared" or not; however, presidents also have rights, such as repelling, and forestalling, even preempting, "sudden attacks." Moreover, while only Congress can authorize a war *de novo*, it cannot do so alone: a congressionally declared war with no president willing to wage it is a meaningless "power." Similarly, presidents do not have unfettered war powers once conflict has started. To pursue any war, Congress must appropriate money and is free to give presidents less, or more, than they request. In determining what funding to provide, Congress can, and has, exercised both limitations and encouragements.

It has done so both poorly and well. During the Civil War a Congressional Committee on the Conduct of the War persistently offered unsolicited, and bad, military advice to President Lincoln and mucked about in how money was to be spent for the war. On the other hand, during World War II, Sen. Harry Truman's Special Committee to Investigate the National Defense, known as the Truman Commission, uncovered waste and fraud in both the executive and legislative branches that impeded the U.S. war effort. Both the public and President Franklin Roosevelt welcomed the exercise, which most historians regard as responsibly executed and helpful to the war effort. In fact, Roosevelt found the Truman Committee positive enough that he asked its chairman to join the 1944 Democratic Party ticket as the vice presidential candidate.

There will be times when Congress or the president, sometimes both, misuse authority or lie down on the job. However, the system is designed to seek to avoid human frailty by permitting one branch, if willing, to check the other. A real problem occurs when one branch or the other has accumulated for itself too much power and the other abdicates its own. In those cases, it takes intelligence and character on the part of someone in the separate but unequal branch to understand the problem and restore the balance. That is what the War Powers Act was all about.

Senators Learning from Their Lessons

When Javits introduced his prototype war powers bill, he did not try to rush the novel and controversial legislation to enactment. Instead, he sought a serious study of the issues and asked the Senate Foreign Relations Committee, where the various bills had been referred, to adopt a resolution, as follows: "Resolved, that the [Foreign Relations] Committee initiate an inquiry into the division of constitutional authority between the Congress and the President respecting military operations amounting to an exercise of the power of the United States to make war."[25]

The committee commenced a two-year effort that involved statements from seventy-seven witnesses for and against the legislation, forty-eight separate reports and studies, and eighteen original historic documents.[26] Many, indeed all, sides and shades of the arguments were heard from, including legal scholars, historians, constitutional experts, executive branch lawyers, cabinet secretaries, and members of Congress. There was a serious attempt to comprehend the issues, rather than to simply pack the deck.

Javits's bill was substantially modified as a result, and it was favorably reported to the full Senate for the first time on 7 December 1971 by a unanimous vote of the Foreign Relations Committee.[27] Included among the supporters were senators one would expect to support the president, such as Republican Leader Hugh Scott of Pennsylvania, and a like-minded James Pearson of Kansas. More predictably, liberal Democratic opponents of the Nixon administration also joined, such as Frank Church of Idaho. When the Committee reported the bill a second time in 1973, the vote was 15–0.[28] A bill that failed to take into account interests of both the president and Congress never would have received this breadth of support.

Javits also put together a unique triumvirate consisting of liberal Democrat Thomas Eagleton of Missouri, who proved to be a thoughtful and intelligent advocate, and the conservative John Stennis of Mississippi.* Stennis's active support was key. His recognition, along with that of Scott, Pearson, and other conservatives, that the bill took legitimate concerns for the president into account made it possible for more than just opportunistic Democratic critics of President Nixon to support the bill. Indeed, after the text had been circulated to all senators, sixty-one ultimately asked to be added as cosponsors.

While the bill rejected the indigestible notion of unfettered presidential war-making powers, it did respect the authorities that scholars, experts, and politicians who supported the president's prerogatives argued were granted to the president through the Constitution. The bill also strived to achieve a mechanism that was practical and practicable in the twentieth century. In this

---

* Behind these senators, a unique group of staffers worked on the bill. In addition to Lakeland on Javits's staff, who subsequently was Republican staff director of the Foreign Relations Committee, Brian Atwood of Eagleton's staff later served President Clinton as a State Department undersecretary and as the director of the Agency for International Development. James Woolsey of Stennis's Armed Services Committee staff later served as an undersecretary of the Navy for President Reagan and as director of the CIA for President Clinton.

regard, the bill had two key sections. Section 3 contained four clauses defining circumstances when presidents were recognized to have authority to introduce U.S. armed forces into hostilities or into "situations where imminent involvement in hostilities is clearly indicated by the circumstances." The section authorized presidents

1. to repel an attack on the United States, its territories or possessions, to forestall "the direct and imminent threat of such an attack," and to retaliate against such an attack;
2. to repel an attack on U.S. Armed Forces outside the United States or its territories and possessions, and to forestall such an attack;
3. to rescue U.S. citizens endangered abroad; and
4. to engage in any other hostilities "pursuant to specific statutory authorization" enacted expressly by Congress before the fact.[29]

Section 5 of the bill permitted the president to engage in the hostilities permitted above for just thirty days, unless Congress authorized continuation of the action. If Congress granted no authorization to continue, the president was given thirty additional days to extract U.S. armed forces. The thirty-day and, if needed, sixty-day deadlines were an effort to resolve "the modern dilemma of reconciling the need of speedy and emergency action by the President in this age of instantaneous communications and of intercontinental ballistic missiles with the urgent necessity for Congress to exercise its constitutional mandate and duty with respect to the great questions of war and peace."[30]

With this mechanism, the authors sought to ensure that no president would take the nation into war without authority from Congress at the front end. And if he attempted to do so without that authority, Congress had an opportunity to require him to extricate U.S. armed forces. As Javits said repeatedly before and after the bill became law, it did not guarantee wisdom on the part of Congress or the president, but, like the original 1787 design, it did require that a decision for the United States to go to war, declared or not, was to be a joint decision by both the Congress and the president.

Taking on the Opponents

The Senate debated the bill for two arduous weeks, from 28 March to 13 April 1972. Opponents, such as Barry Goldwater (R-Ariz.) and Peter Dominick (R-Colo.), took the view that the bill unconstitutionally limited the president's commander-in-chief powers, as defined, of course, by Nixon's lawyers. They mounted several hostile amendments, each of which the three coauthors of the bill beat back during lively debates with senators, going back and forth, responding to the other's points and arguments with their own logic and evidence. There were repeated citations of facts, legal cases, and piles of evidence from both sides. Senators had notes, but they were not speaking just from scripted texts. Some exchanges continued for hours. When it was all finished, the Senate passed the bill by a huge margin, 68–16, easily enough to overcome a presidential veto.

Concurrent with the deliberations in the Senate, the House Committee on Foreign Affairs and the House itself considered what it called war powers legislation. Instead of attempting to define Congress's and the president's authority, or even to establish a mechanism for Congress to consider the question of war, the House bill merely required that the president send a report to Congress when he committed U.S. forces to hostilities. It could be summarized as asking the president to tell Congress when he had taken it to war. So feeble was the legislation, that Nixon's lawyers supported it. This bill passed the House of Representatives, and in the waning days of the ninety-second Congress, the House and Senate protagonists on the issue met in an effort to find a compromise between the two bills.

Neither side was willing to give the ground necessary to produce a compromise bill, and the legislation died at the end of 1972. Neither the House nor the Senate authors were in such a hurry that they were willing to sacrifice their convictions just to get a bill passed. Nor did either side attempt to use the issue in the November 1972 elections or to blame the other for the legislation's failure to achieve final passage. In short, there was no effort to make the issue a political football. (As we will see later, in 2002 the protagonists thought very differently.)

A new Congress convened in January 1973. The Senate reconsidered a bill almost identical to the one it passed in 1972, and endorsed it after another debate—this one lasting just two days—on 20 July 1973, by an even wider margin, 72–18. The House took up an entirely new bill, House Joint Resolution 542, and passed it on 18 July by a vote of 244–170. This new House bill still had no definition of when presidents were authorized to use force, but it did have a mechanism for ending a president's war that Congress did not support. Using a mechanism similar to Section 5 of the Senate bill, the House allowed 120 days before a president needed consent from Congress.

The legislation went to a House-Senate conference to resolve the differences. It was a very arduous series of meetings led by Javits for the Senate and Clement Zablocki of Wisconsin, the Democratic chairman of the House Foreign Affairs Committee, for the House. They argued long and hard over whether Congress could specifically define the president's war making power, as in Section 3 of the Senate bill, or not at all, as in the House bill.

Finally, after several weeks, they came to agreement on a new definition of the president's war powers: "The constitutional powers of the President as Commander in Chief to introduce United States Armed Forces into hostilities, or into situations where imminent involvement in hostilities is clearly indicated by the circumstances, are exercised only* pursuant to (1) a declaration of war, (2) specific statutory authorization, or (3) a national emergency created by attack upon the United States, its territories or possessions, or its armed forces."[31]

The difference between the House and Senate on requiring congressional consent to continue beyond either 30 or 120 days was resolved by providing 60 days, plus an additional 30 if Congress refused consent and the president needed the time to extricate U.S. forces. There were also provisions requiring presidential consultations and reports before and after the initiation of hostilities.

Some felt that Javits and the Senate conferees had given up too much. Others, of course, thought the House had. That some on both sides were unhappy does not make the bill a wise, good, or even fair compromise. Was it a reasonable compromise? Could it pass a fair-minded constitutional test? In Javits's office, we felt so. So did Stennis. Pete Lakeland called some of the constitutional experts consulted throughout the bill-writing process, most prominently Alexander Bickel of Yale, who commanded respect from every perspective. After Pete explained the compromise, Bickel agreed it was reasonable and constitutional.

The third Senate coauthor, Senator Eagleton, disagreed. He believed the bill, as modified, gave the president too much. In the Senate, only James Abourezk, a junior senator from South Dakota, joined with Eagleton, but in the House a sizable faction of like-minded liberal Democrats, about a dozen, also agreed with him.

The new left-wing critics did not give the opponents of the bill a majority. The conference report went back to the House and Senate, passed, and was sent to Nixon, who promptly vetoed it. But, there was a problem. When the House passed the conference report, the vote was 238–123, about eight votes short of the number needed to override Nixon's veto with a two-thirds majority. The liberal Democrats who declared the final bill too weak made the difference. Of these, two of the more vocal were Reps. Elizabeth Holtzman and Bella Abzug of New York. If they continued to oppose the bill, Nixon's veto might prevail. Politics does, indeed, make strange bedfellows.

Two unforeseen developments intervened. First, the veto message Nixon sent to Congress rejecting the bill was so arrogant that it made itself an example of why Congress should oppose the veto:

---

* Several days of debate took place in the conference over whether of not to include this word ("only"). At Javits's insistence, it was included.

The restrictions which this resolution would impose upon the authority of the President are both unconstitutional and dangerous to the best interests of our Nation.[32] . . . Only recently, however, has there been a serious challenge to the wisdom of the Founding Fathers in choosing not to draw a precise and detailed line of demarcation between the foreign policy powers of the two branches [of government].[33]

In other words, my powers are indefinable. "House Joint Resolution 542 would attempt to take away, by mere legislative act, authorities which the President has properly exercised under the Constitution for almost 200 years."[34] Or rather, you're too late boys, bank robbing is now legal and perfectly honorable. "The only way in which the constitutional powers of a branch of the Government can be altered is by amending the Constitution."[35] Unless, of course, you're the president, in which case, you do it by fiat.

The veto message was red meat for Javits and Stennis to use as examples of Nixon's overstuffed doctrine of the imperial presidency. However, they lacked a real event to make it all too painfully obvious to the uncertain in Congress. Nixon handed that event to us: just before the vote on the veto override, the "Saturday Night Massacre" occurred. The Watergate scandal, which was in full bloom at the time, had come to a new crescendo. Nixon wanted Archibald Cox, the independent prosecutor appointed to look into the scandal, fired. He had been too, well, independent. Attorney General Elliot Richardson refused to fire Cox and resigned. His deputy, William Ruckelshaus, the next in line for the task, also refused and resigned. The number three person, Robert Bork, the solicitor general, reluctantly agreed to do Nixon's dirty work. It was one of the more amazing episodes of the ever-escalating Watergate scandal, and it made supporting Nixon's veto of the war powers legislation difficult for anyone sitting on the political fence and even more so for liberal Democrats.

In his statements, letters, and press releases, Javits quoted extensively from Nixon's veto message, pointing out its high-handed, imperious outlook. We went home for the weekend knowing we were on the razor's edge of having, or not having, the votes in the House the following week for the veto override.

The liberal Democratic faction in the House knew the vote on the veto override would be close, and they knew they could make the difference; they refused to say what they would do. When the time came for the House vote on Wednesday, 7 November, Pete Lakeland asked me to go to the House chamber to watch from the gallery and report back the result.[*] The House had just adopted electronic voting, and each member's vote

---

[*] In 1973 the House and Senate proceedings were not televised.

and the running totals showed on an electronic tally board. Immediately before the vote, Abzug said she would vote to override. On the other hand, liberals such as Democrat Ron Dellums of California said they would vote against the bill. The issue was very much in doubt.

As members filed into the chamber and each slipped a plastic card into a machine to vote, I could see that it was, indeed, close. About halfway through the approximate twenty minutes allotted for the vote, I saw Holtzman and Abzug come into the chamber and talk briefly between themselves and then with other liberal Democratic House members. As I watched Holtzman closely, I could see that she kept looking at the tally board as the votes hovered close to the margin needed to override, but were not quite there. As the time for the vote began to run down, Holtzman and a few others still withheld their vote. Then, she put her plastic card above the slot to vote, her eyes still on the tally board. Time was running out, and Nixon was about to win. In the last few seconds, she and several others shoved their voting cards into the slots, and the board showed them voting against the veto; the numbers reached the level needed to override and passed it as some others switched their votes to join the two-thirds majority. The final margin was 284–135—more than enough.[36]

It was a moment of high political drama. Holtzman, Abzug, and others could not bring themselves to cast a vote that would be interpreted as an act of support for Richard Nixon, especially immediately after the "Saturday Night Massacre." It is no overstatement to say that the War Powers Act became law over Nixon's veto thanks to the excesses of Nixon himself. It was an entirely fitting result.

After the House vote, it was all downhill. The Senate took up the measure that afternoon; the vote was 75–18. True to his word, Eagleton reluctantly voted to sustain the veto after a difficult, but respectful, debate with Javits.[37]

After the vote, there was a low note, a sign of the tenor of times to come. Sen. John Tower (R-Tex.), an ardent opponent of the legislation, cautioned that the enactment of the bill had "sent a very dangerous signal to Moscow,"[38] implying that the legislation would make the United States vulnerable to attack. Javits immediately intervened and admonished Tower that such a statement was uncalled for.* Javits also attempted to send a con-

---

* Tower also sent a cheap shot at the legislation during the 1973 Senate debate on the bill after the Foreign Relations Committee reported it. He offered an amendment that stated the bill would "reduce the United States of America to the status of a second rate power." (*Congressional Record*, 93rd Cong., 1st Sess., 20 July, 1973, p. 25103). Such tactics persisted from Senator Tower over the years and did not endear him to his Senate colleagues. During the George H. W. Bush administration, Tower was nominated to be secretary of defense; the Senate rejected his nomination.

ciliatory message to the White House, saying he hoped it would "fully cooperate" with the new law. [39]

It was a forlorn hope.

The Un-Dead Doctrine of Presidential War

When the War Powers Act became law, some may have wanted to declare
the imperial presidency dead and for Congress to successfully reclaim its
lost authority. However, inflated presidential war-making power remained
alive and well, and, despite its lopsided votes in favor of the War Powers
Act, Congress's subsequent reaction to reassertions of the presidential doctrine was incoherent, at best.

Every president since Nixon has "taken the position that [the War Powers Act] is an unconstitutional infringement by the Congress on the
President's authority as Commander-in-Chief."[40] Every president since Nixon
introduced U.S. armed forces into hostilities or situations where hostilities
were imminent* without real consultations with Congress† or without ob-
taining any coherent approval from Congress, sometimes without either, as
required by the War Powers Act.[41]

Even when they asked for and received from Congress a statutory authorization to conduct hostilities, presidents said such action was superfluous. When President George H. W. Bush asked for and received congressional support to conduct military operations against Iraq in 1991, he made
it clear he was asking for political support, not legal authority, and if Congress had voted down the authorization to use force, "I don't need it . . . I
have the authority."[42] Rubbing it in, he later added, "I didn't have to get
permission from some old goat in the United States Congress to kick Saddam
Hussein out of Kuwait."[43]

Clinton redoubled presidential unilateralism when he conducted military operations in Iraq, Somalia, Haiti, Bosnia, Afghanistan, Sudan, and Kosovo
without seeking or receiving coherent congressional authorization.[44] In some
cases, one of the two houses of Congress passed bills or amendments either
approving or withdrawing support for an action already taken by Clinton,
but no joint measure by the House and Senate resulted in any statutory

---

* Carter: Iran, 1980. Reagan: Lebanon, 1982; Grenada, 1983; Libya, 1986. George H. W.
  Bush: Panama, 1989. Clinton: Iraq, 1992, 1993, and 1998; Somalia, 1993; Haiti, 1994;
  Bosnia, 1995; Afghanistan, 1998; Sudan, 1998; Kosovo, 1999.

† To comply with the War Powers requirement that "The President in every possible
  instance shall consult with Congress before introducing United States Armed Forces into
  hostilities. . . . " (from Section 3 of PL 93–148, 93rd Cong., 7 November 1973, as enacted
  over President Nixon's veto), presidents usually quietly notified a few individual
  members of Congress about an action that was about to occur. Presidents and their
  supporters in Congress called that "consultation." It was no such thing. It was
  prenotification.

action as required under the War Powers Act. For example, on 23 March 1999, the Senate passed a nonbinding "concurrent" resolution expressing support for "military air operations and missile strikes in cooperation with our NATO allies against the Federal Republic of Yugoslavia." However, on 28 April 1999, the House defeated the same resolution.[45] The House then proceeded to vote down an amendment to remove U.S. forces from Yugoslavia pursuant to Section 5 of the War Powers Act. Congress could produce no coherent action for or against Clinton's war making, and both it and the president simply ignored the implications under the War Powers Act.

George W. Bush adopted the same posture toward the statute as his father. When Congress passed a broad statutory grant of authority immediately after the September 11, 2001, attacks to authorize "all necessary and appropriate force against those nations, organizations, or persons he determines planned, authorized, committed, or aided the terrorist attacks,"[46] he stated when he signed it into law, "In signing this resolution, I maintain the longstanding position of the executive branch regarding the president's constitutional authority to use force, including the Armed Forces of the United States and regarding the constitutionality of the War Powers Resolution."[47]

Both presidents and Congress adopted their own imaginary postures regarding the War Powers Act. Presidents pretended it was unconstitutional and that they did not really have to observe it; Congress pretended it did not have to do anything under the War Powers Act unless it wanted to. In addition, members other than Bob Dole decided to support or oppose the statute depending on political circumstances. In 1991 Senate Majority Leader George Mitchell (D-Maine) strongly challenged George H. W. Bush's claim that he had the constitutional authority, with or without Congress's authorization, to initiate military operations against Iraq. In 1993, after Clinton had assumed the presidency, fellow Democrat George Mitchell opposed legislation that would have forced Clinton to obtain advance authorization from Congress to send U.S. combat units to Bosnia.[48]

The mechanism for which Javits and others worked so hard in order to give Congress a way to reassert its constitutional rights and responsibilities became something Congress sought to avoid. As Javits said, the act provided a mechanism; it did not provide wisdom—or spine.

A core group of members of the House and Senate labored extensively to make their intellectual convictions bear legislative fruit with the War Powers Act. Unfortunately, Congress has subsequently failed to keep faith with both the intent of the framers of the Constitution and with the mechanism it was handed in the War Powers Act. Congress demonstrated its refusal to take on its constitutional responsibility in 2002, when it went through the motions of the actions called for by the War Powers Act but in truth brought itself to a new low. In doing so, Congress received a great deal of encouragement from President George W. Bush. It is instructive to assess the behavior of both as the president and Congress authorized war with Iraq in 2002.

13

Congress on Its Knees

When the Constitutional Convention was debating the allocation of the war power, George Mason of Virginia said he "was against giving the power of war to the executive, because [it is] not safely to be trusted with it; or to the Senate, because [it is] not so constructed as to be entitled to it." He was, he said, "for clogging rather than facilitating war; but for facilitating peace."[1]

Mason thought it was essential to add the House of Representatives to the decision-making process for war. It could provide a check and a balance not just to the president, but also to the Senate. It was a theory worth trying, but, unfortunately, in 2002 the system broke down completely. The problem was not just that the president deceived Congress, if not also himself, in the manner he pushed for war; it is that no one in a position of responsibility in the House, the Senate, or even the presidency bothered to check into what the president was espousing, thereby denying all the opportunity for the checks and balances in the U.S. constitutional system to operate. The various actors had no time for the safeguards Mason sought; they were all too busy pursuing their political agendas.

President Bush Argues for His War

Bush was very clear about what he wanted and why. In speeches to the United Nations on 12 September 2002 and on national television the night of 7 October, he described what threat from Iraq he sought to deal with:

> Eleven years ago, as a condition for ending the Persian Gulf War, the Iraqi regime was required to destroy its weapons of mass destruction, to cease all development of such weapons and to stop all support for terrorist groups. The Iraqi regime has violated all of those obligations. It possesses and produces chemical and biological weapons. It is seeking nuclear weapons. It has given shelter and support to terrorism and practices terror against its own people. . . .
>
> Iraq's weapons of mass destruction are controlled by a murderous tyrant.
>
> Iraq possesses ballistic missiles with a likely range of hundreds of miles. . . .

Iraq has a growing fleet of manned and unmanned aerial vehicles that could be used to disperse chemical and biological weapons across broad areas. We're concerned that Iraq is exploring ways of using these UAVs for missions targeting the United States. . . .

We know that Iraq and al Qaeda have had high-level contacts that go back a decade.

. . . Iraq has trained al Qaeda members in bomb-making and poisons and deadly gases.

. . . Iraq could decide on any given day to provide a biological or chemical weapon to a terrorist group or individual terrorists. . . .

The evidence indicates that Iraq is reconstituting its nuclear weapons program.

Facing clear evidence of peril, we cannot wait for the final proof, the smoking gun, that could come in the form of a mushroom cloud.[2]

In the face of these loudly proclaimed threats, Bush did not argue publicly that the United States should immediately go to war. Instead, he said he wanted to attempt to resolve the issues peacefully: "I hope this will not require military action. . . . I have asked Congress to authorize the use of America's military if it proves necessary to enforce UN Security Council demands. Approving this resolution does not mean that military action is imminent or unavoidable."[3]

And, he said, he did not want the United States to act alone; he told the American public in his televised address, "We will act with allies at our side."[4] Earlier, he had told the UN General Assembly: "My nation will work with the UN Security Council to meet our common challenge. If Iraq's regime defies us again, the world must move deliberately, decisively to hold Iraq to account. We will work with the UN Security Council for the necessary resolutions."[5]

While the primary emphasis of his speeches was time and time again on acting through the United Nations and with allies, at one point he also intimated that if the United Nations failed to support him, he was prepared to use force against Iraq without UN consent; he told the General Assembly: "But the purposes of the United States should not be doubted. The Security Council resolutions will be enforced—the just demands of peace and security will be met—or action will be unavoidable."[6]

He also told the U.S. public more clearly:

Saddam Hussein has thumbed his nose at the world. He's a threat to the neighborhood. He's a threat to Israel. He's a threat to the United States of America. And we're just going to have to deal with him. And the best way to deal with him is for the world to rise up and say, you disarm, or we'll disarm you. And if not—if, at the very end of the day, nothing happens—the United States, along with others, will act.[7]

These statements left open important questions: Would the United States ultimately act with UN support, or not? How much time and patience was the president willing to give the United Nations? What allies would support the United States with their own forces? With the United Nations? Without the United Nations? In short, President Bush's statements left ambiguous whether U.S. military force was going to be used, and, if so, under what circumstances, when, for how long, and to what end. All of these questions were unknown, if not to Bush, then certainly to Congress, the public, and the world. They were the kinds of things any inquisitive minds in Congress might want to know before they unleashed the dogs of war.

Bush had a different view. Without answering any of these questions, he asked Congress to approve legislation authorizing war against Iraq. The text of the draft bill, written in the White House, was abundantly clear on only one point. After a series of rhetorical "whereas" clauses referring to various offenses by Iraq, it read, "The president is authorized to use all means that he determines to be appropriate, including force, in order to enforce the United Nations Security Council Resolutions referenced above, defend the national security interests of the United States against the threat posed by Iraq, and restore international peace and security in the region."[8]

The open-ended nature of the authority requested from Congress was breathtaking:

- The president was to be permitted to use any means, including military force, not excluding nuclear weapons, as soon as and as long as he—and he alone—determined to be "appropriate."
- The president, and the president alone, would determine what circumstances would prompt war, without any further discussions with Congress, the United Nations, allies, or even Mrs. Bush. The reasons could even include any of the non-core UN Security Council resolutions that dealt with subsidiary issues, such as repatriating Kuwaiti prisoners, records, and property believed to remain in Iraq.
- If none of that was enough, the president was also authorized to go to war to "defend the national security interests" of the United States "against the threat posed by Iraq." "National security interests" is not defined in the text, nor is "the threat posed by Iraq." Both are left to the president to define.
- And if the above somehow was not broad enough, the president was further authorized to go to war to "restore international peace and security in the region." In other words, he was able to use force against anybody in the region as long as it was for restoring "peace and security," as defined, of course, by the president. Thus, if Iraq were to

disarm, return all prisoners and property, observe human rights, convert to democracy, and pose no other perceived threat to U.S. national security interests, Bush could still go to war against Iraq or anybody else if he found anything contrary to "international peace and security" in the Middle East.

In short, the draft legislation stripped away all of the conditions the president said he would observe: the promises about using force only as a last resort and acting with UN support and in concert with allies. It permitted a war initiated by Bush anywhere in the Middle East, against anyone, at any time, to use any weapon in the U.S. arsenal, to do so alone, and for as long as the president saw fit. In previous instances of a declaration of war, or any functional equivalent, such as the Gulf of Tonkin resolution Congress passed to authorize the Vietnam War, there was a charge America had been attacked or the president had already decided to use force. Here, there had been no attack, and the president had as yet made no public decision about war. This would be a first in American history; it was a blank check for a war that the president might or might not want to initiate. Bush was requesting from Congress precisely what the framers of the Constitution sought to deny to the chief executive and to give exclusively to Congress.

War or Politics?

The president's historically unique request for an open door to a war he ostensibly had not yet decided to enter may seem puzzling, but it was nothing strange to the politicians in Washington. Some thought it was brilliant; others were furious. What the president was doing was changing the subject matter of the national political agenda in the run-up to the 2002 "midterm" elections for all 435 seats in the House of Representatives and 34 seats in the Senate. As the *Washington Post* reported: "Republicans believe they will benefit politically if candidates and the public are talking about the war on terrorism, a showdown with Hussein or new domestic security measures in the days leading to the Nov. 5 elections. Bush's political adviser, Karl Rove, has told donors and lawmakers that Republicans will have a better chance of picking up congressional seats this fall if they are talking about national defense."[9]

The Democrats were the furious ones. Usually, elections for the House and Senate in the middle of a presidential term result in gains for the party not in the White House. The year 2002 looked to be no exception. The economy was for the most part in the tank. The Dow Jones Industrial Average had sunk below 8,000. The federal budget had switched from surplus to deficit and was headed further south. And, the Democrats had big plans to bash Republicans for being cold and uncaring on subjects like Social

Security and health care. All the normal signs pointed to the Democrats doing well in the November 2002 elections. With any luck, they would take over the House of Representatives, where the Republicans prevailed by only a few votes, and they could increase their perilous one-vote majority in the Senate. They wouldn't have a shot at the White House until 2004, but they had an excellent chance to control both houses of Congress. So they thought.

The Democrats clearly saw the president's changing the subject to war against Iraq the same way Karl Rove in the White House saw it, as an attempt to influence the elections. As all knew, war and national security are subjects the electorate wants the president, not Congress, to take care of. When international conflict threatens, the voters can be expected to support whoever is president and his party in an election.

Bush started to exploit openly the situation in a fundraising speech in New Jersey on 23 September when he alleged the Democrats were "not interested in the security of the American people."[10] Senate Majority Leader Tom Daschle sternly proclaimed himself outraged that the president called Democrats unpatriotic, but as editorials and news articles in the *Washington Post* made clear, many Democrats were also furious that the subject of the national political debate was being changed from domestic and economic issues to war and homeland security.[11]

The Democrats were angry, but they were also hog-tied. Bush's asking Congress to surrender its war-making authority was an integral part of an election strategy, but the Democrats would only open themselves to charges of being unpatriotic if they complained. What made Bush's stratagem obvious was its timing. He professed to be in no hurry to start the war, just in a hurry to get the legislation he wanted out of Congress. Debating the question of war in the House and Senate permitted no time or opportunity for the domestic subjects the Democrats preferred. And, after the national stage on Capitol Hill was used to debate the war, Congress would adjourn. It was a political masterstroke.

Doctrine Explains Brazen Legislation

Another event in the fall of 2002 further clarified the unique legislation the White House drafted. On 20 September 2002, the White House released a report titled, "The National Security Strategy of the United States." It was an annual report released by every White House that is required by law. Previous examples were uncommonly good cures for insomnia, but this one was not. It announced a new national strategy for war at the whim of the president.

> We will disrupt and destroy terrorist organizations by . . . identifying and destroying the threat before it reaches our borders. . . . [W]e

will not hesitate to act alone, if necessary, to exercise our right of self-defense by acting preemptively. . . . [12]

We must be prepared to stop rogue states and their terrorist clients before they are able to threaten or use weapons of mass destruction against the United States and our allies and friends. . . . [13]

For centuries, international law recognized that nations need not suffer an attack before they can lawfully take action to defend themselves against forces that present an imminent danger of attack. Legal scholars and international jurists often conditioned the legitimacy of preemption on the existence of an imminent threat—most often a visible mobilization of armies, navies, and air forces preparing to attack.

We must adapt the concept of imminent threat to the capabilities and objectives of today's adversaries. . . . [14]

The major institutions of American national security were designed in a different era to meet different requirements. All of them must be transformed. [15]

Three elements of this new view on war against America's enemies are notable.

- It defines an imminent attack *not* as one that is just about to happen: an "imminent" attack is one for which the enemy has "capabilities" that will achieve his "objectives." Put another way, an imminent attack could be years away; it might not even be specifically planned. All that is required is that the enemy is capable of the attack and that an attack would meet his objectives. This was going well beyond the internationally, and constitutionally, recognized right to forestall or preempt an actual attack; it asserted the right to attack in the absence of a truly imminent threat.
- The United States will feel itself free to attack not just to protect itself; it might also attack first to protect its interests, "our allies," and most notably "friends." Presidents used to argue they were free to go to war under certain security treaties, such as the NATO treaty; now, legal structures were no longer needed; war was to be employed if an enemy threatened not just the United States or its treaty allies but now also "friends," who were to be identified, of course, by the president.
- Third, the "major institutions of American national security" are obsolete. What more significant institution of American national security is there than that dusty old Constitution that was "designed in a different era to meet different requirements?" It was much like 1973,

when Richard Nixon's State Department legal adviser declared the Constitution "an old document."

President Bush was reserving the right to attack when he saw a threat in the making, even if others saw no such threat. Such a view attracted a comment from an earlier American politician, who said:

> Allow the president to invade a . . . nation, whenever he shall deem it necessary to repel an invasion, and you allow him to do so, whenever he may choose to say he deems it necessary for such purpose and you allow him to make war at pleasure. Study to see if you can fix any limit to his power in this respect . . . If, today, he should choose to say he thinks it necessary to invade Canada . . . how could you stop him? You might say to him, "I see no probability of [attack]," . . . but he will say to you be silent; I see it if you don't.[16]

Historians of the period recognize the quote; it was Illinois congressman Abraham Lincoln arguing in opposition to war against Mexico in 1848. What Bush was requesting was a classic expansion of presidential war-making authority that had been recognized through history as excessive. It was also a classic time for the checks and balances in the U.S. system of government to operate.

Bush's Weak Case

It was not just Bush's aggressive posture that begged someone to invoke the system of checks and balances. His case for the war was visibly fragile even back then. Time and time again, the president's speeches asserted a threat from Saddam Hussein, even against the United States. However, in the summer and fall of 2002, leak after leak oozed out of U.S. and other intelligence agencies questioning the accuracy of Bush's assertions.

The president linked Iraq to al Qaeda and the attacks of September 11, 2001, by telling the American public that a "very senior al Qaeda leader" had been in Iraq. There were also reports of a pre–September 11 meeting between Iraqis and al Qaeda in the Czech Republic, and Secretary of Defense Donald Rumsfeld called the evidence of the link "bulletproof."[17] However, working-level intelligence analysts from both the CIA and from foreign intelligence agencies made it known to the U.S. and foreign press that these contacts were either transitory or nonexistent.[18] Intelligence agencies found many substantial links between Saddam Hussein and terrorists, but not al Qaeda. Indeed, according to a bastion of Republican politics, the *Wall Street Journal:*

> Mr. Hussein has every reason to keep al Qaeda at arm's length. . . .
> [T]here is little evidence that [Saddam] has been willing so far to

share his biological or chemical weapons with his partners in terror, even during the Gulf War. . . .

The latest example [cited by the administration of Iraq–al Qaeda links] is the case of an al Qaeda operative named Abu Musab Zarqawi, who turned up in Baghdad last summer. The Central Intelligence Agency investigated and learned Mr. Zarqawi was in Baghdad at least partly for personal reasons: He had lost a leg during fighting in Afghanistan and was in the Iraqi capital seeking medical treatment in one of the few places he might escape capture. . . . When the Iraqis were shown what one Jordanian intelligence official called "irrefutable proof" that he was in Baghdad, the Iraqis agreed to investigate. Within days, Mr. Zarqawi was hustled out of Iraq. . . .

In public statements, senior [administration] officials have referred repeatedly to intelligence about al Qaeda–Iraq links that remains largely unverified, intelligence officials say. One incident received special scrutiny: In late 1998, after U.S. cruise-missile strikes on al Qaeda training camps in Afghanistan, Mr. Hussein was reported to have dispatched an Iraqi ambassador to offer sanctuary to both Mr. bin Laden and Taliban chief Mullah Mohammed Omar. But U.S. intelligence officials say that they haven't been able to confirm the meeting and doubt it ever occurred.

An intelligence report passed to the U.S. from officials in the Czech Republic said that one of the leaders of the Sept. 11 hijackers, Mohamed Atta, may have met with an Iraqi intelligence agent last year in Prague. But the meeting has never been verified and most analysts at the CIA doubt it happened, officials say. . . .

An al Qaeda detainee being held at the Guantanamo naval base in Cuba told interrogators that Iraq may have trained some of the group's members in the use of poisons and gases and in explosives. U.S. intelligence officials say it's possible but that they haven't confirmed the report.[19]

Furthermore, members of Congress publicly reported that the information they heard in classified briefings from the CIA contradicted the public statements of the president and his administration. For example, word leaked out in early October that aluminum tubes imported by Iraq were most probably not intended for any Iraqi nuclear program, as alleged by the administration, and that Iraq was not months, but years (perhaps even more), away from developing a nuclear weapon on its own.[20]*

---

* Events during the war and the first year of the occupation would show that the tubes were for conventional missiles and the Iraqi nuclear program did not exist.

In a remarkable letter released to the public in early October, a second-tier official at the CIA took issue with the president's formulation that Saddam posed the threat of a mushroom cloud over the United States. Deputy CIA director John McLaughlin signed a letter on behalf of director George Tenet to the chairman of the Senate Intelligence Committee divulging that a "senior intelligence witness" stated at a Senate hearing that "in the foreseeable future" the likelihood of any attack by Saddam Hussein on the United States was "low," unless the United States attacked him first—in which case, the likelihood became "pretty high."[21] In other words, if he chose war, the president might provoke what he said he sought to prevent.

These and other leaks that found the president's evidence weak provoked a reaction, but not the appropriate one. Little to nothing happened to probe the president's evidence, but there was an effort to stifle the dissonant information. Reports began to appear of a campaign to have CIA director George Tenet fired and commence a new intelligence operation under the control of the war advocates in the Defense Department to produce "better" evidence. The reports were dutifully, but unconvincingly, denied by those same Pentagon officials who were the likely basis of the threats against Tenet and others at the CIA.[22]

However, the CIA was not the only problem. One of Saddam's "imminent" threats was said to be an Iraqi unmanned drone aircraft program able to deliver chemical or biological weapons. Regarding it, the president said, "We're concerned that Iraq is exploring ways of using these UAVs for missions targeting the United States."[23] The aircraft-drone described was analyzed by the press to be, in fact, physically incapable of reaching America from Iraq.[24] Even a plot, said to be engineered by Saddam, to assassinate President George H. W. Bush when he visited Kuwait in 1993—described by President George W. Bush as—"He tried to kill my dad"—may have been a hoax. A *New Yorker* article by investigative journalist Seymour Hersh, published in November 1993 and re-released in September 2002, convincingly argued that the alleged plot might have been a setup by Kuwait in its eagerness to maintain U.S. hostility toward Iraq.[25]

The "bulletproof" evidence cited by the president and his administration had many holes, all evidenced in newspaper articles readily available in October 2002. When advocating war in the absence of an actual attack, or one that is clearly imminent, it is reasonable to expect a compelling case, rather than assertions that one's own intelligence community undermines and that some in the press find weak. The point is not that the president's evidence was proved wrong; it was, however, shown to be uncertain and questionable in early October 2002. And yet, no one pursued the obvious issues, demanded hearings in Congress to get to the bottom of it all, asked GAO to perform an urgent classified inquiry, or egged on the press to look for more.

The unquestioning atmosphere predominating in the highest levels of the U.S. government in October 2002 made it unthinkable for anyone to ask the question which in hindsight is so obvious: What weapons of mass destruction? The remarkable failure to find any weapons of mass destruction in Iraq a full year after the war, after massive searching, prompts the question, Were there any signs of this absence before the war? Of course, there were: in the efforts of Hans Blix and the UN to establish their presence. Blix and the UN sought more time to uncover any if they existed, but America brushed such sentiment aside on the presumption that only an obstructionist or an appeaser to Saddam would question what everyone knew for certain—that Saddam hoarded massive stocks of chemical and biological weapons. Secretary Rumsfeld declared he even knew where they were[26] and that an attack against the United States or its "friends" was literally imminent.

The U.S. Constitution provides protections against wars urged by presidents with weak evidence, giving Congress all the tools needed to stand up to the president. In October 2002 Congress's leaders, especially Democrats, got a little confused; they did not stand up. They got on their knees.

Congress Kowtows to the Idol of Presidential War

When the Democratic leaders in Congress saw in September 2002 the unprecedented war-making authority Bush was seeking, they knew they had a problem. Some surely had real reservations about the war Bush was seeking or the authority he wanted to pursue it, or both. Some also did not want to hurt their chances for winning control of Congress in the November elections by showing any daylight between themselves and the president on a question of war. On the other hand, they also knew they could hurt their relationship with their own political base, and all-important voter turnout in the elections, if they endorsed such a blatant blank check for George W. Bush, the same George Bush so many Democratic Party regulars reviled after the 2000 election debacle in Florida. The leaders in Congress knew they had to appease their political base, but they also knew they had to keep themselves joined at the hip with Bush on the question of war: a tricky posture, but one that skilled politicians know how to assume.

The desired stance was achieved on 2 October. That day, in a ceremony in the Rose Garden of the White House, Bush announced bipartisan agreement on revised legislation on the question of war with Iraq with congressional leaders from both parties. Standing beside him at the podium were Republican Speaker of the House Dennis Hastert and Senate Republican Leader Trent Lott. In addition, there was Democratic Leader of the House

Richard Gephardt and Sen. Joe Lieberman, who while not a titular Democratic party leader, was certainly a prime catch.*

The new legislation was the product of masterful politics and draftsmanship. The insignificant, rhetorical "whereas" clauses in the front of the legislation showed many changes, all of them meaningless. In the part of the legislation that mattered, three new sections were added: (1) Congress stated its support for efforts to work with the UN Security Council; (2) the president was required to report to Congress no later than forty-eight hours after he went to war with Iraq that diplomatic means weren't working and hostilities against Iraq would not impede the war against other terrorists; and (3) reports every sixty days, as already required by the War Powers Act and other laws, had to be submitted.

The key section of the legislation that opened the door to war, as originally drafted by the White House, had alterations as well. The language still read that the president was "authorized to use the Armed Forces of the United States as he determines to be necessary and appropriate," but he could do so only to "defend the national security of the United States against the continuing threat posed by Iraq; and enforce all relevant United Nations Security Council resolutions regarding Iraq." Gone was the language that authorized the president to go war to "restore international peace and security in the region."

Now, Bush couldn't go to war against anyone in the Middle East whom he might deem to impede "international peace and security." An objective he was not seeking was withdrawn; the objective he was seeking was left completely intact.

The new language urged, but did not require, working through the United Nations and using peaceful means. The only reports required were those on efforts to solve problems through diplomacy and to continue the rest of the war against terror. Any competent White House, State Department, or DoD staffer could write those reports whenever they were required. The changes in the legislation were pure window dressing. The president had retained every bit of freedom of action he could ever want.

In addition, the new language added the word "continuing" to the phrase "threat from Iraq." With this revision, supporters of the new "compromise" legislation were openly conceding that the threat was both preexisting and extant; it could thus be assumed to be "imminent" as defined by the new doctrine. The president had achieved not only endorsement of an open door to war, but also, arguably, of his new doctrine.

---

* Senate Majority Leader Tom Daschle was prominently missing; he was undecided at that moment and had walked away from the ceremony as its principals gathered.

The changes were utterly meaningless but they were also useful. Enough new wording appeared for the Democrats, such as Gephardt and Lieberman, to pretend they obtained some meaningful concessions. The new text threw words at the desirability of working through the United Nations and with allies and taking the best shot at diplomacy. Gephardt and Lieberman and any who joined them could claim they had added this dimension to the president's policies. It was a dimension the president remained free under the statutorily binding parts of the legislation to discard totally, if he cared to. In reality, the Democratic leadership extracted no meaningful concession whatsoever from the president's original draft resolution.

Thus, because each and every change in the legislation was accepted by the president (he would have been a fool not to), the Democrats remained joined at the hip with him against Saddam Hussein in the run up to the November mid-term elections. They got to stand tall publicly with the president on the vital question of national security just before the elections while simultaneously bending on their knees on every substantive issue pertaining to the war George Bush could ever want.

Because there is no more onerous question than whether to make war against another nation, one would hope the senators and representatives would give the issue their most profound consideration and rise above exploiting the issue to seek political advantage. Even if it were to be the "cake walk" some prognosticators glibly predicted,[27] war against Iraq would still hold awful consequences for the families and loved ones of military and civilian personnel killed and injured. And, the ramifications for America's role in the world, peace in the Middle East, the ongoing war against terror, and the U.S. budget would clearly all be very significant, as indeed they turned out to be.

Up to the day Congress started its debate on the question of going to war with Iraq, hearings were conducted and even opponents to the impending war testified. However, it was all for show. None of the questionable evidence for the war was addressed in any serious manner; to do so would open the questioners to the charge of not supporting the president in a national security crisis. As these politicians saw it, it would be unpatriotic for them to exercise the system of checks and balances the Constitution expected them to operate.

That political appearances were far more important than the merits was about to become all too obvious.

14

The Week of Shame

Congress's vote on 10 October 2002 to authorize President George W. Bush to go to war against Iraq, and the debate that preceded it, explains how seriously present-day members of Congress take the responsibility to decide on the question of war, as assigned in the Constitution and the War Powers Act.

The debate on the war against Iraq started on Thursday, 3 October, and ended on Thursday, 10 October 2002. The Senate used all six of those business days; the House used just three, from Tuesday, 8 October, to Thursday afternoon.

In the House, there never is much real debating. Because there are 435 voting members, the leadership has to exercise strict control over who talks and for how long. If the rules permitted members to talk as often and as long as the matter at hand requires—as in the Senate—little would be done, and none of it in a timely or efficient fashion. As a result, members can speak for only a few minutes, often just two or three. Only the floor managers, appointed to shepherd the legislation for both sides of the debate to a vote on final passage, can speak longer and more often. Moreover, there rarely is any real give and take or exchange between proponents and opponents of the measure they are considering. There may be rhetorical questions and answers, but debates in the House are more like a series of speeches, alternating between those for and those against the proposition at hand. It is unfortunate, but it is necessary if the House is to get anything done.

The Senate is different. With only one hundred members and a tradition of full debate, most senators take great pride in the moniker "World's Greatest Deliberative Body." When I first started working for Javits in 1971, debates—with senators going back and forth, directing their remarks to the points made by their opponents—were typical. While members sometimes had notes, usually, but not always, prepared by staff, to assist them, they almost always spoke extemporaneously. Only on special occasions, such as a new senator's "maiden speech" or to explain especially long and complicated legislation, would a member deliver his or her remarks from a staff-written speech, more or less verbatim. Any member who relied too much on prepared texts to make his or her points would not command the respect, or sometimes even attention, of the other members and the staff. Such senators, of which there were only a few in the early 1970s, were derided by many staff, and presumably senators as well, as more like windup dolls too doltish to utter words not scripted by staff.

Thirty-one years later, when the Senate started its deliberations on the legislation to go to war against Iraq, things were different. On the first day of the debate, Senators Lott and Daschle, the leaders for both parties, made introductory remarks. Both were quite solemn. Lott stated, "I believe the Senate will, once again, show why it is called 'the greatest deliberative body.'"[1] Daschle joined in, "I want very much for this debate to be respectful, to recognize our solemn obligation as Senators to debate, and our role in providing advice and consent on issues of this import."[2] Then, there was a vote on a procedural matter; then nothing happened. No debate, no talking, not even scripted speeches—nothing.

With no one wanting to talk about Iraq, the Senate quietly moved on to other legislation, an irrelevant appropriations bill, and other miscellaneous issues, including statements on the one-hundredth anniversary of the 4-H Club by my former boss, Domenici, on the Future Farmers of America chapter in Caldwell County, Kentucky, by Sen. James Bunning, and on the one-hundredth anniversary of the city of Mountain View, California, by Sen. Barbara Boxer. At 6:25 PM, the Senate finished for the day.

On Friday, 4 October, the Senate went into session at 9:30 AM and immediately after the morning prayer and pledge of allegiance, turned to the Iraq legislation. For a major debate like this, one would expect a senior member, such as the chairman of the Foreign Relations or Armed Services Committees, or the ranking Republican from either, to start things off. Instead, a junior senator, Bunning of Kentucky, initiated the day's debate for the simple reason that when the time came to talk about Iraq, he was the first in line. Shortly after that, the chairman of the Finance Committee, Sen. Max Baucus, spoke, but he did not want to speak about Iraq; he spoke about a tax bill. Then, Sen. Tom Harkin of Iowa spoke about an education bill; then Baucus spoke again, but this time about a Medicare bill; then Sen. Ron Wyden on energy policy; then, Baucus, again, but now on a U.S.–Chile trade agreement; then, Sen. Christopher Dodd on election reform legislation, and so on. Throughout this, there were only three interruptions, when Sens. Carl Levin, John Warner, and George Voinovich actually did talk about the Iraq question. (That afternoon, Warner and Sen. Robert Byrd of West Virginia spoke at length on Iraq, but more on that later.)

When the Senate resumed on Monday, 7 October, the senators resumed talking about the Iraq legislation, but they were not debating it. Instead, there began a long series of senators coming to the chamber, delivering prepared remarks, and disappearing. The *Washington Post* observed of this performance, ". . . the 'debate' was actually a sequence of prepared speeches involving little if any give and take between lawmakers."[3] The *Post* was accurate.

There was an exception of a specific matter that popped up from time to time and was truly debated, sometimes quite hotly: it was the subject of who gets to speak when, and for how long. At several points, Sen. Henry Reid, who as deputy majority leader—or "whip"—for the Democrats, tried to keep the parliamentary trains running, complained that senators were not showing up to speak when they were scheduled to do so. At one point on Wednesday, 9 October, tempers began to get testy, and it took about half an hour just to decide who would talk next and about what.[4] By Thursday, more and more senators privately and openly expressed dismay that they were not being allowed time to deliver their prepared speeches when they wanted to. At one point, Joe Biden, chairman of the Foreign Relations Committee, could be heard through his microphone calling the "debate" that had been arranged "ridiculous," but the remark was not printed in the *Congressional Record*.[5]

For the Republicans, McCain, who was one of the more outspoken proponents of war, was anxious to keep things moving. As he explained in the *Record,* all the parliamentary skids had been greased to have the legislation passed quickly and in the precise "compromise" form the White House and the congressional leadership in both the House and Senate had already agreed on. McCain was anxious that no one collect the votes to change even a single word of the legislation's text: "We intentionally introduced [in the Senate] the exact same language [as was being debated and passed in the House] so that when the other body [the House] passes it and we pass it, it will be the exact same message. Modifying that agreement could reopen issues that otherwise have been resolved and would unnecessarily slow down consideration of a resolution that the President has requested and made clear is an urgent priority for his administration."[6]

Staff and senators knew exactly the parliamentary situation McCain was describing. When the Senate and House pass different versions of the same legislation, even if just one word is changed, they must resolve the difference in a House-Senate "Conference Committee," consisting of the senior members of the committees that generated the legislation. Those conferences can take hours, days, weeks, or sometimes months depending on the character of the differences between the two bodies and just how insistent the protagonists are in trying to maintain their respective positions.

If anything changed in the Senate version of the Iraq legislation, a House-Senate conference would have been required, and that would have presented multiple opportunities for obstruction to emerge. In the Senate, just appointing the Senate's conferees can be held up; in the conference, the Senate's Democrats would outnumber the Republicans, thereby giving them an opportunity, should they choose to exploit it, to insist on real changes. When the conference is a done deal, the whole thing has to be debated, yet again, in both the House and Senate, with all the attendant opportunities for things to fall apart, or at least be filibustered and delayed yet again in the Senate. Only after both houses pass identical legislation is it sent to the White House for the president's signature and enactment into law. McCain and the other supporters of the Iraq legislation knew they wanted to avoid this labyrinth if at all possible.

By Thursday, McCain was clearly losing his patience with the slow progress. He talked about "invoking cloture" to kill off any chance of a filibuster and to set a time limit of no more than thirty additional hours of consideration. So anxious was McCain to be finished that he objected when Sen. Mark Dayton (D-Minn.) asked for consent to be allowed just thirty more seconds to finish his remarks. [7] It may have been effective parliamentary tactics to rush things along for McCain's side of the issue, but to give speakers the "bum's rush" so America can go to war with nary a thirty-second delay was not an uplifting moment for a body that calls itself "the world's greatest deliberative body."

A Brief, Shining Moment on the Road to War

Interjected between the statements on the 4-H club, trade agreements, and the heated exchanges on who gets to speak when, there was a brief interlude when an actual debate on the war occurred. It was 4 October, and being a Friday, most senators had left town—as is the modern custom—for politicking in their home states or other business out of Washington. As a result, there were only a few senators around to carry the ball. Luckily for those who remember when the Senate chamber did provide a forum for real debates, the members in the chamber that Friday afternoon included long-timers Byrd and Warner.

They actually debated. They went back and forth, disagreeing on both the policy the president had adopted and who in the American government had the authority to go to war. Warner, a "floor manager" for the legislation, said: "the President of the United States, as I read the Constitution, has the authority, at this very moment, to employ the men and women of our Armed Forces in the defense of our Nation. . . . we don't have to pass this [legislation]." [8] And later, "This President, as well as any other President, could act tomorrow without the specific authority of Congress, if he felt it was necessary to use the troops to defend the security interests of this country." [9]

Eighty-five-year-old Robert Byrd (D-W.Va.) could not disagree more; both the specific legislation supporting war and any supposition that the president had any authority to initiate war on his own were completely wrong.

> Here we are today; we have rubber spines, rubber legs, and we do not have backbones. This branch of Government, under the Constitution, is the branch . . . to declare war.
>
> The Framers were very wise when they determined that these two matters—the decision to go to war and the making of war—should be in two different places. The decision, the determination to declare war, should flow from this branch . . . and the matter of making war should be in the hands of a unified commander, the Commander in Chief.
>
> What are we doing? In my view, if we accept this resolution as it is written, we are saying both of these vital functions would be placed in the hands of one man.[10]

Byrd was also an effective showman. He would periodically pull a dog-eared copy of the Constitution from his vest pocket and read from it, his voice, and his hands, quivering from his apparent passion, and his years. Later on, he would do the same, holding his family Bible.

These exchanges were a joy to watch. The senators were passionately stating their case and arguing real differences out. Yet, they treated each other with genuine respect. There were no cheap shots implying that opponents of the president were not patriotic, or that his supporters were warmongers. Neither gave the other the bum's rush or sought some minor tactical advantage by denying the other the opportunity to talk as long as he sought, but neither abused the privilege. It was about two hours of the kind of deliberation that gave meaning to Lott's and Daschle's high expectations.

Then, at the end of the day, Byrd and Warner expressed their respect for each other, shook hands, and left the chamber. After this brief but uplifting interlude, it was back to business as usual.

The World's Greatest Deliberative Body
Gets Down to Business

On Monday, 7 October, the Senate quickly brought itself back to what the *Washington Post* had described as a "sequence of prepared speeches." When a senator delivered his or her remarks, there were usually very few members in the chamber, and even fewer of them were listening. Instead, they were waiting, some of them impatiently, for their turn to deliver their own prepared remarks, and when finished, they usually left the chamber.

On Tuesday, the House started its "debate," which was, as usual, also in the mode of prepared scripts seriatim. While these addresses in the House and Senate were basically in a random order of who arrived when to read from his or her papers, a pattern did ultimately emerge. Each of the speeches could be put into one of three categories:

- Senators and House members supporting Bush on the question of war who described accurately the legislation they were going to vote on, mostly Republicans.
- Senators and House members opposing Bush on the question of war who described accurately the legislation they were to vote on, mostly Democrats.
- Senators and House members saying they supported Bush on the question of war but who described the legislation they were to vote on as something radically different from what was actually before them. These were both Republicans and Democrats.

The Straightforward Proponents and Opponents

Several members of the House and Senate made it clear they supported Bush's policies and the specific legislation before them. In their own words, they were willing to make known their support for unilateral war against Iraq if and when Bush decided for any reason he chose. For example, Warner explained the latitude he was willing to grant the president: "The principal purposes [of this] resolution is to authorize our President to use that force if, and I repeat, if he deems it necessary to remove the threat of those weapons [of mass destruction] for the security of our nation and other Nations." And that the force authorized was not limited, "This resolution also authorizes the President to use all necessary means."[11]

McCain understood and made it clear that neither the president's new doctrine of war whenever he wanted nor the legislation required there be a threat of imminent attack: "Iraq today clearly does not meet the . . . standard of threatening imminent, sudden, and direct attack upon the United States [or] our Armed Forces"[12]

In the House, the Republican Chairman of the International Relations Committee, Rep. Henry Hyde of Illinois, explained the potential for unilateralism: "We have no choice but to act as a sovereign country prepared to defend ourselves with our friends and allies, if possible, but alone if necessary. There can be no safety if we condition our faith on the cooperation of others."[13]

While they saw things differently, but no less patriotically, various opponents to the president and his legislation read the text the same way. His description of the legislation as a "rag" may have been unkind, but Byrd also said less heatedly: "We are voting on this new Bush doctrine of preventive strikes—preemptive strikes. . . . This resolution, S. J. Res. 46, we are about to vote to put the imprimatur of the Congress on that doctrine. That is what the Bush administration wants us to do. They want Congress to put its stamp of approval on that Bush doctrine of preemptive strikes."[14]

Sen. Ted Kennedy (D-Mass.) made the same—and more—clear: "[We are] effectively yielding the decision-making power of making war or peace—effectively unilaterally turning that over just to the decision of the president of the United States. . . . The [legislation's] language says they can take unilateral action without a Security Council mandate to defend against a threat posed by Iraq. It talks about the test to defend against the continuing threat from Iraq."[15]

Understanding what was before them, some members sought to change the legislation. Levin, the Democratic chairman of the Armed Services Committee, offered an amendment to require that the president could use force only if the UN Security Council authorized it, or failing that, only after a subsequent vote of Congress.[16] Recognizing that the legislation permitted unilateral action without UN support, Levin and his amendment presented one of the central issues very clearly: "The issue that is in dispute is whether unilateral force should be authorized by Congress at this time . . . whether we should authorize the President now to go it alone."[17] His amendment failed to pass.

Opponents in the House also recognized the unhindered unilateralism that was before them, and they attempted to change it. Democratic Rep. John Spratt of North Carolina offered, and failed with, an amendment much like Levin's. Democratic Rep. Dennis Kucinich of Ohio attempted, and failed, to send the legislation back to the International Relations Committee with instructions to rewrite the bill to require reports from the president on the likely costs and consequences of going to war against Iraq with or without allied or UN support.[18]

In short, there were a number on both sides of the debate who read and understood that the legislation permitted unilateral, preemptive hostilities against Iraq, with or without an attack or even an imminent attack, at some unknown point in the future. Many were willing to grant the president authority to go to war, but only under very different circumstances: whenever the president chose under conditions he alone selected, or only under circumstances that had not yet been realized, such as UN support or a clearer understanding of other circumstances, such as cost.

Not All Senators Can Read

Others thought they had a better idea. There were a substantial number of members, in both the House and Senate, consisting of both Republicans and Democrats, who were squeamish about unilateral war without an attack or an imminent threat but were also skittish about permitting any political daylight between themselves and Bush on the war issue. Some members described this dilemma to the *Washington Post:* "More than a dozen Democrats, who requested anonymity, have told the *Post* that many members who oppose the president's strategy to confront Iraq are going to nonetheless support it because they fear a backlash from voters. A top party strategist said every House Democrat who faces a tough re-election this fall plans to vote for the Bush resolution."[19]

And from senior political commentator David Broder, again in the *Washington Post,* who found: "a squad of embattled incumbents who do not want to impair their re-election prospects by challenging the president on his strength as commander in chief. Senators such as Max Cleland in Georgia and Tim Johnson in South Dakota and challengers such as Erskine Bowles in North Carolina and Alex Sanders in South Carolina want no daylight between themselves and Bush on the Iraq issue."[20]

Said another way, such members of Congress believed it more important that they be elected, or re-elected, than the United States avert a war they did not support. The lives of the American soldiers and Iraqi civilians who would die were less valuable, in these people's minds, than their re-elections.

These politicians handled the "dilemma" in which they felt themselves by voting in favor of the legislation, but by explaining their vote with words describing legislation that did not exist. They said they were voting only for acting through the United Nations and with allies, and that hostilities must be an act of last resort. They further said the legislation and their vote were in opposition to the doctrine of preemption, unilateralism, or unlimited presidential power. So blatant was the contradiction between these descriptions of the legislation and the actual text of the legislation that one Republican admonished his fellow senators that they needed to read the bill. Sen. Don Nickles of Oklahoma said: "I heard some people debating this resolution as if they had not read it. . . . I encourage my colleagues to read the resolution."[21]

The *Congressional Record* shows who these people are; they included Democrats, especially very senior ones and some harboring presidential ambitions, and also a few Republicans. Their prepared speeches demonstrated a chasm between the text of the legislation they voted for and what they said they were voting for. For example, perennial presidential hopeful and the Democratic leader in the House, Richard Gephardt of Missouri, explained his vote in favor of the bill.

> Exhausting all efforts at the U.N. is essential. . . . We must do everything we can to get the U.N. to succeed. . . . Completely bypassing the U.N. would set a dangerous precedent that would undoubtedly be used by other countries in the future to our and the world's detriment. It is too high a price to pay.[22]

Why then would he vote for, even be a coauthor of, legislation that invites the president to ignore the United Nations?

He also said, "This resolution also limits the scope and duration of the President's authority to use force."[23] It does not. It throws verbiage at these ideas by requiring reports and determinations by the president, but in the final analysis, the authorization to use force is unlimited in the nature of weapons the president can use, the length of time he may use them, and the reasons he is free to select for going to war. Gephardt also said: "In my view, [the legislation] is not an endorsement or an acceptance of the President's new policy of preemption. . . . But the acceptance of such a momentous change in policy must not be inferred from the language of this resolution."[24]

By permitting the use of preemptive war, as specifically defined by the doctrine, the legislation cannot be understood as anything but an approval of the doctrine. As one of the authors of the legislation, Gephardt had an opportunity to alter the text of the legislation with just a fig leaf to declare the precedent of this war not to constitute congressional approval of the doctrine, but he failed to do even that. It was simpler just to describe the resolution inaccurately.

Gephardt was hardly alone. One of the primary supporters of the legislation in the House was Rep. Tom Lantos (D-Calif.), who was also the top-ranking Democrat on the House International Relations Committee:

> It is not the application of the doctrine of preemption we are considering here. We are dedicating U.S. power and prestige to upholding, not challenging, international law. We are devoting our efforts to strengthening, not weakening, the international system. . . . Let us be clear. We seek to preserve peace, not to provoke war; we seek to maintain international order, not to disrupt it.[25]

A strange description, indeed, for a legislation that authorizes a president to ignore the United Nations; to go to war without a single ally's assistance; and to do so in the absence of an attack, even an imminent one, against the United States, its armed forces abroad, or even its allies or friends.

The gap between rhetoric and reality was at least as wide in the "world's greatest deliberative body." Presidential candidate John Kerry said:

> If we do wind up going to war with Iraq, it is imperative that we do so with others in the international community, unless there is a showing of a grave, imminent—and I emphasize "imminent"—threat to this country which requires the President to respond in a way that protects our immediate national security interests. . . . Let there be no doubt or confusion about where we stand on this. I will support a multilateral effort to disarm [Saddam Hussein] by force, if we ever exhaust those other options . . . but I will not support a unilateral U.S. war against Iraq unless that threat is imminent and the multilateral effort has not proven possible under any circumstances. . . .
>
> Nor is the grant of authority in this resolution an acknowledgement that Congress accepts or agrees with the President's new strategic doctrine of preemption. Just the opposite. This resolution clearly limits the authority given to the President to use force in Iraq, and Iraq only.[26]

One wonders if Kerry had read either the text of the legislation he was voting for or the White House's document proclaiming the preemption doctrine, especially how it defined "imminent." If Kerry had read these documents, one then wonders if, to him, words in print have any meaning other than what a U.S. senator wants to pretend they mean.

Daschle, Lieberman, and Sen. Hillary Clinton (D-N.Y.) all made the same kind of statement. According to Daschle: "The President's desire to wage war alone, without the support of our allies . . . was wrong. . . . I now commend the administration for changing its approach and acknowledging the importance of working with our allies."[27]

Of course, the legislation he was voting for permitted the president "to wage war alone." Daschle went on to argue for cooperation with the United Nations, and with allies, and to use force only as a last resort, all things the legislation rendered null and void as preconditions for war. He then concluded: "If the administration attempts to use the authority in this resolution without doing the work that is required before and after military action in Iraq, the situation there and elsewhere can indeed get worse. We could see more turmoil in the Persian Gulf, not less. We could see more bloodshed in the Middle East, not less. Americans could find themselves more vulnerable to terrorist attacks, not less."[28]

If one wants to require a president to do "the work before and after military action" to make a possible war palatable, why would one support legislation that requires no such thing?

Lieberman wrote in a commentary for the *Wall Street Journal*: "Our resolution does not give the president a blank check. It authorizes the use of U.S. military power only to 'defend the national security of the United States against the continuing threat posed by Iraq' and to 'enforce all relevant United Nations Security Council Resolutions regarding Iraq.'"[29]

According to this logic, a blank check is not a blank check. He continued in this make-believe vein in the Senate chamber:

> . . . the United States will not go it alone. . . .
>
> If we come to that moment where we have no other choice but war, then it is clear that we will have allies in good number at our side. That was one of the items we added to the resolution. . . .
>
> This is limited to the duration of authority necessary to address the current and ongoing threats posed by Iraq.[30]

Lieberman was one of the authors of the resolution; he went to the White House to stand in front of the cameras with the president to endorse it. One wonders if he can read and understand legislation or whether he was simply dissembling.

Senator Clinton had the wishful thinking disease worse than most others:

> Today, Mr. President, we are asked whether to give the President of the United States authority to use force in Iraq should diplomatic efforts fail to dismantle Saddam Hussein's chemical and biological weapons and his nuclear program. . . .
>
> Some people favor attacking Saddam Hussein now, with any allies we can muster. . . . However, this course is fraught with danger. . . . If we were to attack Iraq now, alone or with few allies, it would set a precedent that could come back to haunt us. . . . a unilateral attack . . . is not a good option. . . .
>
> I believe the best course is to go to the United Nations for a strong resolution. . . .
>
> I believe international support and legitimacy are crucial. . . .
>
> My vote is not, however, a vote for any new doctrine of preemption or for unilateralism or for the arrogance of American power or purpose, all of which carry grave dangers for our Nation, the rule of international law, and the peace and security of people throughout the world. . . .
>
> So it is with conviction that I support this resolution as being in the best interests of our Nation. A vote for it is not a vote to rush to war.[31]

It is hard to imagine a more perfect contradiction between the text and meaning of the legislation and what Clinton said she was voting for and why.

There were other Democrats pretending the legislation did not say what it said, including Max Cleland of Georgia,[32] Ben Nelson of Nebraska,[33] Evan Bayh of Indiana,[34] Bill Nelson of Florida,[35] and Christopher Dodd of Connecticut.[36] There were also some Republicans, including Voinovich of Ohio and Chuck Hagel of Nebraska, who said: "A regional and international coalition is essential. . . . America must understand it cannot alone win a war against terrorism. It will require allies, friends, and partners. . . . If we do it right and lead through the U.N., in concert with our allies, we can set a new standard for American leadership and international cooperation."[37]

He Who Hesitates and Then Gets Lost

In reviewing the House and Senate "debates," I found only one member who seemed genuinely undecided about how he was going to vote. This was the Democratic chairman of the Senate Foreign Relations Committee, Joe Biden of Delaware. In his initial statements, he described the issues aptly:

> The President said he has not decided whether or not we are going to go to war. He said it is his hope that we not go to war. It is his hope it can be avoided. Yet, for the first time in the history of the United States of America, the President of the United States is asking for the Congress to give him the equivalent of a declaration of war—to go to war—before the President has made up his mind.[38]

He also clearly understood the new preemption doctrine:

> The President always has the right to act preemptively if we are in imminent danger. If they are coming up over the hill, he can respond; . . . if missiles are on their way, we can respond. But that is not the way I hear it being used here. We are talking about preemption [without an actual imminent attack], as if we are adopting a policy. As [former Secretary of State] Dr. [Henry] Kissinger said before our committee, that will undo an agreement the Western World made in the early 1640s at the end of the religious wars in Europe, which said no country has a right to preemptively move against another country because they think they are going to be bad guys.[39]

In addition, Biden later expressed his concern that legislation that, in effect, permitted the use of the preemption doctrine was, in fact, an endorsement of that doctrine:

I find myself supporting this resolution but worried that supporting this resolution will get us into real trouble. . . .

I hope we don't walk out of here . . . and somebody 6 months from now or 6 years from now will say we have the right now to establish this new doctrine of preemption and go wherever we want anytime.[40]

Biden, as chairman of the Foreign Relations Committee, was in a position to lead a serious effort to amend the resolution to bring it into conformance with his, and others', views on acquiring UN support before the United States goes to war. He ultimately decided to do nothing. Biden simply switched to describing the unaltered legislation in ways very different from what he had been saying. Among the last flurry of prepared speeches on the last day of the "debate," he said: "This is not a blank check for the use of force against Iraq for any reason. It is an authorization for the use of force, if necessary, to compel Iraq to disarm, as it promised after the Gulf War."[41]

Incorrect: the resolution authorized the use of force against "the continuing threat posed by Iraq" as determined by the president. Saddam Hussein's alleged weapons of mass destruction were one of those "continuing" threats, but there were others as expressed in fifteen different UN resolutions, none of which the president had to invoke under the text of the legislation Biden was now endorsing. Indeed, the force was authorized against any threat from Iraq the president deemed to exist, real or unreal. Therefore, if Biden were to say to Bush, as Lincoln prophesied in 1848, "I see no probability of [Saddam attacking] us," Bush would be fully within his rights under the text of the legislation to say, "Be silent; I see it, if you don't."

On 10 October the Senate voted 77–23 to go to war against Iraq without changing even a single word of the legislation.

Probing for the Bottom of the Gutter

Some Republican candidates for the Senate in the elections occurring shortly after 10 October apparently felt compelled to outdo the contorted behavior of the prominent Democrats.

As we know, some Democrats felt they would be vulnerable if they voted their beliefs and opposed the war. Those who voted against their own thinking probably thought they had escaped cheap, war-related political shots from Republicans. They were wrong. Some Republicans could not deny themselves the opportunity to engage in true gutter politics, even after the target Democrats had cast their vote in favor of the president's war. In what became a nationally reviled example, the Republican candidate for the Senate in Georgia, Rep. Saxby Chambliss, ran a television ad picturing Osama bin Laden while the narrator talked about the Democratic candidate, incumbent Max Cleland. Cleland voted for the war legislation, but he also opposed Bush's position on federal personnel policies in a homeland security bill. Chambliss equated Cleland's support for federal hiring and firing rules in the new Homeland Security Agency to be equivalent to aiding Osama bin Laden. Having worked under these employment rules in the GAO for nine years, I can say they do, indeed, favor sloth and bureaucratic clog, but to equate them to the wanton slaughter of innocents is the lowest form of belly crawling I have seen in three decades of work for politicians. Just to make Chambliss's slander even more revolting, it should be noted that Cleland was a veteran of the Vietnam War, who lost both legs and an arm in the war.

In an ad campaign that did not attract, but should have attracted, the same level of national disgust, Republican candidate John Thune in South Dakota tried much the same thing by linking his Democratic opponent, Tim Johnson, to Saddam Hussein because Johnson voted against Bush's budget request for missile defense.

The voters in Georgia rewarded the proponent of these vile tactics with an electoral victory. In South Dakota, guttersnipe Thune narrowly lost. One wonders how much lower the Republican candidates would have been willing to go if the Democratic candidates who ducked had voted their conscience on the war. It is entirely possible that the Republicans had already hit the bottom of the gutter, and had the targets of these attacks stood up, steadfast in their convictions, they might have done better.

Of course, it was not just the Republicans who used revolting tactics on the question of war and security. In South Carolina, Democrat Alex Sanders slandered his Republican opponent, Lindsey Graham, for voting against the death penalty for terrorists, even though Sanders himself was an opponent of the death penalty. On 9 October, during the House consideration of the Iraq legislation, Democratic Rep. Pete Stark of California went beyond disagreeing with Bush and criticizing his policies and engaged in a crude ad hominem attack. "Rich kids will not pay [for the war against Iraq]; their daddies will get them deferments as Big George did for George W."[42] This and other personal slurs earned Stark a reprimand from the presiding (temporary) speaker of the House, which—while not unheard of—is rare.[43]

In Congress, and elections for Congress, appalling behavior is a bipartisan exercise.

Some Pearls among Swine

Beyond the bright spot of the real and respectful debate between Senators Warner and Byrd on Friday, 4 October, there were some Democrats and Republicans in the House and Senate who rose above crass self-interest and voted against what conventional wisdom held was the smart thing to support . Democratic Sens. Richard Durbin of Illinois, Carl Levin of Michigan, Jack Reed of Rhode Island, and Paul Wellstone of Minnesota were all up for re-election and, therefore, were potential targets for Saxby Chambliss–style attacks. These senators nonetheless voted against final passage of the Iraq legislation. Wellstone was particularly notable in this group. Durbin, Levin, and Reed were not facing serious challenges in their re-election bids; they had politically competent Republican opponents running against them, but polling in October made it clear their opposition was getting no traction with the electorate.[44] Wellstone was running behind his opponent and was clearly vulnerable. He probably expected his opponent to exploit, one way or another, his voting against the legislation, but he had nonetheless done so. Wellstone and members of his family were killed in an airplane crash shortly after the Iraq vote when he returned to Minnesota to campaign. Wellstone courageously stood alone as one who held on to and voted for his convictions on the Iraq legislation, even when he probably knew it would hurt him politically.

Also notable was Republican Sen. Lincoln Chafee of Rhode Island. He was not up for re-election, but as the only Republican voting against the legislation in the Senate, he was not winning any new friends in the White House or among the Republican congressional leadership. The same is true of Republican Reps. Connie Morella and Jim Leech, and a very few others, in the House. Morella and Leech's cases were especially notable because they were in close races in the elections.[*] Their districts were both politically liberal, and some might argue that their political advantage was to vote as they did. That may or may not be the case; however, on a question as important to Bush as war with Iraq, it took some real guts to vote against a president in one's own party on an issue so important to him.

These Democrats and Republicans are worth remembering; they should win awards as "Pearls among Swine" for 2002.

Time and again I have heard senators and their staff tell visitors to the Capitol building that the U.S. Senate is "the world's greatest deliberative body." It is clearly a title that fits the senators own image of themselves.

---

[*] To his credit, Morella's Democratic opponent, Maryland State Sen. Chris Van Holland, did not attempt to exploit her vote on the war.

The reality is different. The moniker is a figment of their egos, not an accurate description of what occurs these days in the Senate chamber.

In arguing for the War Powers Act, Javits constantly said the bill would not guarantee that Congress would act wisely, just that it gave the members a mechanism to exercise their constitutional responsibilities. When Congress acted on the Iraq legislation, it was only going through the motions of the decision-making framework the War Powers Act established; the legislation and behavior of too many members was utterly devoid of the spirit behind the Constitution and the War Powers Act.

One is tempted to recoil from today's Congress and think the advocates of the presidency are right that the power to decide war should be seated with the president. However, Bush's exploitation of the issue of war for political purposes in October 2002 amply demonstrates that the executive is just as capable as the Saxby Chamblisses in Congress to use an issue as terrible as war for selfish political advantage. The framers of the Constitution were right to deny the presidency the war power.

One is also tempted to declare a pox on all their houses and to judge the House, the Senate, and the presidency all unfit for treating serious questions in a serious manner. However, even if the U.S. constitutional system failed to produce an unpolitical result on the question of war with Iraq in October 2002, the failure was much more one of human nature than of the Constitution.

There is reason for some hope based on the performance of the few members in today's Congress and from the more numerous of the past. Perhaps, the trick to rid us of the Chamblisses of the political world is to figure out a way for the Javitses and the other worthies to predominate. There is no way to guarantee that result, but there are some things to do to make it more possible.

Conclusion: Twelve Not-So-Easy Steps to a Sober Congress

A nd so it goes. Today's members of Congress work tirelessly, like unrepentant drunks, at their own bad behavior. The last appropriations bills for fiscal year 2004, including an $87 billion supplemental for occupation and reconstruction in Iraq and Afghanistan and a gigantic omnibus bill to fund several civilian agencies, were festooned yet again with pork. And, Senator McCain again delivered eloquent lectures to his colleagues and did nothing. The House and Senate were working hard to match their record-breaking $8.5 billion pork bill in the defense budget the previous year.

At the Defense Department, senior civilians and military officers still fail to present the public with complete and accurate descriptions of the cost of systems and the size of budgets. When Congress stuffs bills with junk, the Pentagon's leaders continue to remain silent and condone the transfer of billions of dollars from military readiness to pork.

Thanks to some very competent oversight work by Senator McCain and his staff—at the Senate Commerce Committee, not the Armed Services Committee—the Boeing air refueling tanker deal began to stink badly enough for many in the press, Congress, and even the Pentagon to notice. By extracting incriminating e-mails out of Boeing, McCain established the basis for a criminal investigation of wrongdoing by a former Air Force official hired by Boeing after she allegedly shared with the company proprietary cost data from a possible competitor (Airbus). An April 2004 DoD Inspector General report found that with its leasing proposal, the Air Force had relied on "an inappropriate procurement strategy" costing additional billions and that, overall, the deal should be delayed until multiple problems were resolved.[1] A May 2004 study by the Defense Science Board put the final nail in the coffin by finding no urgent need for the new tankers and a real requirement for the analysis of alternative possibilities—the very study cancelled by the Air Force in 2002. Secretary of Defense Rumsfeld capitulated to all the studies and the adverse politics by announcing in May that he was deferring any decision until that restarted study was available.

Sadly, however, Senator McCain continued his practice of talking more strongly than he acted. He endorsed, even coauthored, a deal for Boeing in late 2003 and early 2004 wherein the company would still build the tankers; the only change being that the first twenty would be leased and the next eighty purchased incrementally. While proclaiming that this deal would save billions compared to the original deal Senator Stevens shoved past him in December 2001, McCain did not divulge two elements of his "solution" that made it almost as bad an idea as the first Stevens plan.

First, as assessed by the CBO, the new deal was written as an entitlement program, meaning that unspecified funding was heretofore authorized for any Boeing tanker configuration the Air Force and Boeing decided on. Under the terms of the legislation, any and every bell, whistle, and bauble the Air Force and Boeing decided they wanted to add could be added to the tankers, and given that no exact dollar amount was legislated, the price could soar to any new Olympian height the advocates decided.[2] This was an open door to abuse hardly justified by the behavior demonstrated by Boeing and the Air Force on the matter, and it was an element the press consistently failed to reveal, despite several explanations of it to journalists by not just this author but also the CBO and congressional budget committee staff.

Second, the new deal permitted the Air Force to pay for the second batch of eighty tankers incrementally rather than in the up-front "full funding" mode that had been the practice in DoD acquisitions for several decades. It is a seemingly minor point, but piles of GAO, CRS, CBO, and other reports over those same decades had proven amply that by failing to establish a total cost baseline, incremental funding proved itself to be another open door to procurement abuse and a methodology that made Congress's already feeble oversight even more difficult.

When Secretary Rumsfeld announced his deferral of a decision on the tankers, the House Armed Services Committee wrote legislation sent to the Senate that insisted the deal go through. At the time of this writing, there was no indication from Senator McCain of what, if anything, he would do to spike the House intent to proceed. Yet again, after divulging and saying all of the right things about others' poor behavior, Senator McCain failed to elevate his own behavior to the level of his own rhetoric. It was the same story of his failing to achieve his own considerable potential by talking tough, but failing to act in a manner consistent with his self-expressed standards.

The biggest indicator of the corrosion of American security occurs where some might think the apparatus to have worked rather well—in the fighting with Iraq. It is a subject fully worthy of its own extended analysis, but consider the following: The lopsided victories of U.S. armed forces against Iraq in 1991 and 2003 were against an opponent that, with only a few exceptions, behaved in combat like a tethered goat led by a military jackass.* Once ground operations began in Operation Desert Storm in 1991, "The few Iraqi units that tried to fight proved themselves so ill-trained as to be almost helpless."[3] Referring to the Iraqi armed forces in the second war in 2003, some authorities asserted them to be the worst in the world.[4] A draft of the U.S. Army's own study of Operation Iraqi Freedom found Iraqi incompetence to be the critical element in the victory.[5]

And yet, the remnants of these same incompetent forces posed problems the U.S. military services and political leadership were unable to solve in 2004. After Saddam Hussein's armies melted away during Operation Iraqi Freedom, a second phase of guerrilla operations began. It was inspired mostly by the ham-handed, culturally insulting manner in which the Washington leadership insisted that the American-led occupation be conducted. Accordingly, the overdue capture of Saddam Hussein in December 2003 changed virtually nothing; daily U.S. fatalities continued, sometimes increasing dramatically, as they did in April and May 2004.[6] By mid-2004 the anti-U.S. violence in Iraq remained high.

There also erupted a national dishonor: the scandal of the American treatment of Iraqi detainees in Abu Ghraib prison and elsewhere in Iraq. As this book went to print, the civilian leadership of the Pentagon, the Army, and the Senate Armed Services Committee held inquiries in the attempt to limit the scope of wrongdoing to enlisted personnel. Meanwhile, some in the press uncovered evidence to make it clear there was much to the scandals the American public and the world were yet to learn about. Others were merely conducting a whitewash. The absence of competent oversight by the Senate Armed Services Committee was outdone only by the refusal of the House Armed Services Committee to conduct any inquiry at all. Whitewashing and refusing to bother even with that, it was the wastrels of defense at their worst.

The Ghost Senator and the Unthinking President

Meanwhile, the Democratic Party selected a nominee for the presidency I can only characterize as a "ghost senator."

When walking through the Capitol Hill complex on a normal workday, I would frequently stumble upon senators performing their own daily tasks.

---

* The term "tethered goat" was coined by the commander of allied air forces in Operation Desert Storm in 1991. U.S. Air Force Gen. Charles Horner was referring to the ease with which the allied air component overcame Iraq's air defenses and was able to find and attack targets on the billiard-table-like terrain of the theater. Longtime military analyst of the Middle East, Anthony Cordesman, at the Center for Strategic and International Studies, termed Saddam Hussein a "military jackass" for the quality of his control of Iraqi military operations in Operation Iraqi Freedom in 2003.

I would see them on the elevators, on the trolley that connects the Senate office buildings with the Capitol, and, of course, on the Senate floor, especially during votes. It was always considered out of place for staff to address any senator that was not one's own boss, even a friendly, but respectful, "How are you, senator?" But in these silent encounters, I would usually register a personal recognition of the member I had come upon. Some of these members commanded from me some respect because they were major actors on the national security issues I followed. For example, even if he only rarely translated his knowledge and prestige into meaningful legislative action, Sen. Sam Nunn (D-Ga.) was one whom I could instantly associate with something that stuck with me as significant. Similarly, while I was no fan of his politics, Sen. Jesse Helms (R-N.C.) was one for whom I felt a begrudging respect as a Washington "heavy."

But then, there was also another type of senator I would run across in the elevator or see in the chamber—the ones I could never associate with any deed or even articulated thought that had any lasting effect. The thought would dash through my head, "Oh, yeah, he's a senator too; forgot that he was even still around here." John Kerry was such a senator. He was duly elected to a full term (actually, in his case, several), and he was even a long-term member of the Foreign Relations Committee, thereby affording himself the opportunity to be a player on national security issues. He had all the physical trappings of a senator: the mane of graying hair, the deep, rich voice, the intent stare, and the appropriate physical posture. But, Kerry never seemed to make any difference. It was almost as if he was both a member of the Senate and yet not a member, at least not one that mattered. He was a "ghost senator"; he had all the form, but none of the substance.

As such, Kerry seemed a nearly perfect foil for his Republican opponent. Inarticulate without a script and one who once boasted, "I don't do nuance," President Bush presents a stark contrast to the more elegant, articulate, complicated Kerry. All too clearly, the president is not someone who permits himself to get lost in thought too often. More palpably a man of action, Bush has had a real impact. The problem to this writer's way of thinking, however, is that those actions have created a huge mess: a deficit even deeper than the pit Ronald Reagan dug for the nation and a conflict in Iraq that is isolating us from our natural allies, strengthening the resolve of our enemies, and leaving Americans divided and wondering how to bring it to an end.

It is not a pretty choice for Americans to make in the voting booth, but it is the inevitable result of the political behavior we, as citizens, have permitted to flourish. One can hope for new politicians with a determination to end business as usual. However, there seems no such individual or group on the horizon. Given the way America currently conducts its political business, there seems little prospect either party will produce a leader willing to challenge the status quo with anything beyond rhetorical bromides.

Solutions are not likely to be easy or quick in coming. In the absence of dramatic new alternatives, we will have to find a way to work with what we have.

Solutions?

The unhappy performance of Congress notwithstanding, it is important to appreciate that there exist members who demonstrate occasional spasms of character. It is they who offer a glimpse of hope. For example, between his hunts for more pork for New Mexico, Senator Domenici has risen to laudable heights by resisting gigantic spending for unevaluated and indiscriminate benefits to military retirees. Similarly, Senator Byrd, who has never been shy to shove all manner of pork into West Virginia, rose to statesman stature when he interposed himself between a presidential war and a herd of senators rushing headlong into it. While this work reserves its greatest contempt for those who pose as Horatius at the bridge, "busting pork," while simultaneously pointing out the ford downstream for the plundering members, even Senator McCain has shown real merit by tabulating the pork Congress shovels into defense bills and by having the wit to appreciate the wrongness of others' actions.

These senators and others are not purebred "wastrels" but mixed breeds. Even among the worst on Capitol Hill, surely there are many who do not kick their dogs every single day.

It is to the higher, better side of the mixed breeds that the nation should turn for change. Perhaps there will be one who selfishly realizes that there is great political self-benefit in real reform. Perhaps there will be one with a sincere aspiration to lead the Congress back toward its constitutional responsibilities. In either case there is a void in Congress waiting to be filled with better, if not perfect, leaders.

As with recovering alcoholics, reform does not require replacing the sitting members; instead, it can be accomplished by changing how the current ones think and act. Redemption requires many difficult changes, none of them easy or guaranteed to work, either alone or even altogether. But, if change does start in Congress, if the central organism of the American constitutional system of democracy rises to its responsibilities, others in government will have no choice but to take notice. If Congress makes itself accountable, the rest will find accountability imposed on them.

Thus, a series of recommendations are set forth below. They are loosely based on the "Twelve Steps" to a sober life posited by Alcoholics Anonymous. They are what the author believes is an appropriate framework for congressional reform. Today's politicians, their staff, journalists, and observers of Congress may want to contemplate the following ideas for change.

Twelve-Step Program for Recovering Wastrels

Step One: Decision. Alcoholics Anonymous says the first step to a sober life is to admit that life as it is has become unmanageable.[7] In politics, public self-actualization starts with a speech: dissecting the problem and its consequences with all the elegance hundreds of speechwriters in Washington know how to convey, once instructed to do so.

Announcing how terrible the problem has become is the easy part. The hard part is living a political life consistent with a set of principles a true reformer has set out for himself or herself and that are going to be applied to the rest of Congress if it is willing, or despite their howls of protest.

Step Two: Action, Not Just Words. The leader of reform and his or her cohorts—if any— must be prepared to be utterly alone, but also unafraid.

Because of the Senate's unique parliamentary rules, it is the easier place to start. The emerging leader of reform can be young, old, new, senior, Democrat, Republican, liberal, conservative, moderate, or Buddhist. The only real requirement is that he or she be fully willing to employ the tools already at hand.

The first step is the simple act of publicly pointing out the games other members play every single time they occur; Senator McCain does this rather effectively today. The second step is for the leader of reform to refuse to play the games, again much as Senator McCain does. The third is to force malefactors to live by their own rules, which Senator McCain and all others in Congress consistently refuse to do. Budgetary and procedural rules in the Senate, less so in the House, provide a rich menu for any member to make business as usual an exercise in parliamentary agony.

Here are just a few ways to do it.

Huge new entitlement programs that have not been assessed in honest hearings with their costs and consequences fully exposed by competent analysis are sometimes vulnerable to Budget Act points of order requiring the advocates to summon three-fifths of the Senate (sixty votes) to overcome. Even in the many cases where the objecting senator cannot summon even the forty-one votes needed to prevail, just raising the objections achieves two important goals: what the members are doing is exposed (spending untold billions without bothering to understand the consequences) for the press—if awake—to notice, and the opportunity is presented for more than just a little discussion of the matter.

Budget Act points of order are "debatable motions." Even without the votes to win, a budget-conscious member can make his or her colleagues work for their pandering. The objecting member may lose, on a motion to impose cloture or on a point of order, but the public will be made aware of what is going on, and the rest of the Senate might come to learn that the next time some member seeks to pour billions of dollars into the yawning gullet of a selected constituency, it will take a little more time and a little more energy than it does now.

Of course, one does not need a Budget Act point of order to hold up the Senate with a filibuster. Almost every time someone is talking about something in the Senate, a member can start an "extended discussion" and persist until sixty senators counteract with cloture (it will take a few days) or the dilatory member gets some sort of accommodation, such as taking some of the worst of the pork out of the bill at hand. On 9 December 1998, Senator McCain, and two other senators joining with him, wrote to Senator Stevens threatening to "employ all legislative tactics at our disposal, consistent with the rules of the Senate" (that's parliamentary lingo for a filibuster) whenever a new defense spending bill came to the Senate loaded with pork.[8] Since the date of that letter, Senator McCain has counted at his own Web site more than $35 billion in pork in defense appropriations and authorizations bills, but he has yet to carry out his very appropriate threat. It is time for him to do so. If he cannot, someone else should do it for him, and perhaps McCain will come along later.

Only the ignorant and unimaginative in the Senate think a filibuster is the only way to slow things down until a problematic member gets an accommodation. A single member can force the Senate to listen to a clerk read every word of a bill (the porkiest ones are hundreds of pages long) simply by objecting that the reading be dispensed with. In the ill-attended Senate chamber, a single member can insist on quorum calls, sometimes taking hours, until enough senators are in the room to constitute a quorum. There are the Senate's own parliamentary rules to be enforced (such as against "immaculate conceptions"). A single member can raise an objection to conferees being appointed to meet with House members to resolve differences in a bill and permit it to move forward.

The list goes on and on. One does not even have to be a parliamentary expert to exploit the rules; both the Republican and Democratic parliamentary staffs on the floor of the Senate know all the pitfalls a member can heave the Senate into. If these staffers' bosses instruct them not to cooperate, the Senate's parliamentarian is available, and if he or she is forced by the majority leader to make himself or herself unhelpful, there are former parliamentarians all over Washington, D.C., who know the ropes and who can help, with or without a fee.

The problem is not lack of opportunity, it is lack of will.

Step Three: Steeling Resolve. Setting new standards will not be fun. In both the House and Senate, there are many ways to isolate, punish, and ridicule members who do not go along with the crowd.

The member who seeks to change business as usual would need to value his or her goals above their personal career and be prepared to endure hard fights, frequent defeats, and the disapprobation of many. Members can become irate when they are blocked from unraveling American defenses with pork, passing bills written without decent oversight, or rushing into ill-justified wars. Things can get a little nasty, and they can get even worse behind closed doors. Hot-tempered members like Senator Stevens will come to the chamber and yell. In private, he will make threats: for example, to de-pork appropriations bills of "member items" for the state of the problem senator. If the miscreant senator holds a committee or subcommittee chairmanship, that will be threatened. If he or she does not have a chairmanship (or even if they do), party contributions for the next campaign will be threatened. Perhaps, most telling of all, in the club atmosphere of the House and Senate and its party caucuses, the problem member will be shunned: a minor-sounding problem perhaps, but in politics where groups are key elements of survival and success, it is important.

The problem member will at some point come to a crisis whereupon he or she will either rejoin the fold or press on, perhaps utterly alone, demanding a change in the culture. Members contemplating becoming a genuine reformer should check their own gut before setting forth on this program. In the initial stages there may be lots of press kudos, but as the campaign wears on, the loneliness and the pressures can take their toll. This is not a program for the faint of heart or the opportunistic; those types will crumble and fail and make the effort even harder for a real reformer, if ever one emerges.

But in Washington, where ethics are relative, a point of comparison at a new, higher level, even when set by a single lonely—but genuine—member, can be a powerful device to alter the behavior of others. In the fishbowl environment of Congress, no one wants to compare poorly to a new and higher standard.

It is a simple proposition, but sometimes the simplest things are the hardest to do.

Step Four: End Documentary Lying. Steps one, two, and three are the hard part; the rest is easier.

It would be a nice rhetorical flourish to demand an end to lying in politics, but enforcement would just not be workable, and it could be an open door to far worse. It should not be too much, however, to require that Congress present itself to the public as it is, rather than covered by several layers of deception.

First, the *Congressional Record,* the official transcript of the proceedings of the House and Senate, should be an accurate record of what actually happens in the House and Senate chambers. Today, it is no such thing. Members and their staff alter the transcript every hour of every day. An accurate transcript would mean the prohibition of the practice—now widespread—of inserting written, undelivered speeches into the record of proceedings "as if read." It takes only a single member to object any time another asks "unanimous consent" to do so. With things that were never actually said a part of the official transcript, members can, and have, made statements others would sharply object to, and the legislative history of a bill passed by the body can be altered, and has been, without any other member having the opportunity to correct the misleading insertion. Furthermore, in both houses, members and staff should be denied access and the ability to make any changes to the transcript before it is printed; today, staff can be found in a basement office of the Capitol busily altering even the words that were spoken.

For historians and for lawyers trying to understand Congress and interpret its intent in legislation, and for any press who bother to read the *Record,* the official transcript of proceedings should be what was actually said, not what members and staff permit to be shown. The same should be required for the transcripts of committee hearings and any other official business of Congress where a transcript is made.

Step Five: Reality TV on Capitol Hill. The television cameras in the House and Senate chambers present an interesting problem. Many who remember real debates, especially in the Senate, before the cameras were permitted, blame their presence as irresistible motivation to members to pander more aggressively to constituencies with highly scripted speeches, to posture incessantly with much form and little substance, and to use simplistic and hopelessly biased "show and tell" posters to pretend substantiation on the television screen.

The cameras may be the source of these ills, but they also give the voters a live, real-time picture of what is occurring in the national legislature. In a functional democracy that is invaluable; it is for the better that the cameras are there to stay.

Instead, the cameras should be permitted to present an accurate picture of what is and is not going on in the House and Senate chambers. For, in truth, the members have found a way to distort real-time transmission. Current House and Senate practices require the camera to be up tight on whoever is speaking.* The televised images show nothing of the almost-empty chambers during all but the rarest sessions. And, even in those instances where there are more than half a dozen members in the House or Senate chambers, the cameras are prohibited to show the uninterested members, the ones chatting among themselves, not listening, or staring at the ceiling impatiently waiting for their turn to read off a staff-written speech—or insert it in the record as if read.

The public would achieve a far more useful understanding of what is and is not occurring in the House and Senate chambers if the cameras were controlled consistent with professional newscasting precepts. That is, if a control room were permitted to direct the cameras to the empty desks, the snoozing octogenarians, the non-listening chatterers, and all the rest in the chambers, the public would be able to see its legislature as it is.† The behavior might improve. Members would be distressed at images of themselves shown talking to empty chairs, blank faces, and members' backs. If left unable to alter their appearances, they would surely seek a solution to the unhappy self-image making; some might lock on to the actual debate of legislation. They used to do it; they need a little encouragement.

There would be a very serious issue of who would control the cameras. There would be great influence in showing members of just one party or faction snoozing, perpetually absent, or behaving poorly.

Today's Senate and House television cameras are small, unobtrusive, and remotely controlled. Management of them could be distributed to existing networks, selected by party leaders, for airing to networks and the existing C-SPAN system. Or, the camera feed to C-SPAN could be on a rotating basis. Or, if party leaders can find one entity both sides could trust (at least for the duration of a specific contract); they could jointly appoint a single electronic journalist to control the cameras. During national telecasts of the president giving his State of the Union message in the House chamber, the cameras frequently wander from the podium to show members approving or disapproving what is said, reading papers, and checking

---

* During roll call votes and quorum calls, when no one is speaking, the cameras are allowed to step back and show the wells of the chambers where members mill around and talk with each other during votes.

† Today, the public can see all this, but only from the gallery above the chamber. The proposed change would only broaden the audience.

their watches. It is only a short step from this level of camera digression to a format accurately portraying regular House and Senate sessions.

The members will not like it, but the public will.

Step Six: A Professional Staff. Members of Congress need to be confronted with better information and analysis for the national security decisions they contemplate in legislation. The availability of objective, reliable, accurate data and analysis to inform members will not guarantee better decisions in Congress, but it will enable decisions with members' eyes open to the costs and the consequences. That is usually not the case today.

There is no such thing as a Republican F-16 or a Democratic aircraft carrier. Then, why do the Armed Services Committees and the Defense Appropriations Subcommittees hire separate Democratic and Republican staffs? It is to interject partisanship into national security issues, especially at the base information level. There is only one set of reliable and valid data on the performance and cost of fighter aircraft, ships, and armored vehicles. The information should not come in Democratic or Republican slants to members.

All too often, the politicized staffs on Congress's national security committees are too preoccupied with seizing a political advantage, or they are professionally ill-equipped to find and assess reliable data, or they are both. In other cases, they are too busy chasing down members' pork requests. Sometimes, the staff are too anxious to secure a major job with the Pentagon or in the industry to perform unbiased oversight. The reasons are many; the effect is all the same: there is no competent oversight on national security issues on Capitol Hill. A major reason is the poor quality or absence of oversight work by the staff.

Congress needs a truly professional staff for its national security committees. Such a staff would have the following characteristics:

- The individuals would have demonstrated competence not just in the subject area assigned to them, but also formal training or experience in evaluative techniques, such as auditing or program evaluation. All too often, I have seen staffers who have large amounts of the wrong expertise. Members of Congress frequently hire ex-service pilots as aviation "experts," but while such individuals may have the considerable brains and skill to fly modern fighter aircraft or transports, they have no knowledge or experience in how to buy or evaluate them.*
- The professional staff would work for members on both sides of the aisle. They would be hired and fired only by a joint decision of both the senior Democrat and Republican on the committee itself.

They would also be afforded the aggressive whistle-blower protection they are now specifically denied.

- The staff's memoranda on oversight issues would be public documents, when they are not by necessity classified, and in all cases their memoranda should be distributed to all members in the House and Senate. It can be amazing how exposure to readers on more than one side of an issue and to the public can make a staffer think longer, harder, and better before he or she communicates with a member of Congress. Moreover, all members of Congress, not just those on the Armed Services Committees, would benefit greatly by objective, professional analysis of Pentagon issues from the staff of the defense committees appointed to serve Congress.

Today, the Armed Services and Appropriations Committees do make public their recommendations in the form of committee reports on legislation. As analysis of the issues, these are pitiful documents. When there is any analysis, it is one-sided. For many issues, the reports are mute for the simple reason the members want to keep the public and other senators in the dark. Most of the pages in Appropriations Committee reports are taken up with tabular listings of pork the committee is instructing the Defense Department to buy.

A truly professional staff would feel itself insulted by such a public work product.

Step Seven: Spike the Revolving Door on Capitol Hill. The biggest revolving door problem on Capitol Hill is not the members; it is the staff.

Being politicians, members of Congress will often allow unrelated or inappropriate considerations to influence their vote on an issue. One of those can be, has been, and will always be, How might my vote influence my career, including after I leave Congress? That is the nature of politics. For any member who sells his or her vote for a job with Boeing or Lockheed, good riddance. The Congress will be better off without them, and the company foolish enough to hire them is wasting valuable office space.

For professional staff, it is a very different question. The job of professional staffers is to provide information and advice to members to help them make a decision. Human nature is all too frail to permit Boeing, Lockheed, or any large or small defense manufacturer to dangle the prospect of future

---

*. Many of them are also very biased in favor of the military services from which they stem and find it difficult to believe their parent service could choose poorly. In this regard, it is notable that the most successful aircraft in the Air Force and Navy inventories today (the F-15, F-16, F18, and A-10) were initially designed or selected over the strenuous opposition of those same services and many in the pilot communities among them.

employment before, during, or after a staffer provides his or her analysis of the pros and cons of candidates for a multibillion-dollar defense contract.

The prospect of employment with DoD is just as problematic. Presidents and their Pentagons are every bit as eager as the commercial manufacturers to influence data and advice in Congress. I have seen staffers conform their advice to what the military services or the Pentagon's civilian leadership want far more frequently than simply selling out for a fat job with a manufacturer. Moving on to a senior job in the Pentagon is high in the career ambitions of many Armed Services and Appropriations Committees' staffers, and some staffers behave accordingly.

To keep things simple, staffers should be prohibited to take any job with the Defense Department or any defense manufacturer for at least five years after they leave Capitol Hill. Period. No exceptions. For those who think that is unfair or it will inhibit their career, leave now and good riddance.

Some might worry that such a prohibition will prevent Congress from attracting "good" people. While I hardly think so, it should help to offer better pay. There is no reason, other than members' egos, not to offer many key national security staff jobs a salary up to and above the $150,000 a member of Congress currently draws. If members want good advice, they should be willing to pay for it.

Step Eight: Shrink the Personal Staffs. Committees constitute less than a fifth of the staff who work directly for members; the vast majority work on personal staffs of members. It is a vast horde, and it is remarkable how few qualifications some have for the lofty positions they hold. If there were a higher quality and less biased professional staff on committees with their data and analysis available to all members, there would be less need for the redundancy on personal staffs there is today, where every member has one or more staffers devoted to national security issues.

There is an important reason, beyond thrift, to reduce the size of members' personal staffs. With fewer eager-to-please staffers tugging at the member's pant leg or skirt with their latest idea to involve, and impress, the boss, members would have an opportunity to focus themselves on a smaller number of activities. For example, rather than having a bill or amendment on every hot political subject under the sun, with fewer personal staff, a member would have to focus limited resources on the issues he or she most wanted to be involved in. Nothing would guarantee that the member would choose wisely or appreciate the benefits of doing better work on a smaller number of issues. But, a major reduction in the size of personal staffs, perhaps as much as 50 percent, would reduce the incessant nibbling for members' time and attention.

Furthermore, members would no longer have as large a herd of personal servants rushing off to pick up his or her laundry, walk the dog, or hassle with the member's health-care provider. It would be useful for members of Congress to participate in the day-to-day life activities citizens do. It would tend to discourage Congress's continuing as a self-established aristocracy.

At worst, it would all save a few million dollars each year, and it would not reduce the quality of Capitol Hill staffing one iota.

Step Nine: End Federally Paid Campaign Workers. An unknown number of members of Congress exploit their federally paid personal, and sometimes committee, staffs for political benefit in one of two ways, if not both. Members permit, and at times encourage, their staff to work on their political campaigns on weekends and vacation time. It is legal and is permitted by contemporary House and Senate ethics rules, but in truth, it is little more than an expansion of a member's campaign staff with "volunteers" who may feel little choice in the matter and to whom the non-incumbent political opponent has no access. These "volunteers" are frequently highly paid professionals with skills and usefulness to a campaign well beyond stuffing envelopes and joining phone banks to get out the vote. Duties such as writing speeches and appearing in front of voter groups are common.

In some cases, a member will expect a personal staffer to do some of these things even on a normal Senate or House workday. Writing speeches that members use during the re-election campaign and authoring bills and amendments that respond to campaign issues are commonplace. These activities permit sitting members a significant advantage over their non-incumbent opponents.

Congress should declare vacation and weekend "volunteering" for an employer's re-election campaign to be a violation of House and Senate ethics rules. Once a member declares his candidacy for re-election, all committee and personal staffers should be prohibited from writing any speech to be delivered in the member's state or district. It is more problematic to prohibit staff from writing legislation; restricting the subject matter to issues actually debated in the House or Senate might be feasible. A violation might usefully incur a disqualification of an elected member's credentials to sit as a member of the House or Senate, if re-elected.

To protect staff who point out transgressions and for many other reasons, Congress should adhere to the recommendations of its own Office of Compliance and write strict and meaningful whistle-blower protection rules to apply to itself.

Step Ten: Conduct Oversight. With a competent professional staff, oversight should be a relatively easy matter.

The problem might be to convince the chairmen of committees to hold hearings with witnesses from more than one side of an issue. Today, only the Defense Department or other advocates of weapon systems are usually heard. Another problem will be to hold more than one hearing on major subjects, such as the solitary hearing the Defense Appropriations Subcommittee holds each year to "consider" the entire budget for the Navy and Marine Corps. Finally, something is needed to interest members in questions on subjects other than pork for their states.

With professionally written staff memoranda distributed to all members, chairmen would be under some public and intra-Congress pressure to probe the issues raised by the staff more thoroughly than today. Moreover, with a competent staff and public distribution of their memoranda, there would be less of a requirement to conduct oversight only via committee hearings. Competent memoranda will comprise a form of oversight in themselves.

To interest members in something other than pork at oversight hearings, chairmen could easily schedule hearings devoted to pork and nothing else and instruct committee members to hold such questions for them. In the likely event of members who insist on pork questions at oversight hearings, chairmen should be entitled to rule them out of order and move on to another member to ask questions. It will probably cause an eruption; it should be fun to sit in the audience as a member of an Armed Services Committee insists on the right to ask a witness about their local base's need for a new day care center. With any luck, the not-so-patiently waiting witness will be a secretary of defense who takes the opportunity to tell the porcine member that his or her idea of how to spend defense dollars lacks merit.

Indeed, if chairmen of defense committees were willing to hold pork-only hearings, that would be an excellent opportunity for members to learn how to conduct oversight. Political show trials pointing out the evils of pork would not be necessary; evaluation of the projects members seek to stuff into authorization and appropriation bills is. The defense-related committees need to erect reasonable hurdles for pork projects to climb over to win insertion into legislation. These could include the following:

- An estimate from the CBO on the cost of the project, including not just costs in the first year but over ten years. Today, such estimates are avoided like the plague; they force advocates to pony up to what they are pushing, and they inform others of the consequences of going along. Members sometimes say their pork projects are just small one-time items; that is almost never the case. Many are just annual increments of ongoing projects; others have operating-cost tails attached to their snouts.

- A statement from DoD on the merits, or lack thereof, of the specific project being sought. This statement could be delivered orally at hearings, or more usefully in the form of a document signed by the head of the office in DoD that would be responsible for carrying out the project. In other words, base commanders, program managers, and weapon system advocates in the civilian bureaucracy and military services would have to publicly put themselves on the line as informing Congress whether it should depart from the president's budget and endorse the project. If endorsed, they should explain where the extra money should come from and whether it is a good idea to raid O&M or any other part of the president's budget to pay for it. This should provide some interesting statements from those who in the past have been waving this spending through behind the backs of secretaries of defense.

Step Eleven: Lobbyists to Find Honest Work. Senator Javits had a rule that many of us on his staff loved to enforce. The rule was that Javits would perform casework only for constituents from New York State. In other words, we did not work for lawyers on K Street downtown or even ones from New York representing clients. We would act only in response to letters signed by constituents, not lawyers or lobbyists, and we would meet only with constituents. The constituent could hire a lobbyist or a lawyer and even bring them to meetings or ask them to draft the letters they signed. But in most cases, they learned they were wasting their money: Senator Javits would help what he judged to be meritorious requests for help with or without the pricey lawyers, and if there was a need for expertise in the legislative process, we almost always had more of it than the lawyer/lobbyist. And besides, we were free. The lawyers/lobbyists hated it, but it did not bother either us or the New York state constituents.

Of course, today's members of Congress will not like this idea either; it will cut down a major source of campaign contributions.

Step Twelve: Help the Press Do Its Job. None of the ideas listed here will come to anything if the press does not bring positive and negative examples to the public's attention. Politicians live and die based on what the press writes and says. Politicians crave media coverage as much as a homeless alcoholic craves a cheap muscatel.

The problem is that too many in the press are doing their job poorly, or not at all. Newspapers and electronic media do, for example, write many stories about pork and other obvious transgressions, but they rarely go beyond what they are fed by predictable sources. A journalist writing about congressional pork will invariably go to Senator McCain, acquire a copy of his latest, and very lively, listing of foolishness that Senators Stevens, Inouye, Byrd, and others have added to a bill, quote some blistering statements from the Arizona senator—all of them very appropriate and, of course, newsworthy—and write a news article. Just as the *Washington Post* printed only part of the story about "the night pork did not die" (in chapter 4), the complete story (the reformer's posturing, the failure to live up to his own promises, his enablement of what he professes to oppose) goes undescribed.

The consequences extend well beyond wasting money. The second war against Iraq is a classic example. As noted in chapter 13, there were many straws in the wind in October 2002 that there was something suspect about President Bush's assertion that unless war were to be declared quickly against Saddam Hussein, a "mushroom cloud"[9] might materialize somewhere over the United States. Congress failed to look seriously into those issues and resolve them, but that is no excuse for the press to fail to do the same. Instead, an atmosphere seemed to pervade the major newspapers and the television media that it was the right thing to do to support the drive to war and that it was pushing things too far to question seriously possible weaknesses for fear that a paper or newscaster might be labeled by the war advocates as unpatriotic. Just as the president failed the nation by hyping his case for war and most in Congress failed by swallowing it all whole, too many in the U.S. press also stuck a wet finger into the air to check the wind, rather than dig into the facts.

Some of the steps listed above should help the press: the accurate transcripts, the publicly available professional memoranda, and the attempts at competent oversight. In the final analysis, our democracy relies on a press that is not just free to print what it wants but that is more competent and better informed.

A Congress Our Grandchildren Deserve

America's constitutional checks and balances, the safeguards placed to protect liberty, to promote good government, and to provide for and maintain American armed forces are failing. They are failing because today's politicians want them to, and too many in the press and the electorate seem okay with that.

The problem is not that political "machines" have prevailed—either the traditional state or local ones, such as the one in Frank Capra's *Mr. Smith*

Goes to Washington, or the twenty-first-century, election-financing ones. Nor is it the triumph of impersonal, formulaic entities, such as the "military-industrial complex" or what some now term the "Iron Triangle" (which adds Congress to the bipolar "complex"). It is certainly not a failure of the American constitutional system, which provides all the tools that willing stalwarts need to prevail. Instead, it is simply a failure of individuals. Things—complexes and triangles, or even political machines—do not engage in ethical failures; people do.

None of the steps listed above is guaranteed to work, and other ideas may be better. These ideas are, however, the result of more than thirty years of observation of and participation in both the lows and highs of a system that today is clearly broken. There is really only one thing that will force members of Congress to perform as best as they are able. That is for the public to have the information to distinguish the good from the bad and the phonies from the sincere.

Notes

PREFACE

1. Michael Coleman, "Domenici Staffer Fired over Essay," *Albuquerque Journal,* 19 May 2002.
2. Howard Kurtz, "McCain, Rising Up against 'Spartacus'," *Washington Post,* 13 May 2002, C-1.

CHAPTER 1. WHAT IS THE PROBLEM?

1. Quote based on an eyewitness to the meeting and as told to the author.
2. David Isenberg, "The Not-so-friendly Reality of US Casualties," *Asia Times,* 22 October 2003.
3. *Congressional Record,* 26 September 2001, p. D944.
4. Ibid., p. D944.
5. *Congressional Record,* 24 September 2001, p. D926.
6. *Congressional Record,* 1 October 2001, p. D953.
7. *Congressional Record,* 26 September 2001, p. D944.
8. See *Congressional Record,* 7 December 2001, pp. D1219–24.
9. *Congressional Record,* 7 December 2001.
10. Military Construction Bill, 2002, Report of the Senate Committee on Appropriations, Report 107-68, 25 September 2001, p. 16.
11. Section 8124 of Conference Report to the Fiscal Year 2003 DoD Appropriations Act, HR 5010, House Report 107-732, p. 50; Senate Report to Fiscal Year 2003 Military Construction Appropriation Bill, S. 2709, Senate Report 107-202, p. 17.
12. Department of Defense Appropriations Bill, 2003, Report to Accompany HR 5010, Senate Report 107-213, 18 July 2002, p. 224.
13. Ibid., p. 66.
14. Remarks of Sen. John McCain, *Congressional Record,* 7 December 2001, p. S12595–99.
15. "Senate Passes Defense Appropriations Bill," Analysis of the Council for a Livable World, 10 December 2001, available at www.clw.org/milspend/fy02approppass.html.
16. Report of the Senate Appropriations Committee to accompany HR 5010, Senate Report 107-213, p. 5.
17. For example, see Conference Report to accompany HR 4185, Making Appropriations for the Department of Defense for the Fiscal Year Ending September 30, 1984, House Document 98-567, 18 November 1983.

CHAPTER 2. EGO IS AT THE HEART OF THE TROUBLE

1. Patricia Connell Shakow, "The 'Family' Javits," *Washington Post,* 10 March 1986, p. A15.
2. Joseph McLellan, "The Launching of Captive Nations Week," *Washington Post,* 19 July 1978, p. E3.
3. Ibid.
4. For example, see, "Kassebaum to Propose Cuts in Defense Budget," *Kansas City Times,* 8 April 1981; "Kassebaum Asks for Major Defense Cuts," *Topeka Capital-Journal,* 9 April 1981; and "Kassebaum Wants to Cut 'Absurd' Defense Request," *Kansas City Star,* 9 April 1981.
5. For example, see "Getting Our Money's Worth," *Topeka Capital-Journal,* undated xerox.
6. See Steven V. Roberts, *New York Times,* 11 July 1983, p. A12; and Charles Mohr, *New York Times,* 12 October 1983, p. B6.
7. See *Houston Post,* 28 December 1983
8. See *Defense Week,* 30 April 1984.
9. Copies of multiple memoranda and letters are in the author's files and are the basis for the details related here.
10. *DoD Statistical Report on the Military Retirement System,* Fiscal Year 2000, Office of the Actuary, Department of Defense, RCS No. DD-P&R (PI) (1375), p. 21.
11. *Congressional Record,* 12 October 2000, p. S10369.
12. *Congressional Record,* 20 June 2002, p. S5825.
13. *Congressional Record,* 26 June 2002, p. S6089.
14. Ibid.
15. Ibid., p. S6090.
16. Ibid.
17. Ibid., p. S6102.
18. Ibid., p. S6103.
19. Ibid., p. S6090.
20. Ibid., pp. S6106–12.
21. Ibid., p. S6105.

CHAPTER 3. WAR IS NOT HELL: IT'S AN OPPORTUNITY

1. Remarks of Sen. Dianne Feinstein, *Congressional Record,* 26 September 2001, p. S9828–29.
2. Remarks of Sen. Carl Levin, *Congressional Record,* 21 September 2001, p. S9565.
3. Remarks of Sen. John Warner, *Congressional Record,* 21 September 2001, p. S9569.
4. See *Congressional Record,* 1 October 2001, p. D953.
5. Ibid.
6. Pat Towell, "Changes to Defense Bill Modest Despite Focus on Anti-Terrorism," *Congressional Quarterly Weekly,* 20 October 2001, pp. 2484, 2485.
7. Helen Dewar, "Defense Bill Passes: Base Closings Delayed," *Washington Post,* 14 December 2001, p. A43.

8. Remarks of Sen. John McCain, *Congressional Record,* 7 December 2001, p. S12595.

9. See *Congressional Record,* 7 December 2001, pp. D1219–24.

10. "Senate Passes Defense Appropriations Bill," Analysis of the Council for a Livable World, 11 December 2001, available at www.clw.org/milspend/fy02approppass.html.

11. Author's analysis of the amendments considered on 7 December 2001 and described on pp. D1219–24 of the *Congressional Record* of 7 December 2001.

12. Ibid., p. S12655.

13. Ibid., p. D1223.

14. Ibid., p. S12664. The text of the amendment leaves unclear the precise intent, and it is not explained at any point in the *Congressional Record* or other materials relevant to the bill.

15. Stevens amendment 2450, *Congressional Record,* 7 December 2001, p. S12665.

16. Analysis provided by OMB analysts to the author.

17. The memo, titled "NO21—KC-135E Recapitalization (U)" is in the possession of the author.

18. The CBO analysis is in the possession of the author.

19. CBO letter from Douglas Holtz-Eakin, director, to Sen. John W. Warner, chairman, Senate Armed Services Committee, 16 October 2003, available at ftp://ftp.cbo.gov/46xx/doc4629/tanker2.pdf.

20. Letter of OMB Director Mitchell E. Daniels Jr. to Hon. Kent Conrad, chairman, Committee on the Budget, U.S. Senate, 2 November 2001.

21. Letter of OMB Director Mitchell E. Daniels Jr. to Hon. John McCain, U.S. Senate, 18 December 2001.

22. Public statements of Senators Domenici and Stevens at the Defense Subcommittee "markup" of HR 3338 on 5 December 2001, Dirksen Senate Office Building.

23. Remarks of Sen. John McCain, *Congressional Record,* 7 December 2001, p. S12595.

24. Remarks of Sen. Phil Gramm, *Congressional Record,* 7 December 2001, p. S12600.

25. This description is based on an eyewitness account.

26. Department of Defense Appropriations Bill, 2002, and Supplemental Appropriations, 2002, Report of the Committee on Appropriations to accompany HR 3338, House of Representatives, House Report 107-298, p. 119.

27. Juliet Eilperin, "Plane Lease Deal to Cost U.S. Extra," *Washington Post,* 26 December 2001, p. A1; and "At Annual VIP Jetliner Jam, the Beat Goes On," *Defense Week,* 2 January 2002, p. 3.

28. "Conferees Reach Bipartisan Accord on Fiscal Year 2002 Defense Authorization Bill," Press Release, House Armed Services Committee, Bob Stump, chairman, 12 December 2001, p. 1.

29. *Congressional Record,* 13 December 2001, p. S13124.

30. Conference Report to accompany HR 3338, Making Appropriations for the Department of Defense for the Fiscal Year Ending September 30, 2002, and for Other Purposes, House Report 107-350, 19 December 2001, p. 188.
31. Ibid., p. 192.
32. Ibid., p. 193.
33. Ibid., p. 177.
34. Department of Defense Appropriation Bill, 2002, and Supplemental Appropriations, 2002, Report of the Committee on Appropriations to accompany HR 3338, Senate Report 107-109, p. 38, 5 December 2001.
35. Conference Report to accompany HR 3338, Making Appropriations for the Department of Defense for the Fiscal Year Ending September 30, 2002, and for Other Purposes, House Report 107-350, 19 December 2001, p. 170.
36. Author's tabulation from the table inserted by Senator McCain in the *Congressional Record*, 7 December 2001, p. 12597–99.
37. Statement of Administration Policy, 28 November 2001, Department of Defense Appropriations Bill, FY 2002, Executive Office of the President, Office of Management and Budget, available at www.whitehouse.gov/omb/legislative/sap/107-1/HR3338-h.html.
38. Statement of Administration Policy, 6 December 2001, Department of Defense Appropriations Bill, FY 2002, Executive Office of the President, Office of Management and Budget, available at www.whitehouse.gov/omb/legislative/sap/107-1/HR3338-s.html.
39. Defense Bill Signing Statement, Statement by the President, 10 January 2002, available at www.whitehouse.gov/news/releases/2002/01/20020110-8.html.

Chapter 4. Mr. Smith Is Dead

1. A copy of this statement is in the author's files.
2. See the remarks of Senator McCain, *Congressional Record*, 20 December 2001, p. S13837.
3. Ibid., p. S13839.
4. Ibid., p. S13838.
5. Ibid., p. S13841.
6. Ibid., p. S13842.
7. Ibid.
8. Ibid.
9. *Congressional Record*, 6 June 2002, p. S5179.
10. Ibid.
11. Ibid.
12. *Congressional Record*, 6 June 2002, p. S5181.
13. Ibid., p. S5182.
14. Ibid., p. S5183.
15. Senate amendments 3718 and 3719, *Congressional Record*, 5 June 2002, p. S5093.
16. *Congressional Record*, 5 June 2002, p. S5090, and 6 June 2002, pp. S5181–82.

17. *Congressional Record,* 6 June 2002, p. S5182.
18. Ibid., p. S5184.
19. *Congressional Record,* 4 June 2002, p. S4943.
20. *Congressional Record,* 5 June 2002, p. S5077.
21. *Congressional Record,* 6 June 2002, p. S5119.
22. Ibid., p. S5120.
23. Ibid., p. S5124–26.
24. Ibid., p. S5135.
25. Ibid., p. D573.
26. Report to accompany S. 2551, Senate Report 107-156, p. 149.
27. *Congressional Record,* 6 June 2002, pp. S5174–75, S5177, and D571–72.
28. Ibid., p. S5173.
29. Ibid., p. S5174.
30. Compare the amendment as introduced to that as passed; see *Congressional Record,* 5 and 6 June 2002, pp. S5071, S5180.
31. *Congressional Record,* 5 June 2002, p. S5073.
32. *Congressional Record,* 6 June 2002, p. S5174.
33. Ibid., p. S5177–78.
34. Billy House, "McCain Misses Defense Spending Vote," *Arizona Republic,* 18 October 2002, available at www.azcentral.com.
35. Helen Dewar, "Divisive Climate Stymies Work of Conference Committees," *Washington Post,* 10 June 2002, p. A19.

Chapter 5. Confessions of a Pork Processor

1. Thomas E. Ricks, "Naval Battle: Awarding of Contracts Irks Senate's Lott," *Wall Street Journal,* 21 April 1997, p. A24.
2. Ibid.
3. Ibid.
4. Thomas E. Ricks, "Lott Aide Pushes Sweeping Agenda on Shipbuilding," *Wall Street Journal,* 23 April 1997, p. B2.
5. Ibid.
6. Discussion involving the author, Senator Cohen, and other senators in 1996.
7. *Congressional Record,* 8 June 1999, p. S6719.
8. Philip Dine, "Senate Seeks 4 More Boeing F-15 Eagle Jets," *St. Louis Post-Dispatch,* 9 June 1999, p. C1.
9. Text of amendment 587, *Congressional Record,* 8 June 1999, p. S6719.
10. The quote and this entire example is fully described in a Franklin C. (Chuck) Spinney "blaster," no. 284, "The Win-Win Power Game . . . or . . . Why Working the Troops Overtime is Good for St. Louis and the Nation," at www.d-n-i.net.
11. "Defense Projects Funded," *Morgan Messenger,* 23 October 2002.
12. Dan Morgan, "With Spending Bill, Credit in Advance Lawmakers Tout Projects in Measure that Congress Has Not Passed," *Washington Post,* 27 October 2002, p. A4.

13. Ibid.
14. Robert Holzer and Mark Walsh, "Services' Wish List Hits Hill," *Defense News*, 24–30 March 1997, p. 1.

CHAPTER 6. PORK LOWS AND HIGHS

1. Jack N. Rakove, *Original Meanings: Politics and Ideas in the Making of the Constitution* (New York: Alfred A. Knopf, 1996), p. 49.
2. For a fuller description, see John Steele Gordon, "USS Boondoggle," *American Heritage*, February/March 1993, pp. 20–22.
3. William Roberts, "The Struggle for Subsidies: Defense Bill Sheds Key Maritime Parts," *Journal of Commerce*, 29 October 1997, p. 1.
4. Warren B. Rudman and Gary Hart, "We Are Still Unprepared," *Washington Post*, 5 November 2002, p. A25.
5. Dan Morgan, "Senate GOP Prevails in 1st Test on Spending," *Washington Post*, 17 January 2003, p. A10.
6. Dan Morgan, "Senate GOP Wins Again on Spending Package," *Washington Post*, 18 January 2003, p. A4. After Senator Stevens threatened to remove pork from the bill to fund the FBI at a higher level, this *Washington Post* article stated, "Sen. Robert C. Byrd (D-W.Va.) dared Stevens to make good on the threat." Stevens did no such thing; nor did Byrd offer his own amendment to strip out pork to pay for more FBI funding. In sharp contrast to their words, the senators' actions made their priorities clear. The *Washington Post* credited Byrd with "daring" Stevens to fulfill his threat, but it failed to write that Byrd did not make good his own "dare" by offering his own amendment to effect the result he professed he wanted—higher FBI funding at the expense of pork.

CHAPTER 8. WATCHDOGS, LAPDOGS, AND DISTORTED LENSES

1. "Congressional Staff and Management; Historical Overview," *Final Report of the Joint Committee on the Organization of Congress*, December 1993, p. 9. Data for CRS staff is from CRS Annual Report for FY 2001 as summerized to the author by a CRS representative.
2. "Congressional Staff and Management; Historical Overview," *Final Report of the Joint Committee on the Organization of Congress*, December 1993, p. 11. The *Final Report* cites only a limited exemption for Congress; however, at staff orientation and other meetings while the author worked at the agency, GAO management frequently explained GAO had no authority, or desire, to investigate Congress. After a scandal involving the House sergeant at arms in the early 1990s, some GAO auditing of congressional accounts was begun.
3. Paul Dwyer and R. Eric Petersen, "Legislative Branch Employment: Trends in Staffing," Congressional Research Service Report, 21 June 2001, Order Code RL30996, pp. 9–10.
4. Letter of Congressional Budget Office Director June E. O'Neil to Strom Thurmond, chairman of the Senate Armed Services Committee, 17 May 1996.

5. "Reaching Globally, Reaching Powerfully: The United States Air Force in the Gulf War," U.S. Air Force, September 1991, p. 55.

6. "We Own the Night," *Lockheed Horizons* 30, May 1992, p. 57.

7. Statement of Lt. Gen. Charles A. Horner, USAF, and Brig. Gen. Buster C. Glosson, USAF, , Department of Defense Appropriations for 1992, Hearings of the Subcommittee on the Department of Defense of the Committee on Appropriations, House of Representatives, 102nd Cong., 1st sess., 30 April 1991, p. 468.

8. While numerous sources asserted the achievement of "one bomb, one target" effectiveness, prominent claimants included defense manufacturers, such as Texas Instruments, which produced LGBs, and Lockheed, which produced the F-117. Such claims were made in both advertisements and in annual ("10-K") reports to stockholders.

9. Author's recollection of BBC TV reporting from Baghdad during the war, as rebroadcast by CNN.

10. An assertion in "Tomahawk: A Total Weapon System," brochure by McDonnell-Douglas.

11. See Department of Defense, "Conduct of the Persian Gulf War, Final Report to Congress pursuant to Title V of the Persian Gulf Conflict Supplemental Authorization and Personnel Benefits Act of 1991," Appendix T, Performance of Selected Weapons Systems, April 1992, p. T-201.

12. Joint Chiefs of Staff estimate from April 1991, according to Joint CNA/DIA Research Memorandum 93-49, *TLAM Performance During Operation Desert Storm: Assessment of Physical and Functional Damage to the TLAM Aimpoints,* Vol. 1: Overview and Methodology, March 1994, p. 21.

13. *Operation Desert Storm: Evaluation of the Air Campaign,* U.S. General Accounting Office, June 1997, GAO/NSIAD-97-134, p. 137.

14. Ibid., p. 147–48.

15. Ibid., p. 139–43.

16. Ibid., pp. 78–82.

17. Ibid., pp. 78–82.

18. Ibid., pp. 177–93.

19. See first released GAO report, *Operation Desert Storm: Evaluation of the Air War,* GAO/PEMD-96-10, p. 5.

20. See "Senator Calls for Declassification of GAO Data on Gulf War Munitions," *Inside the Air Force,* 12 July 1996, pp. 10–11; and "DoD Officials Promise Secrecy Review of Gulf War Report," *Defense Week,* 15 July 1996, p. 2.

21. Tony Capaccio, "GAO Deflates Glossy Gulf War Weapons Claims," *Defense Week,* 22 July 1996, pp. 5, 11; see also above cited GAO report (pp. 144–45) and the refutations of DoD officials' statements footnoted on pp. 133, 138.

22. For ads, see advertisements in *Aviation Week & Space Technology* in 1991: e.g., "TI Paveway III: One Target, One Bomb," cited on page 145 of GAO's 1997 report. For pundit articles, see *Aerospace America,* October 1994 and "Defense in an Age of Hope," by former Secretary of Defense William J. Perry, *Foreign Affairs* 75, no. 6, November/December 1996, p. 76–79.

23. Letter of Deputy Assistant Secretary of Defense, Requirements and Plans, DoD to Acting Assistant Comptroller General, Program Evaluation and Methodology Division, GAO, dated 4 September 1996, p. 2.

24. Letter of the Under Secretary of Defense, Acquisition and Technology, DoD to Assistant Comptroller General, National Security and International Affairs Programs, GAO, dated 29 July 1996, p. 3.

25. See "One Target, One Weapon," Paul Kaminski, *Air Force Magazine* 79, no. 8, August 1996, p. 80, and Mr. Kaminski's 2 May 1996 Ira C. Eaker Distinguished Lecture on National Defense Policy at the U.S. Air Force Academy, Colorado Springs, Colorado.

26. Tim Weiner, "'Smart' Weapons Were Overrated, Study Concludes," *New York Times,* 9 July 1996, p. A1.

27. Pat Cooper and Robert Holzer, "Debate Swirls Around F-117," *Defense News,* 23–29 September 1996.

28. John Diamond, "GAO Study Takes Aim at Gulf War Weapons," *Washington Post,* 1 July 1997.

29. "'Smart' Bombs, Smart Choices," *Washington Post,* 15 July 1996, p. A18.

30. Michael Vickers, "Dumbing Down Defense Debates," *Washington Times,* 19 July 1996.

31. Eliot Cohen, "A Bad Rap on High Tech," *Washington Post,* 16 July 1996, p. A15.

32. "Operation Desert Storm: Evaluation of the Air War," GAO/PEMD-96-10, p. 4.

33. Ibid., pp. 11–12.

34. Counted from the Senate Armed Services Committee's Web site at http://www.senate.gov/~armed_services.

35. See GAO's Web site at http://www.gao.gov. As this book went to press, GAO had changed the format for the presentation of its year 2000 reports at its Web site. Just 118 "National Defense" reports are listed for the calendar year 2000. The author's original count also included some of the reports now listed in other topic categories.

36. After PEMD was abolished, an NSIAD identifier was attached to PEMD's second Desert Storm report when it was printed and released.

37. Ralph Nader, "Axing GAO Diminishes Government's Accountability," *Liberal Opinion Week,* 26 May 1996. In addition, the *New York Times* wrongly reported that PEMD was "destroyed by budget cuts imposed by Congress" in "Selling Weapons: Stealth, Lies, and Videotape," by Tim Weiner, *New York Times,* 14 July 1996, p. E-3.

Chapter 9. Beyond Nonfeasance: The Utility of Distortion

1. "Department of Defense Authorization for Appropriations for Fiscal Year 1997 and the Future Years Defense Program," Hearings before the Committee on Armed Services, U.S. Senate. 104th Cong., 2d sess. on S. 1745, Part 1, 5, 6, 12, 13, 14, 19, 21, 26, 28 March and 16 April 1996, p. 36.

2. Ibid, p. 77.

3. Ibid.

4. *Congressional Record*, Remarks of Senator Bumpers, 23 May 1996, p. S5510.

5. Charts and graphs used during the Senate's debate are not reproduced in the *Congressional Record*. The figure shown here is reproduced from the author's memory.

6. "FY 2000 Defense Budget," briefing to Senate staff, February 1999, William J. Lynn, Under Secretary of Defense (Comptroller), p. 3.

7. DoD News Briefing, Tuesday, 11 April 2000, 1:30 PM, EDT, Office of the Assistant Secretary of Defense (Public Affairs) transcript downloaded from DoD Web site "DefenseLINK News: DoD News Briefing . . . Adm. Craig R. Quigley, USN, DA" http://www.defenselink.mil/news/Apr2000/t04112000_t411dasd.html.

8. Ibid., p. 10.

9. Ibid., pp. 9–10.

10. Ibid., p. 6.

11. Ibid., pp. 9–10.

12. Ibid., p. 9.

13. Ibid., p. 9

14. Selected Acquisition Report (RCS: DD-A&T [Q&A] 823) PROGRAM: V-22 (OSPREY), as of date: 31 December 1999, p. 1.

15. Ibid., p. 8.

16. Ibid., p. 9.

17. Ibid., p. 8.

18. On page 10 of the 11 April 2000 DoD transcript, General McCorkle admits, "The ones that we got in '99 I think were somewhere in the area of $57 million." In 1999 the Navy paid—just in procurement costs—$603.9 million to acquire seven V-22s. That comes to $86.3 million per copy, not counting any R&D, and not counting $60 million provided in advance procurement for those specific aircraft the previous year. (See "Procurement Programs [P-1]," Fiscal Year 2001, February 2000, Office of the Under Secretary of Defense [Comptroller], p. N-2.)

19. Found at http://www.af.mil/newspaper/v1_n21/v1_n21_s4.htm. "News; U.S. Air Force ONLINE News," AF separates F-22 facts from myths.

20. "Emergency Spending under the Budget Enforcement Act," Congressional Budget Office, December 1998, p. 1. Subsequent to the writing of this passage in the draft manuscript, Congress moved the provision involving emergency spending to a different statute and then allowed it to expire in 2002. Subsequently, procedural rules controlling emergency spending were written into annual congressional budget resolutions; however, it is unclear whether they will expire again due to squabbling among House and Senate Republicans over spending rules and tax cuts in the FY 2005 congressional budget resolution.

21. For a discussion of congressional and executive branch rules and practices on emergency spending, see "Emergency Spending under the Budget

Enforcement Act," CBO Memorandum, December 1998, Congressional
Budget Office, and "Budget Bulletin: A Weekly Bulletin produced when the
Senate is in session," Senate Budget Committee Majority Staff, 15 Septem-
ber 1998.

22. *Congressional Record,* 30 June 2000, p. S6226.

23. "National Defense Budget Estimates for FY 2001," Office of the Under
Secretary of Defense (Comptroller), March 2000, p. 216.

24. CIA World Factbook at http://www.cia.gov/cia/publications/factbook/
geos/iz.html.

25. "U.S. Drives World Military Spending Up Sharply in 2002," SIPRI Reports,
DefenseNews.com, 17 June 2003.

26. See "Auditors Seek 'Lost World' of Miscounted Billions," *Defense Week,* 28
April 1997, p. 1, and "Statement of Eleanor Hill Inspector General, Depart-
ment of Defense before the Subcommittee on Government Management
Information Technology, Committee on Government Reform and Over-
sight, House of Representatives, on Department of Defense Financial
Management," Report Number 98-118, delivered 16 April 1998, and
"Defense Financial Management," Statement of Donald Mancuso, acting
inspector general, Department of Defense, before the Subcommittee on
Government Management Information and Technology, House Government Reform Committee, U.S. House of Representatives, 4 May 1999.

27. "Internal Controls and Compliance With Laws and Regulations for the DoD
Agency-Wide Financial Statements for FY 1999," DoD Inspector General,
Report No. D-2000-091, 25 February 2000, p. ii. It is notable that $6.9
trillion in adjustments were recorded in FY 1999; of these, $2.3 trillion were
unsupported; another $2.0 trillion were not reviewed because of time
constraints; of the $6.9 trillion, just $2.6 trillion were supported by an audit
trail.

28. "DoD Looks to Accountants to Sort Out Books," *Jane's Defence Weekly,*
2 August 2000.

29. "Independent Auditor's Report on the Department of Defense, Fiscal Year
2002, Agency-Wide Principal Financial Statements," Department of Defense
Inspector General, 15 January 2003, (Project D2002FI-0104.000), pp. iii–225.

CHAPTER 10. THE ENGINE OF CONGRESSIONAL GOOD AND EVIL: THE STAFF

1. Paul Dwyer and R. Eric Petersen, "Legislative Branch Employment: Trends
in Staffing, 1960–2000," CRS Report for Congress, Congressional Research
Service, 21 June 2001, p. 4.

2. Norman J. Ornstein, Thomas E. Mann, and Michael J. Malbin, *Vital Statistics
on Congress, 2001–2002* (Washington, D.C.: The AEI Press, 2002), p. 126.
Figures given are for 1999.

3. For a brief biography of Jackson, see *Soldier-Statesmen of the Constitution* by
Robert K. Wright Jr. and Morris J. Macgregor Jr. (Washington, D.C.: Center
of Military History, U.S. Army, 1987) pp. 127–29.

4. Ibid., p. 127.

5. Ibid., p. 129.

6. Jack N. Rakove, *Original Meanings: Politics and Ideas in the Making of the Constitution* (New York: Alfred A. Knopf, 1996), p. 13.

7. "Congressional Staff and Management; Historical Overview" *Final Report of the Joint Committee on the Organization of Congress,* December 1993, p. 1.

8. "Senate Chronology," U.S. Senate Web site at www.senate.gov/pagelayout/history/one_item_and_teasers/chronology.htm.

9. "Congressional Staff and Management; Historical Overview" *Final Report of the Joint Committee on the Organization of Congress,* December 1993, pp. 1, 4.

10. "Senate Committees, Operations, Staffing," U.S. Senate Web site at www.senate.gov.artandhistory/history/common/briefing/Committees.htm#4. A hard copy of this Web site's material is in the author's files.

11. "Congressional Staff and Management; Historical Overview" *Final Report of the Joint Committee on the Organization of Congress,* December 1993, p. 1.

12. "Senate Chronology," U.S. Senate Web site at www.senate.gov/pagelayout/history/one_item_and_teasers/chronology.htm.

13. "Congressional Staff and Management; Historical Overview," *Final Report of the Joint Committee on the Organization of Congress,* December 1993, p.1.

14. Ibid.

15. Ibid.

16. Ibid., p. 4.

17. The author has never seen an objective analysis to document this assertion; however, the assessment was prevalent on Capitol Hill shortly after the Rayburn and Hart buildings were constructed.

18. "Congressional Staff and Management; Historical Overview," *Final Report of the Joint Committee on the Organization of Congress,* December 1993, p. 4.

19. Ibid., p. 14.

20. Ibid.

21. E-mail from Assistant Senate Historian Betty K. Koed to the author, 13 February 2003.

22. "Congressional Staff and Management; Historical Overview," *Final Report of the Joint Committee on the Organization of Congress,* December 1993, p. 2.

23. "Senate Chronology," U.S. Senate Web site at www.senate.gov/pagelayout/history/one_item_and_teasers/chronology.htm.

24. "Congressional Staff and Management; Historical Overview," *Final Report of the Joint Committee on the Organization of Congress,* December 1993, p. 2.

25. Data analysis extracted from *Report of the Secretary of the Senate,* from 1 April 2002 to 30 September 2002, Part II, pp. B-2-1–B-2-215.

26. "The Congressional Committee System; Historical Overview," *Final Report of the Joint Committee on the Organization of Congress,* December 1993, p. 3.

27. Ibid., p. 2.

28. Norman J. Ornstein, Thomas E. Mann, and Michael J. Malbin, *Vital Statistics on Congress: 2001–2002,* p. 135; and from U.S. Senate and House of Representatives Web sites at www.senate.gov and www.house.gov.

29. *Military and Civilian Personnel Assignments to Congress,* Audit Report, Office of the Inspector General, Department of Defense, Report No. 97-186, 14 July 1997, pp. 6–7.

30. Report of Senate Appropriations Committee on FY 1998 Department of Defense Appropriations Bill, Senate Report 105-45, p. 144–45.

31. *Military and Civilian Personnel Assignments to Congress,* Audit Report, Office of the Inspector General, Department of Defense, Report No. 97-186, 14 July 1997, p. 10.

32. Based on a conversation with a member of the Senate Armed Services Committee staff.

33. "Congressional Staff and Management; Historical Overview," *Final Report of the Joint Committee on the Organization of Congress,* December 1993, p. 2.

34. Norman J. Ornstein, Thomas E. Mann, and Michael J. Malbin, *Vital Statistics on Congress: 2001–2002,* p. 126.

CHAPTER 11. HILL LIFE AND DEATH

1. Federalist Paper No. 57, by James Madison as reproduced in *The Federalist: The Famous Papers on the Principles of American Government,* ed. Benjamin Fletcher Wright (University of Texas: Metrobooks, 1961), p. 385.

2. "Application of Laws to Congress—Laws that Do Not Apply to Congress," *Final Report of the Joint Committee on the Organization of Congress,* December 1993, p. 1.

3. Ibid., p. 7.

4. Ibid., p. 1.

5. "Application of Laws to Congress—Congressional Exemptions and Special Rules" and "Application of Laws to Congress—Laws That Do Not Apply to Congress," *Final Report of the Joint Committee on the Organization of Congress,* December 1993, pp. 1–2.

6. Office of Compliance Manual, Introduction, p. 1.

7. "Office of Compliance: Reports and Studies," Section 301(h) Report, *Report to Congress,* 2002, p. 13 at www.compliance.gov/reports-studies/sec301h/sec301h_2002.pdf.

8. Final Board Decisions of the Office of Compliance are listed on the office's Web site at www.compliance.com/decisions/decisions.html.

9. Reports and Studies Conducted by the Office of Compliance, "Report to Congress on the Use of the Office of Compliance by Covered Employees," Office of Compliance, January 2003, p. 14. The report notes that of the thirteen formal complaints filed in 2002, eleven contained the notation that the complainant experienced "retaliation for opposing practices made unlawful by the [Congressional Accountability Act]."

10. "Office of Compliance: Reports and Studies," Section 102(b) Report, December 2002, pp. A-3, A-4.

11. Ibid., p. B2.

12. Ibid., p. 1.

13. Ibid., p. 5.

14. Bill Miller and Juliet Eilperin, "Obscure Labor Issues Block Homeland Security Agency," *Washington Post*, 23 September 2002, p. A8.

15. *Congressional Record*, 20 June 2002, p. D650.

16. *Congressional Record*, 27 June 2002, p. D700.

17. "Summary of Hearings on Congressional Staff and Management," *Final Report of the Joint Committee on the Organization of Congress*, December 1993, p.1.

18. "Congressional Staff and Management," *Final Report of the Joint Committee on the Organization of Congress*, December 1993, p.1.

19. Norman J. Ornstein, Thomas E. Mann, and Michael J. Malbin *Vital Statistics on Congress: 2001–2002*, p. 126.

20. Julia Malone, "A Century of Congressional Expansion," Cox News Service, 1999, p. 1.

CHAPTER 12. POLITICIANS AT THEIR BEST

1. Discussion of the author with a participant of the luncheon meeting in 2003.

2. Jack N. Rakove, *Original Meanings: Politics and Ideas in the Making of the Constitution* (New York: Alfred A. Knopf, 1996) , p. 263.

3. *War, Foreign Policy and Constitutional Power,* Judge Abraham Sofaer, American Bar Association, 1976, p. 31, as quoted in "The War Powers Resolution: Necessary and Legal Remedy to Prevent Future Vietnams," Albert A. Lakeland Jr. in Steven P. Soper, ed., *Congress, the President, and Foreign Policy,* American Bar Association Standing Committee on Law and National Security, American Bar Association, 1984, p. 154.

4. Ibid.

5. Ibid.

6. Ibid.

7. From *The Writings of James Madison,* vol. VI, ed. Gaillard Hunt, (New York: G.P. Putnam's Sons, 1906), as quoted in *War Powers Legislation,* Hearings before the Committee on Foreign Relations, U.S. Senate, 92nd Cong., 1st sess., on S. 731, S.J. Res. 18, and S. J. res. 59, 8, 9, 24, 25 March, 23, 26 April, 14 May, 26, 27 July, and 6 October 1971, p. 154.

8. *The Writings of Thomas Jefferson* 123 (Paul Leicester Ford ed., 1895) as quoted in "Congressional Abdication: War and Spending Powers," by Louis Fisher, *Saint Louis University Law Journal* 43, no. 3, Summer 1999, p. 938.

9. Letter from James Madison to Mr. Monroe (Nov. 16, 1827), in *3 Letters and Other Writings of James Madison* (Philip R. Fendall ed., 1884), as quoted in "Book Review: The War Powers of the President and Congress: Who Holds the Arrows and Olive Branch?" by Jacob K. Javits with Winslow T. Wheeler, *New York University Law Review* 57, no. 4, October 1982, p. 851.

10. Statement of Prof. Alexander Bickel, 26 July 1971, "War Powers Legislation," Hearings, p. 553.

11. Benjamin F. Wright, ed., *The Federalist*, p. 446.

12. Ibid., p. 446.

13. From the National Archives as quoted in "The War Powers Resolution: Necessary and Legal Remedy to Prevent Future Vietnams," Albert A.

Lakeland Jr. in Steven P. Sober, ed., *Congress, the President, and Foreign Policy*, American Bar Association Standing Committee on Law and National Security, American Bar Association, 1984, p. 155.

14. "Major U.S. Armed Actions Overseas, with Relevant Congressional Action, 1789–1970," and "Instances of Use of United States Armed Forces Abroad, 1798–1970," as reproduced in *War Powers Legislation,* Hearings before the Committee on Foreign Relations, 92nd Cong., 1st sess., on S. 731, S.J. Res. 18, and S. J. Res. 59, March through October 1971, pp. 298–316.

15. "National Commitments," Report of Committee on Foreign Relations to accompany S. Res. 85, 91st Cong., p. 25, as cited in "War Powers," Report of Committee on Foreign Relations to accompany S. 2956, 92nd Cong., U.S. Senate document 92-606, p. 19.

16. Testimony of Charles N. Brower, acting legal adviser, Department of State, 13 March 1973, Hearings before the Subcommittee on National Security Policy and Scientific Developments of the Committee on Foreign Affairs, House of Representatives, 93rd Cong., 1st sess., 7, 8, 13, 14, 20 March 1973; "War Powers," p. 145.

17. Based on statement of Raoul Berger, Charles Warren Senior Fellow in American Legal History, Harvard Law School, 11 April 1973, in *War Powers Legislation,* 1973, Hearings before the Committee on Foreign Relations, United States Senate, 93rd Cong., 1st sess., on S. 440, 11 and 12 April 1973, p. 10.

18. Thomas M. Franck, "Constitutional Practice until Vietnam," in Steven P. Soper, ed., *Congress, the President, and Foreign Policy,* American Bar Association Standing Committee on Law and National Security, American Bar Association, 1984, p. 21.

19. Albert A. Lakeland Jr., "The War Powers Resolution: Necessary and Legal Remedy to Prevent Future Vietnams," in Steven P. Soper, ed., *Congress, the President, and Foreign Policy,* American Bar Association Committee on Law and National Security, American Bar Association, 1984, p. 159–60.

20. Ibid., p. 160.

21. Ibid.

22. As quoted in ibid., p. 161.

23. William M. Goldsmith, "Separation of Powers and the Intent of the Founding Fathers," in Steven P. Soper, ed., *Congress, the President, and Foreign Policy.,* American Bar Association Committee on Law and National Security, American Bar Association, 1984, p. 8,

24. Thomas M. Franck, "Constitutional Practice until Vietnam," in Steven P. Soper, ed., *Congress, the President, and Foreign Policy,* American Bar Association Committee on Law and National Security, American Bar Association, 1984, p. 15.

25. "Documents Relating to the War Power of Congress, The Presidents Authority as Commander-in-Chief and the Indochina War," Committee on Foreign Relations, U.S. Senate, July 1970, p. iii.

26. See "Documents Relating to the War Power of Congress, The Presidents

Authority as Commander-in-Chief and the Indochina War," Committee on Foreign Relations, U.S. Senate, July 1970; *War Powers Legislation,* Hearings before the Committee on Foreign Relations, 92nd Cong., 1st sess., on S. 731, S.J. Res. 18, and S. J. res. 59, March through October 1971, and "War Powers Legislation, 1973," Hearings before the Committee on Foreign Relations, U.S. Senate, on S.440, 11 and 12 April 1973.

27. "War Powers," Senate Report 92-606, 9 February 1972, Committee on Foreign Relations, p. 10.

28. "War Powers," Senate Report 93-220, 14 June 1973, Committee on Foreign Relations, p. 7. One member voted "present."

29. Section 3 of S. 440, as introduced by Senators Javits, Stennis, Eagleton, and others on 18 January 1973 in the 93rd Congress.

30. Remarks of Sen. Jacob Javits, *Congressional Record,* 18 July 1973, 93rd Cong., 1st sess., p. 24541.

31. Section 2(c) of PL 93-148.

32. "Vetoing House Joint Resolution 542, A Joint Resolution Concerning the War Powers of Congress and the President," Message from the President of the United States, 25 October 1973, House Document 93-171, p. 1.

33. Ibid.

34. Ibid.

35. Ibid.

36. *Congressional Record,* 7 November 1973, 93rd Cong., 1st sess., p. 36221.

37. Ibid., pp. 36188–89.

38. Ibid., p. 36198.

39. Ibid., p. 36198.

40. "War Powers Resolution: Presidential Compliance," Richard F. Grimmett, Foreign Affairs, Defense, and Trade Division, Congressional Research Service, Library of Congress, Issue Brief for Congress, 24 March 2003, p. CRS-2.

41. For a detailed discussion, see "The War Powers Resolution: After Twenty-Eight Years," Richard F. Grimmett, Foreign Affairs, Defense, and Trade Division, Congressional Research Service, Library of Congress, CRS Report for Congress, 15 November 2001, pp. 11–45.

42. "Declarations of War and Authorizations for the Use of Military Force: Background and Legal Implications," David M. Ackerman, American Law Division, and Richard F. Grimmett, Foreign Affairs, Defense, and Trade Division, Congressional Research Service, Library of Congress, CRS Report for Congress, 27 September 2001, p. 13.

43. Ackerman and Grimmett, p. 14.

44. Louis Fisher, "Congressional Abdication: War and Spending Powers," *St. Louis University Law Journal.* 43, no. 3, summer 1999, p. 942.

45. "War Powers Resolution: Presidential Compliance," Richard F. Grimmett, Foreign Affairs, Defense, and Trade Division, Congressional Research Service, 24 March 2003, pp. CRS 4–5.

46. Text of S. J. Res. 23, as passed by the Senate on 14 September 2001, Sec. 2(a).

47. "President Signs Authorization for Use of Military Force Bill," Statement by the President, The White House, 18 September 2001, p. 1, at www.whitehouse.gov/news/releases/2001/09/20010918-10.html.

48. Louis Fisher, "Congressional Abdication: War and Spending Powers," *St. Louis University Law Journal* 43, no. 3, summer 1999, p. 977.

CHAPTER 13. CONGRESS ON ITS KNEES

1. *War Powers Legislation,* Hearings before the Committee on Foreign Relations, U.S. Senate, 92nd Cong., 1st sess., 8, 9, 24, 25 March, 23, 26 April, 14 May, 26, 27 July, and 6 October 1971, Statement of Alexander M. Bickel, professor of law, Yale University, 26 July 1971, p. 550.

2. Excerpts from "President Bush's Address on Iraq," *Washington Post,* 8 October 2002, p. A-20.

3. Ibid.

4. Ibid.

5. "President's Remarks at the United Nations General Assembly," 12 September 2002, White House Web site at www.whitehouse.gov/news/releases/2002/09/20020912-1.html.

6. Ibid.

7. "President Stresses Need for Strong Iraq Resolution," Excerpts from 1 October 2002 Presidential Remarks following Meeting with Members of Congress, from White House Web site at www.whitehouse.gov/news/releases/2002/10/20021001-2.html.

8. "In Bush's Words: 'Use All Means' on Iraq," *New York Times,* 20 September 2002, p. A1.

9. Jim VandeHei, "Daschle Angered by Bush Statement," *Washington Post,* 26 September 2002, p. A1.

10. Ibid.

11. David S. Broder, "Still Reeling from Vietnam," *Washington Post,* 9 October 2002, p. A31; Mary McGrory, "Mistaken Patriots," *Washington Post,* 17 October 2002, p. A21; Jim VandeHei, "Daschle Angered by Bush Statement," *Washington Post,* 26 September 2002, p. A1.

12. "The National Security Strategy of the United States of America," Office of the President of the United States, 17 September 2002, p. 6, available at www.whitehouse.gov/nsc/nss.pdf.

13. Ibid., p. 14.

14. Ibid., p. 15.

15. Ibid., p. 29.

16. As quoted in an 1848 admonition in connection with the Mexican-American War, from "War Powers," Report of the Senate Foreign Relations Committee to accompany S. 440, Senate Report 93-220, 14 June 1973, p. 29.

17. Thom Shanker, "Rumsfeld Denies Rift Exists between Pentagon and CIA," *New York Times,* 25 October 2002, p. A15.

18. Warren P. Strobel, Jonathan S. Landay, and John Walcott, "Officials' Private Doubts on Iraq War," *Philadelphia Inquirer,* 8 October 2002, p. A1; Julian

Borger, "White House 'Exaggerating Iraqi Threat' Bush's Televised Address Attacked by US Intelligence," *The Guardian,* 9 October 2002, p. 1; Sebastian Rotella, "Allies Find No Links between Iraq, Al Qaeda," *Los Angeles Times,* 4 November 2002, p. A1.

19. David S. Cloud, "Bush's Efforts to Tie Hussein to al Qaeda Lack Clear Evidence; US Intelligence Can't Affirm Claims Despite His History with Other Terror Groups," *Wall Street Journal,* 23 October 2002, p. A1.

20. Warren P. Strobel, Jonathan S. Landay, and John Walcott, "Officials' Private Doubts on Iraq War," *Philadelphia Inquirer,* 8 October 2002, p. A1.

21. Letter of John McLaughlin for George Tenet to Hon. Bob Graham, chairman, Select Committee on Intelligence, U.S. Senate, 7 October 2002, reprinted in *Congressional Record,* 9 October 2002, p. S10154.

22. Bradley Graham and Dana Priest, "Pentagon Team Told to Seek Details of Iraq–al Qaeda Ties," *Washington Post,* 25 October 2002, p. A24; Thom Shanker, "Rumsfeld Denies Rift Exists between Pentagon and CIA," *New York Times,* 25 October 2002, p. A15; Warren P. Strobel and Jonathan S. Landay, "Pentagon, CIA in Bitter Dispute on Iraq," *Philadelphia Inquirer,* 28 October 2002.

23. Excerpt from President Bush's Address on Iraq, *Washington Post,* 8 October 2002, p. A20.

24. Dana Milbank, "For Bush, Facts Are Malleable," *Washington Post,* 22 October 2002, p. A1.

25. See "A Case Not Closed," by Seymour M. Hersh, *New Yorker,* 1 November 1993.

26. Statement made on the ABC television show *This Week* on 30 March 2003.

27. See comments of Kenneth Adelman, in Howard LaFranchi "US Seeks Right Equation to Topple Saddam," *Christian Science Monitor,* 1 March 2002.

CHAPTER 14. THE WEEK OF SHAME

1. *Congressional Record,* 3 October 2002, p. S9892.

2. Ibid., p. S9893.

3. Helen Dewar and Juliet Eilperin, "Iraq Resolution Passes Test, Gains Support," *Washington Post,* 10 October 2002, p. A16.

4. *Congressional Record,* 9 October 2002, p. S10189–91.

5. The author heard the remark and located the point in the debate on page S10288 on 10 October when it was made but was not able to find it in the *Record.*

6. *Congressional Record,* 9 October 2002, p. S10160.

7. *Congressional Record,* 10 October 2002, p. S10245.

8. *Congressional Record,* 4 October 2002, p. S9959.

9. Ibid. p. S9960.

10. Ibid., p. S9955.

11. Ibid., p. S9948.

12. *Congressional Record,* 10 October 2002, p. S10249.

13. *Congressional Record,* 8 October 2002, p. H7196.

14. *Congressional Record,* 4 October 2002, p. S9957.

15. Ibid., p. S9963.
16. *Congressional Record,* 9 October 2002, p. S10191.
17. Ibid., p. S10192.
18. *Congressional Record,* 10 October 2002, pp. H7796–99.
19. Jim VandeHei, "Daschle Angered by Bush Statement," *Washington Post,* 26 September 2002, p. A1.
20. David S. Broder, "Still Reeling from Vietnam," *Washington Post,* 9 October 2002, p. A31.
21. *Congressional Record,* 8 October 2002, pp. S10100–101.
22. *Congressional Record,* 10 October 2002, p. H7778.
23. Ibid., p. H7778.
24. Ibid., p. H7779
25. *Congressional Record,* 8 October 2002, p. H7195.
26. *Congressional Record,* 9 October 2002, p. S10174.
27. *Congressional Record,* 10 October 2002, p. S10241.
28. Ibid., p. S10242.
29. Joe Lieberman, "Our Resolution," *Wall Street Journal,* 7 October 2002, p. A26.
30. *Congressional Record,* 8 October 2002, p. S10104.
31. *Congressional Record,* 10 October 2002, pp. S10288–90.
32. *Congressional Record,* 7 October 2002, p.S10010.
33. Ibid., p. S10028.
34. *Congressional Record,,* 8 October 2002, pp. S10067–68.
35. Ibid., p. S10099.
36. *Congressional Record,* 9 October 2002, p. S10177.
37. Ibid., pp. S10175.
38. *Congressional Record,* 9 October 2002, p. S10183.
39. Ibid., p. S10184.
40. *Congressional Record,* 10 October 2002, pp. S10249–50.
41. Ibid., p. S10290.
42. *Congressional Record,* 9 October 2002, p. H7333.
43. Ibid., p. H7334.
44. Assessment based on polling data for all candidates received via e-mail periodically on all 2002 Senate races from Council for a Livable World, 332 4th Street, NE, Washington, D.C., 20002 at www.clw.org.

CONCLUSION: TWELVE NOT-SO-EASY STEPS TO A SOBER CONGRESS

1. Andy Pastzor, "Pentagon Blasts Air Force Contract for Boeing Tankers," *Wall Street Journal,* 30 March 2004, p. A6.
2. For details of the procurement arrangement, see Congressional Budget Office Cost Estimate H.R. 1588, National Defense Authorization Act for Fiscal Year 2004, 25 November 2003, pp. 2–4.
3. "What Great Victory? What Revolution?" by William S. Lind, essay written in the aftermath of the 1991 Gulf War, in the author's files.

4. Thomas Withington, "What If We Battled a Real Army?," *Long Island Newsday,* 6 August 2003.

5. Tom Bowman, "US Technology, Inept Enemy Led to Iraq Victory, Army Says," *Baltimore Sun,* 13 October 2003, p. 1A.

6. See "Casualties in Iraq," at http://www.globalsecurity.org/military/ops/iraq_casualties.htm and http://lunaville.org.warcasualties/summary.aspx.

7. See "The Recovery Program" on the Alcoholics Anonymous Web site at http://www.alcoholics-anonymous.org/.

8. Letter signed by Sens. John McCain, Chuck Robb (D-Va.), and Chuck Hagel (R-Nebr.) to Hon. Ted Stevens, chairman, Committee on Appropriations, U.S. Senate, dated 8 December 1998. The three-page letter was sent on McCain's stationery, noting him as the leader of the exercise.

9. Remarks by the President on Iraq in Cincinnati, Ohio, 7 October 2002, available at www.whitehouse.gov/news/releases/2002/10/20021007-8.html.

List of Abbreviations

ABM	antiballistic missile system
AWACS	airborne warning and control system
CBO	Congressional Budget Office
CIA	Central Intelligence Agency
CRS	Congressional Research Service
DAISUMS	daily intelligence summaries
DIA	Defense Intelligence Agency
DoD	Department of Defense
GAO	General Accounting Office
GDP	gross domestic product
IADS	integrated air defense system
IFF	"identification, friend or foe"
IG	Inspector General of the Department of Defense
IRS	Internal Revenue Service
JCS	Joint Chiefs of Staff
LGB	laser-guided bomb
NSIAD	National Security and International Affairs Division
O&M	Operations and Maintenance
OMB	Office of Management and Budget
OSD	Office of the Secretary of Defense
OTA	Office of Technology Assessment
PEMD	Program Evaluation and Methodology Division
PSI	Permanent Subcommittee on Investigations
SAR	Selected Acquisition Report
SASC	Senate Armed Services Committee
UN	United Nations

Index

About the Author

Winslow T. Wheeler worked on national security issues for thirty-one years for members of the U.S. Senate and for the U.S. General Accounting Office. In the Senate, Wheeler worked for Jacob K. Javits (R-N.Y.), Nancy L. Kassebaum (R-Kans.), David Pryor (D-Ark.), and Pete V. Domenici (R-N.Mex.). He was the only Senate staffer to work simultaneously on the personal staffs of a Republican and a Democrat.

As a Senate staffer, Wheeler worked extensively on hundreds of bills and amendments that are now U.S. law. These included the War Powers Act and multiple proposals to reform Pentagon procurement and to require more realistic weapons tests.

In 2002 he was pressured to resign from his position with the Senate Budget Committee because of an essay he wrote, under the pen name "Spartacus," criticizing Congress's reaction to the September 11 attacks. He is now a Visiting Senior Fellow at the Center for Defense Information in Washington, D.C.